Design
Leadership

Design
Leadership

Securing the strategic value of design

Raymond Turner

Routledge
Taylor & Francis Group

LONDON AND NEW YORK

First published 2013 by Ashgate Publishing

Published 2016 by Routledge
2 Park Square, Milton Park, Abingdon, Oxfordshire OX14 4RN
711 Third Avenue, New York, NY 10017, USA

First issued in paperback 2016

Routledge is an imprint of the Taylor & Francis Group, an informa business

British Library Cataloguing in Publication Data
Turner, Raymond, 1946-
   Design leadership : securing the strategic value of design.
   1. Industrial design--Management. 2. Product management.
   3. Strategic planning.
   I. Title
   658.5'7-dc23

   ISBN: 978-1-4094-6323-8 (hbk)

The Library of Congress has catalogued the printed edition as follows:
Turner, Raymond.
   Design leadership : securing the strategic value of design / by Raymond
Turner.
      pages cm
   Includes bibliographical references and index.
   ISBN 978-1-4094-6323-8 (hbk.)
   1. Leadership. 2. Industrial
design--Management. I. Title.
   HD57.7.T887 2013
   745.20968'4--dc23

                                                                2012045376

ISBN 13: 978-1-138-24763-5 (pbk)
ISBN 13: 978-1-4094-6323-8 (hbk)

For Patricia

Contents

Design drivers for business

Design spend, the largest single sum of money the board knows the least about

Design provides a clear, practical, link between the strategic discussions in the boardroom and the daily activities of business

Design leadership helps define the future, design management provides the tools for getting there

Putting design into the DNA of business maximizes shareholder value from the investment

Corporate reputation is built on customer experience, design helps create it

Design is a business tool that makes strategy visible

Design leadership is a commercial imperative

Design investment increases brand value and reduces development costs

About the author

Raymond Turner is an internationally recognized authority on design leadership and management, and their strategic value to business, government and society. He has worked in the design industry for 40 years as a designer, design manager, consultant and corporate director of design leadership. Now he is an independent consultant helping clients realize maximum value from their design investment through strategic design direction and design implementation planning.

He works for large corporations and small to medium-sized businesses across a wide range of industries including transportation, local and national government, city planning, public broadcasting, household and leisure product manufacturing, and construction. He is also a non-Executive Director of Image Now, Ireland's leading branding consultancy.

During his career he has held a number of key design posts including:
- Founding Director of Raymond Turner Associates, design leadership and management consultants;
- Group Design Director of BAA, the world's largest private airport company;
- Design Director of Heathrow's new fifth air terminal and Heathrow Express, the high speed rail link between Heathrow and central London;
- Principal design management consultant to Eurotunnel;
- Managing Director of Wolff Olins, international corporate identity consultancy;
- Design Director of London Transport;
- Assistant Chief Executive of Kilkenny Design Workshops, a multidisciplinary design practice working on behalf of the Irish government;
- Senior Creative Designer for Gillette Industries.

Other responsibilities have included:
- Design advisor to the Bank of England Printing Works;
- Chair of Design Dimension, an educational trust;
- Chair of the Design Business Association's Design Effectiveness Awards;
- Member of the Advisory Council of the Design Management Institute, USA.

He has a First Class Honours degree in Industrial Design; is qualified in mechanical and electrical engineering; is a Fellow of the Chartered Society of Designers (UK) and a member of the Design Management Institute (USA). He has an Honorary Doctorate in Technology from London City University; an Honorary Master of Arts Degree from University of the Creative Arts and is Honorary Research Fellow at Lancaster University. Raymond is regularly invited to speak on the strategic value of design to business, design management, and frequently contributes papers for international design journals. Raymond is married and lives in Dublin and Winchester.

Acknowledgements

This book is almost entirely based on my own experience of working in the design industry for many decades. During that time my thinking about design leadership, design management and the challenge of making design work has developed, changed and in most instances become clearer. Colleagues, clients and friends alike have helped this to happen through discussion and sometimes argument but always to a fruitful end. To them all I express my most sincere thanks for putting up with my endless meandering on the journey to better understanding.

I would like to acknowledge here everyone who has helped me get this far although I am sure to forget some. To those I apologize in advance and will try to correct the omission at the next opportunity.

Special thanks go to Peter Gorb who first helped me put some structure to my early thinking on design management; to Dr Tony Ridley of London Underground who made me realize that behavioural style was as much a key to making design work as technical expertise; and to Wally Olins with whom I worked for five years and during that time enabled me to develop a better understanding of the progression of design's influence in business.

Aiden Grennelle of Image Now provided the design concept for the book, and I am most grateful to him for making it look so engaging. Paul Dowd and Stephen Browne, also of Image Now, undertook the exacting task of producing artwork for every page with meticulous care and precision. Tom Lockwood has not only provided a thought-provoking Foreword, but has put the subject of design leadership into an even wider context. And thanks also to Peter Evers for the author's photography.

Professional colleagues and associates from different parts of the world have helped me develop my thinking on the subject. Particular thanks go to Clive Grinyer – CISCO, James Berry – Woods Baggot, Joe Ferry – InterContinental Hotels, Darrell Kavanagh – Image Now, David Griffiths, Michael Wolff – Michael Wolff and Company, Tim Selders and Frans Joziasse – PARK, Barry Weekes – BAA, John Lloyd – ex Lloyd Northover, SeymourPowell, Paul Priestman – Priestman Goode, David Kester – Design Council, Tom Karen – ex Ogle Design, Frank Duffy – ex DEGW, Keith Perry – Nononsence Design, Roland Laycock – Eglin Concourse International, Jen Kavanagh – London Transport Museum, Helene Cargo – Eurotunnel , Alan Lamond – Pascall and Watson, Miquel Angel Munar – Roca, Jim Dowdell – GloHealth, Gerry O'Hagan – Bord na Móna, Chantell Bramley – New West End Company, Mai Britt Mitchley – Niels Torp, Sean Curtis – Curtis Consulting, Roisn McDaid – KSi Faulkner Orr, and Eryl Smith – ex BAA.

Deborah Dawton of the Design Business Association has been generous in allowing me to use many of its short case examples that appear in the book. My thanks also go to Deborah's colleague,

Natallie Maher, for her single-mindedness in securing many of the illustrations from the design companies that have submitted their work for the DBA's Design Effectiveness Awards – and to these businesses for allowing me to reproduce their images and for being engaged in design effectiveness in the first place. Without these contributions the book would be much the poorer.

Many clients have been especially generous in letting me reflect on the experiences we have had together in resolving, sometimes very difficult, business issues through design leadership. Others who have helped and influenced me in this project are Rachel Cooper of Lancaster University, Sue Gordon who critiqued my early draft, Eilis McNulty of Dolmen and Darrell Kavanagh of Image Now who acted as conscientious readers of the manuscript, and to Sean McNulty, a colleague of many years standing, whose knowledge and insight with respect to the part dealing with innovation was especially valuable.

And to Patricia Turner who has provided unending encouragement and endless patience during the whole process of unsociable working hours, researching, compiling, writing and re-writing; and even during those, albeit not too frequent, periods when I have thought 'why am I doing this?' – a very special thank you.

Despite all the advice given and debate that has taken place during the writing of this book I, of course, take full responsibility for its contents, opinions expressed and conclusions drawn.

Raymond Turner

Foreword

Every now and then something strikes a true note with me. Let's say not just being in alignment, but in harmony. *Design Leadership* does just this for me. It resonates. It is in balance. Perhaps because it is not theoretical, it is real; not subjective, but objective; and most of all because it helps clarify one of the most important topics to me – the strategic value of design in business and society.

I don't make such claims often, because our world today is so full of false claims. And it seems now that design is so hot, so to speak, just about everyone is an expert about it. This could be good, if we subscribe to the premise of Thomas Watson Junior, the former chairman of IBM, and the famous graphic designer Paul Rand, that 'good design is good business'. Yes, this statement is reality, and now that it seems everyone 'plays' design today, my question is, who leads design? And today it seems everyone claims that design sells, but my question is, 'How do you know the value of design?' And lastly, today it seems everyone claims to participate in concept designing, collaboration, co-design, and design thinking, but my question is, 'How do you know the best methods of design as a process for strategic business success?'

That's why *Design Leadership* is so relevant to me. It answers these difficult questions, and more. It sheds light on design management and design leadership, design strategic value and design processes.

I particularly enjoy the fact that Raymond Turner bases this book on his first– hand experience in industry. With all due respect, Raymond is not a theorist or an academic researcher, but rather he is a practising design manager. He has dedicated a robust career encouraging colleagues everyday in the business and public sector communities about the virtues of good design as a process, product or service. In fact, he is a pioneer in articulating the differences between design management and design leadership, and one of the foremost authorities on this subject. Personally, I have learned a great deal from Raymond Turner.

Another reason that *Design Leadership* resonates with me is that today I see almost global design parity. Have you noticed how similar some products are becoming? A Tesla and a Lotus, that's an easy one. But I'm talking about the similarities between seemingly disparate objects, like an Audi car and Oakley sunglasses, a 3M stapler and an Alessi teapot, or a Starbucks café and your local bank lobby. Consumers love cool design, and companies are catching on.

I am typically asked to be a design judge several times each year, for many of the world's leading competitions, such as the Industrial Design Society of America, IDSA, the Good Design award in China, the Taiwan Design Centre awards, Good Design in Australia, and the Red Dot design award in Germany. Design judging has been particularly interesting because, with Red Dot for example, there were over 5,000 entries from 60 countries, and it is a great way to keep up with the changing landscape of design quality. It is clear that good design is becoming the norm – just a few years ago some of the design entries I evaluated were laggards. But recently I have been positively impressed by the quality overall. This means, of course, that the bar of design quality is rising all over the world, and any company that wants to compete internationally must have very good design quality.

I also have noticed the presence of a design status quo; we may be reaching design parity. Because everything is pretty good already, at least in these types of design competitions, it is getting harder to stand out. It's tougher to recognize the brand, or even the country of origin by the design. Design is reaching equilibrium all over the world. This is both good and bad: good because the bar is rising, and bad because with parity of design, it's almost as if good design is becoming good enough.

Therefore, if formal design is not a differentiator, what is? I think the future will be about competition in design leadership; companies in which design is part of corporate strategy, that manage to integrate design thinking throughout the organization, that build effective design competencies both internally and externally, that take responsibility for service design and the entire customer experience, and that strive to use design to solve the right problems; these are the companies that are succeeding, and will reap the advantages in the years to come. And the many examples in Raymond's book bring this insight to life.

In the past, some companies found success by competing with good design against bad design, and it was easy to win. But the future is becoming a competition of good design against good design. So every company has to up their design game just to stay even, not to mention gain preference. Imagine – what if IKEA and Nike were direct competitors? Or Audi and Apple? Or Dyson and OXO? Or Coach and BMW? Then we would see even better design, and more design innovation, more quickly. I believe it is competition on this level that the future holds, and this takes design leaders.

In addition, investing in the design can be a sustainable business advantage, because it leads to five benefits; creative collaboration, innovation, differentiation, simplification and customer experience.

For starters, designers tend to collaborate with each other, other disciplines, and users to generate new ideas, explore alternatives, and create new objects; products, web sites, brands, stores, and so on. The process of design thinking, co-creation and design as creative collaboration can help companies move beyond their norms and create new markets. Companies like P&G, Intuit and Four Seasons have changed their corporate culture and embrace such collaborative processes. Intuit created a Design for Delight process, 'D4D', which they use for problem solving and has led to launching new mobile products and services quickly, based on employee involvement and nurturing a design-thinking culture.

This cross-pollination can be the path to innovation. Design helps bring innovation to market – just take away the design part of any innovative idea and see what you're left with. What would a Dyson Airblade hand-dryer be without its unique usability?

In addition to being a collaborative path towards innovation, design is a way to differentiate a brand's products from its competitors'. This goes beyond logo, graphic design and branding to enabling user and customer experiences that cannot be easily copied. And when P&G wanted to gain preference in the generic mop category, it asked Continuum Innovation to look into mopping. Continuum developed a waterless solution called Swiffer that has now become a branded product asset and nearly a billion-dollar business.

We live in an experience economy, and design is key to creating meaningful customer experiences. Case in point: Philips Lighting wanted to sell more light bulbs, but the products have developed to the point where differentiation is hard to achieve, so they've improved the retail experience by connecting with Engine Service Design to create new software and a service platform that helps their retailers manage their lighting and media assets across their stores. The simple light bulb became differentiated through service design and the retailer experience.

Lastly, design simplifies. We live in complexity, and there is nothing like using the sensibilities of design to unpack wicked problems. The data-storage company StorageTek used to have completely different parts for each of their different servers and data-storage product lines, mostly due to legacy issues and business unit independence. The design department created a common platform strategy using shared components – just as Toyota Highlanders and Sienna minivans share the same chassis platform. The move not only saved StorageTek millions of dollars in just a few years but also was the environmentally responsible thing to do. Design simplifies and should enable reuse and ecological solutions.

In 1953, Neil Borden, the president of the American Marketing Association, helped define the value of marketing by coining the term 'Marketing Mix', which subsequently led to the famous 4 Ps of marketing (product, price, place and promotion). As the past president of the Design Management Institute, I gave it a try and proposed that Collaborate, Innovate, Differentiate, Simplify and Customer Experience become the 'Design Mix'.

As this book points out, there is significant value in integrating strategy and design when evaluated in light of the 'triple bottom line', from an economic, social and environmental viewpoint. I would argue that no other business discipline or function has greater potential to affect that triple bottom line than design. As stated above, when one considers the values of design as a process, an artifact or service, its benefits are virtually unlimited. But this is just the tip of the iceberg. I trust you will find the ideas, case studies and hands-on real-world experience Raymond has presented in *Design Leadership* to be a real value to business, government and our wider community. He has clearly shown how to secure the strategic value of design. I hope it resonates as true with you as it has with me.

Thomas Lockwood, PhD
Founding Partner
Lockwood Resource
President Emeritus, Design Management Institute

Introduction

The fundamental tenet of this book is that design is a commercial and social imperative and its management and leadership are integral parts of what can make business successful, government effective and society safer and more enjoyable for everyone. The reverse is also true.

When companies ignore its relevance and potential they are depriving owners and shareholders a full and proper return on their investment in design. There are similar disadvantages when governments ignore its social enhancing potential.

Even though we hear the word 'design' used everyday – magazines feature it, thousands of book pages are written about it, TV programmes are dedicated to it and international competitions extol the virtues of it, very little of substance has been published about the leadership of it. Senior practitioners in business and design struggle to understand what is involved in leading by, and through, design.

These are hard words, but the reality is that unless a business capitalizes on every resource available it will not sustain differentiation, create competitive advantage, maximize employment opportunity or evolve into a world-class performer. One of the most undervalued resources is design, and none of these wider ambitions are achievable without fully utilizing it's potential across the organization and down through its management layers.

For every company directing and managing design to help deliver its corporate ambitions, for every one ensuring all design activity addresses real business issues, for every design consultancy that rigorously delivers the full weight of its creative capability through strategically focused design responses, there will be an improvement in business performance as a result.

Key to making design effective in any organisation is the critical need for everyone concerned with the work to understand 'what success looks like' before they start. In other words, before designing anything, each person in the team must have a clear understanding of the criteria by which the design proposals, once they have been produced, will be judged. The responsibility for this is ultimately the client commissioning the work; however the designer, or design manager, has the responsibility of ensuring this happens.

Many of the companies whose experiences are touched on in this book have used design to help develop their business strategy or understand the implications of following a particular strategic path. They have found that the need to do this gets greater as the differences between competing companies gets less. As more and more products and services become increasingly similar to each other in what they do, it becomes increasingly more difficult to differentiate between one business and another. Price differential is never the answer in the long run as there is only so much you can do with cost reduction as a point of difference.

All of which leads to the conclusion that, ultimately, design leadership is a commercial imperative that business cannot afford to ignore. Its potential to have an impact on business performance can be so profound that the responsibility for the quality and relevance of every design solution must remain with the business commissioning the work – no business has the luxury of delegating or abrogating responsibility for it.

These beliefs are not based on the premise that design is good simply because designers tell us so. Neither is it based on academic study or extensive research. It is, rather, an overriding conclusion from working at the design 'coal face' for many decades. Experience derived from being a designer, design manager, design director and design leader on large and small projects, covering most design disciplines, for organizations, companies and consultancies in Europe, USA, UAE and the Far East.

How this book works

It is divided into four parts.

Part One – Preparing the ground

The first part is concerned with making an organization fit for using design effectively and getting it to understand the case for putting design on the business agenda.

It deals with some basic issues that must be confronted before design will be considered as an effective business resource. In particular it discusses how to convert the sceptics – those people who see design as a thing rather than a process, or as a tactical rather than strategic resource, or something that is always a cost to the business rather than an investment for greater return, or who never see it as a key mechanism by which an organization's reputation depends or can be enhanced.

Part Two – The how and what of delivery

The second part provides guidance on how to assess the role and value of design to specific circumstances.

It then addresses ways to make design effective and work to advantage. It deals with the different roles and responsibilities of design managers and leaders. It also describes some specific processes for managing and leading design. It examines the behavioural styles needed for effective design management, functional leadership and being a better design client.

Part Three – Looking back to look forward

The third part is about understanding and learning from the past as the basis for understanding and preparing for the future.

It sets out some of the challenges that these people face based on the changing nature of our business and social worlds, including the issue of bridging the gap between what the design industry offers and what business, government and society need from it. It looks at the role of innovation management as an integral part of the design process and how collaborative working is having an impact on design outputs.

Part Four – Case examples

Two types of case examples have been used throughout the book – short ones and longer ones. The short ones are positioned in the narrative where they best serve to illustrate the point being made. The longer ones have been placed together here in this fourth part so as not to interrupt the argument, clarity and flow of the general text. These case examples illustrate many points although their principal focus is captured in the title. All case examples have come either directly from my own experience working as a company design director or consultant in design leadership; or from the winners of the Design Business Association's Design Effectiveness Awards for which I was chair of the judging panel for several years.

Summary of reflections

It summarizes my experience in 13 key mantras of learning, each intended to help future managers and leaders be more effective in managing and leading through design. It reminds the reader of the key arguments covered in the book and leaves them with a final thought.

Part One – Preparing the ground

Part One of this book is concerned with how to prepare an organization so that it can use design effectively and helping it understand the case for putting design on to the business agenda. It deals with some basic issues that must be confronted before design will be taken seriously. This includes bringing the sceptics on board – they are the people who see design as a thing rather than a process, or as a tactical resource rather than strategic one, or something that is always a cost to the business rather than an investment for greater return, or who never see it as a key mechanism by which an organization's reputation depends or can be enhanced.

Why bother with design?

Perhaps we should get this question out of the way first. Why is understanding the role of design so important? Why do we have to bother with it?

The answer is simple. We are surrounded by things, systems, environments and structures. If the natural world did not create them then man did, and part of the process of creating them was designing them! It may not have been called design at the time but the process of creating must have included it, otherwise they would not exist. As will be seen later, design is much more about a process and much less about a thing.

'design is a process not a thing'

Design is not something that can be avoided. We are surrounded by its use, we interact with things as a result of it. The issue we should be concerned with is how effectively has it been used? In other words, how well does it satisfy the brief that required the work to be undertaken in the first place, how well does the design solution satisfy the wider strategic objectives of the organization commissioning it, and to what extent has shareholder value been optimized by its deployment?

These are serious questions, ones which business leaders must learn to address if they are to maximize design's potential as a way of maximizing shareholder value. They are questions which design managers and design leaders are required to confront.

All products and services are dependent on design for their very being – without it they cannot exist, and getting the most from the investment is a challenge, and responsibility, for client and designer alike.

On the one hand, the challenge facing the design client, irrespective of company size or sector, is, 'How do I increase my return on design investment while at the same time reducing the cost of that investment?' On the other hand, the challenge facing the design consultant is, 'How do I ensure that my client sees their commitment to design as an investment not a cost?'

Within this challenging environment every successful client/consultant relationship has, at its core, the overriding objective of using design as a means of adding value, and so giving a return on the investment in it. If 'added value' is not at the core of this relationship, then the inevitable consequence is the design work will be seen as a commodity where the cheapest wins the day – and, by definition, only one supplier can be the cheapest!

In many spheres the term design has become reduced to being part of a sales slogan used to promote 'designer sunglasses, designer chocolates, designer jeans or designer alcoholic pop drinks'. This highly inflated and superficial use of the word design, so common in everyday experience, hides its profound potential contribution to making business more successful and society more enjoyable.

Once all this pretentious unintelligible jargon about 'designerly things' in sales promotion has been stripped away, there is one inescapable conclusion that you are left with, and it is this, design is a key contributor to making organizations successful in what they set out to do, and so ranks as a commercial imperative.

'design is a key contributor to making organizations successful in what they set out to do, and so ranks as a commercial imperative'

This proposition is explored fully in the following pages and the main task in front of any design manager or design leader is to get all other relevant people aligned with this view.

To be successful in this means addressing two critical challenges if the ground is to be well prepared for making design work effectively and to maximize its potential, whether that is within organizations, businesses, government departments or our wider society. These are to:
• create a comprehensive understanding of what is possible with design;
• demonstrate the value that design can bring.

This is not easy work. Much of it is about stepping outside the comfort zone of most design-trained people. It means overcoming some basic prejudices if design is to be taken seriously, if it is to contribute to the transformation agenda facing many businesses today, if it is to deliver lasting strategic value.

I remember my first day as Design Director of London Transport and meeting a senior colleague who was chairman and managing director of one of the main operating businesses. A very warm and welcoming person by nature who, at this first meeting, told me clearly that he had not supported my appointment when it came to the Executive Committee for approval. We had never met before this so his position was not based on a clash of personalities. It was based on an assumption, or a prejudice. He believed I would get in the way of his reinvestment programme by trying to exercise some superficial design judgment or personal taste opinions about what his line mangers were doing with design. I remember being somewhat shaken by his comment. I reacted by saying the first thing that came into my mind – 'You have my reassurance I will not interfere with any design work your managers are engaged in, unless, or course, I don't believe they are getting value for money from it'.

Subsequently, of course, I had to prove my point and, fortunately, was able to do so. We became close colleagues and he was one of my most supportive allies – all because of being able to show how investment in design could be maximized, could be focused on the challenges his business was facing and would improve the quality of service to his customers.

I only tell this story because prejudice can be a serious hindrance to design effectiveness. This first part of the book suggests ways by which these prejudices may be addressed. It makes no assumptions that this will either be a simple task or quick to achieve. What it does do, however, is propose ways of dealing with five of the most commonly encountered prejudices in business about the role of design. Each one represents a hindrance to getting the most out of design. Often the challenge of addressing them is skipped over in the rush to arrive at the, so called, creative aspects of what design can do. However, if you can win over one manager, that win can be infectious. It can lead to other successes within the business. That can also lead to successes in other businesses when those managers move on in their careers. And best of all, it can lead to those managers embracing greater design challenges in their quest for improvement and change.

Chapter 1
The sceptics

The first of these prejudices, or issues, is to do with design sceptics. These are the people, sometimes the clients of design consultants, sometimes line managers in a company that employ staff designers, who think they understand the role and potential of design, but only see its most superficial qualities. They see design as a commodity, a service that can be bought on an ad hoc basis whenever they think it appropriate. They do not see it as something that can contribute to the long-term wealth of the business. If this is the case then those sceptics need to be brought onboard.

The issue of how to deal with those people who remain design sceptics has been around for a long time. Alan Topalian 1980 adopted a very strong position on this issue. He reminded people responsible for design that in this kind of work they were not paid to be nice guys. I have come to a similar conclusion that this is not something that can be solved with subtlety and guile. My mantra is equally to the point, persuade by the authority of your argument, not the argument of your authority.

'persuade by the authority of your argument, not the argument of your authority'

The sceptics view

These business people are easily recognized because they tend to share the general view of many others that design is superficial, something that gets added after the real work has been completed – like the icing on the cake, it's the finishing touch.

They also believe design is expensive, after all designers charge big fees which business people find hard to accept because they cannot quantify the return for the money they spend on it. Also, design is elitist because it is only big businesses that have the opportunity, and the money, to do something with design. Even though, by far, the largest group of businesses in most countries are in the category of small to medium size, design is not for the small guys – and who needs the icing anyway? Not forgetting that designers don't live in the real world – they don't even look like normal people!

And, in the order of things, design is irrelevant because you can't see that it adds any real value. There are far more important things to think about like market share, turnover and profit margin. The fact that these sceptical views are held by so many people is not surprising considering that we are bombarded with the word design wherever we look and this, inevitably, conditions our expectations of it.

The other view

Of course there is the opposing point of view to that of the sceptics which is that design is not about any of these things. This other view holds that design is one of a company's most strategically potent assets which can have a direct bearing on its wealth creating capability – so long as you know how to use it!

Design is not superficial

The counter argument is that design is not superficial nor is it about finishing touches. It affects all parts of the business, it is key to making business strategy at least visible and potentially tangible in many other ways. The argument continues that it is an essential ingredient that can breathe new life into old products and help create innovative new ones. It can be the basis of designing spaces from the inside out for user convenience, improved work dynamics and operational efficiency, rather than from the outside in for the aesthetic value of it. It can be key to differentiation and growth in the marketplace.

Although the dictionary definition of the word 'superficial' describes it as something to do with the surface of things, this does not always mean it is of no significance. Fashion is an area of design which has much to do with appearance, or things so called 'superficial', but that is not to say it is of no importance – far from it. As the following example shows design can go much deeper than this.

Case Example – Dulux Perfect

This proposition is well illustrated by a range of products launched recently by ICI Paints AkzoNobel under the Dulux brand name. See Figure 1.1. Dulux is the company's best known paint brand. In the UK, 50p of every £1 spent on paint is on Dulux. It made sense therefore to expand into Do-It-Yourself (DIY) home decorating accessories, since only one in ten consumers traditionally purchase a paintbrush or roller with their paint.

Figure 1.1 *Part of the Dulux Perfect range of products. In this case the paint brush has a tin opener as part of the handle*

Webb deVlam, a brand strategy and design consultancy, used detailed consumer 'Discovery' sessions to investigate the painting experience through ethnographic studies of DIY activity in the home. This was supplemented by consultations with trade professionals. The project resulted in Dulux Perfect, a comprehensive range of brushes, rollers and trays, each with unique features that enhance the home decorating activity. These features include a tin opener integrated into brush handles, and a triangular brush to make painting edges easier.

After an initial launch in 2009, which resulted in a 5 per cent share of the £160 million home decorating accessories market, the launch of the extended range in March 2010 generated continued success. Annual sales have increased 36.49 per cent and are still growing. Distribution has more than doubled in major accounts and Dulux Perfect won the DIY Week 'Product of the Year' Award.

Design is not expensive

Equally, design is not an expensive new overhead but something that companies are already engaged in and could almost certainly do more cost effectively. Designing the right solution in the first place costs less than designing the wrong solution and then having to manage the fall out from that bad decision. There is well-documented evidence that design can save money, not only by making things easier and cheaper to produce, but also by having a positive affect on the cost of ownership.

Case Example – Eglin Concourse airport seating

Figure 1.2 Eglin airport seating, concept design by Robert Heritage RDI

A good example of designing for 'cost of ownership' is that of the airport seating system manufactured by Eglin Concourse International and design concept by Robert Heritage OBE RDI (1927–2010). See Figure 1.2.

A significant cost in the use, and therefore ownership, of airport seating relates to the time, money and operational disruption caused by the replacement of traditional upholstery. Historically, in many cases the seating used by many of UK's airports required the whole seating unit to be removed from the departure lounges and waiting areas, and taken off site for reupholstery. This was mainly because the fabric and foam were fixed directly to the seating frame and needed the resources of an upholsterer's workshop for their replacement. Consequently, either a stock of additional seating had to be stored somewhere and made available for when those in use needed maintenance, or there would be a shortage of seats for passengers to use while the seats were away for repair. Neither of these options was acceptable to the airport owners nor the passengers.

One of the many requirements of the brief for the redesign of the seating commissioned by BAA, the airport company that owns Heathrow and operates many others around the world, was to address the problem of reupholstery. Others included reducing the footprint to achieve greater seating capacity, minimizing security risk by being able to easily see under it, reducing cleaning cost and weight, making seating layout more flexible. The brief required the upholstery to be replaced insitu and for this operation to cause little or no disruption to service. In addition, any spare parts that needed to be used for this operation should be held by the upholsterer without causing them any significant storage problem.

The resultant design solution, see Figure 1.2, responded to this requirement very well. The seat and back upholstered squabs were held in place on the frame by 'pop' rivets. Once the fabric was

life-expired these squabs could be removed by drilling out a few rivets, on site, in a few minutes. Replacement pre-upholstered panels could then be fixed in place equally quickly. The panels took up very little space at the factory as they stacked easily one on another, there was virtually no inconvenience to passengers and the airport operators did not have to store additional seats or organize for any to be taken away for repair. As a result of addressing the cost of ownership when briefing the designers, BAA was able to significantly reduce the operational cost of seat repairs when compared with the ones they had traditionally used.

Although the design work for this new seat was in response to a brief commissioned by BAA the seats were subsequently made available, directly from the manufacturer, to other airport operators that wanted to buy them.

Design is not elitist

The issue of elitism is never far away when considering the role of design in business. Elitism is generally used when describing attitudes and activities of a small select group of people. In this case the reverse is true. Far from being elitist, design should be inclusive by involving everyone in the company because it certainly will affect them. For example, design is fundamental to creating and managing customer experience and many people in an organization are in a position to make design-related decisions that influence this. For example, designing a building in such a way that it is easy to keep clean is likely to mean that the janitorial staff will have as much affect on the quality of that experience, or the working conditions of staff, as designing for the chief executive's long-term strategic intentions.

Case Example – Airline Moves

Figure 1.3 *Airline Moves at Heathrow*

Terminal 5 at Heathrow consists of three buildings: Terminal 5A, Terminal 5B and Terminal 5C. These buildings are all used for departures and arrivals and are linked by a transit train. It's opening has led to the most complex airline relocation programme ever undertaken. Over a 21 month period ending in January 2010, 50 of Heathrow's airlines moved terminals with a view to reducing cross-airport transfers and accelerating journey times for passengers.

The Team design consultancy was asked to develop an internal communications programme to help support the relocation process. This programme was developed into three key steps, each with its own objective aligned to the overall business target. These key steps involved developing an internal brand for the programme, Airline Moves, with accompanying messaging; briefing sessions; induction and training; and ongoing employee engagement. See Figure 1.3.

Despite numerous challenges, Airline Moves performed extremely well against its Key Performance Indicators, ensuring that no flights were affected by the relocations, and 100 per cent of staff knew what to do on the day. This meant no disruption to operations and a seamless passenger experience. This programme of relocation was successful, not only because the operation was managed effectively, but also because everyone knew what they needed to do and when – largely as a result of the efficacy of the internal communications programme.

Design is not irrelevant

Far from being irrelevant, design can be used to position a company in line with its strategic intent. It can influence how customers and staff experience the products and services of the company, it can make clear what the company stands for. It can overtly manifest its values through what it says about itself and how staff behave; it is key to defining, creating and maintaining differentiation. The case example below, 'Anua, extension or change?' outlines the process one company went through when exploring how best to represent a change from its traditional activities and how design was used to help make these decisions.

Case Example – Anua, extension or change?

A NEW CONTRACT WITH NATURE

Figure 1.4 *The new vision for Bord na Móna*

Bord na Móna was established by the Irish Government to harvest bog peat on a large scale as a principal means of providing power, particularly to rural communities. It has been part of Ireland's heritage for over 75 years. It has provided employment and created communities. Just as Ireland's needs and priorities have changed over that time, so too have those of the company. The core business has expanded beyond the harvesting of peat, the activity that gave the organization both its name and its reason for existence for much of the twentieth century.

As local and global pressure has grown to find more sustainable ways of producing power and conserving resources, Bord na Móna developed many innovative new products and services to meet those demands. These have included producing eco-fuels and environmental systems for cleaning water and purifying waste, waste collection, resource recovery and renewable energy expertise. In addition, water treatment, district heating and ecotourism businesses have also been developed.

The products and services that make up the business are diverse but all share two key characteristics. The first is that they draw directly upon the unique set of skills and insights the company has built up over three-quarters of a century working with nature. The second is that they are specifically designed to serve the present and future needs of its customers, the Irish economy and the planet.

Bord na Móna's attitude towards these non-traditional business activities has been clearly expressed by its Chief Executive Gabriel D'Arcy 2010, 'As a society, we need to forge a new contract with nature which respects both its power and fragility. As a company we have committed ourselves to doing just that. This commitment to sustainability is a journey we began some time ago. It's transforming what we do and ensuring we are respectful in how we do it. It's about operating in a sustainable way now and in the future. It's about delivering products and services that are increasingly environmentally, socially and commercially sustainable.'

'A New Contract with Nature' was adopted as the company's vision. See Figure 1.4. It informs all they do and how they do it. The decision to create an environmental division within Bord na Móna represented one part of manifesting this vision. Image Now, one of Ireland's leading strategic brand consultancies, was engaged to help Bord na Móna evaluate the branding and positioning options for these environmental products and services There were many questions to address. For example, were they to be seen as another division of the current business or something totally different and separate? Or, should they be associated with the main brand and if so, to what degree? Was this move to develop an environmental business to be seen as a business extension for Bord na Móna or a change of direction?

These were challenging questions that, when answered, could help shape the future development of the whole business. The process started by undertaking a significant amount of research, followed by design studies and testing. Collectively this work resulted in a clear direction being taken. These environmental products and services were not seen as core to Bord na Móna's basic remit, but there would be value in them having some level of association with it. The Bord na Móna heritage, its reputation and size, would help to provide reassurance to customers that these new services were endorsed by a company they could trust. This would apply when dealing directly with individual customers or on a business-to-business basis.

The design response was the development of a new endorsed brand that could be seen to represent these discrete environmentally related activities. It was to look different but carry a reassurance that the products and services were being provided by an established company with a well-respected reputation. Creating the new brand included the development of a new name, a motivating proposition for those employed in these non-traditional activities, and a narrative explaining what the brand stood for and why it looked different from the rest of the group.

Figure 1.5 *Anua, the endorsed brand representing Bord na Móna's environmental business activities*

The new name, Anua, is derived directly from the Irish word 'athnuaigh' meaning 'renew'. See Figure 1.5. It was chosen because it represented the effort the company was making to preserve the natural environment that had played such an important part in Bord na Móna's past whilst finding new ways of using it for the benefit of everyone in Ireland. This commitment to renewal fitted in with Bord na Móna's strategic aim to focus on innovation and the processes behind innovation, service excellence and capitalizing on their collective skills in a collaborative and coordinated approach to everything they did.

Gabriel D'Arcy maintains, 'The new areas of innovation in which the organization has become active draws directly on the innovative skills built up over years of working with nature, business, industry and customers. It is this heritage that gives the company both the expertise and the motivation to become a leader in the development of sustainable products and service.'

The new environmental business, Anua, operates as an integral part of the wider group. It is already established in the UK and United States. As more and more of Bord na Móna's activities shift away from the traditional business based on peat harvesting, to those focused on future ones less dependent on non-replaceable resources, the company will face a challenge. Leave the old name behind, along with its traditional associations, perhaps in favour of Anua, or build a new set of associations, products and services around the existing name that will enable it to continue to develop for many years to come. Such are the issues associated with change – in business requirements, concern for the environment's diminishing natural resources and a growing need to provide for an increasing population.

Often the challenge of change can be a two edged sword – uncomfortable to face, but if not faced some businesses will find irrelevance not far away. In the case described here, Bord na Móna squared up to this challenge and used design as an effective tool to explore the alternatives available to it when considering how its environmental division should be seen to operate and relate to the main business.

So, what do you do?

The sceptics will always remain so unless they are brought to a position of understanding the potential breadth and depth of the influence design can have in their organization. If you are lucky to either find a company that has successfully used design before, or a manager that has done so, then the task should be easier. Although it should not be assumed, even then, that 'design will speak for itself'. It must be given a persuasive voice and it is the responsibility of design managers and design leaders to do this. If they don't, nothing will change because there is rarely anyone else within an organization that could, or would, do it instead.

The arguments for design are comprehensive and profound. The Design Business Association, for example, runs an annual Design Effectiveness Award competition. The purpose of this competition is to identify those companies and their designers who have used design effectively to the point of changing their business. They have many examples of how design has had a transforming impact on business, government and society. There will almost certainly be many that resonate with most business situations and most industry sectors.

There is no better advocate for design than the converted sceptic, hence the position taken at the beginning of this section 'convert them with the authority of your argument not the argument of your authority'.

Chapter 2
Deliver strategy

The second issue concerns the blind spot that many people have about the role design can play in helping realize corporate strategy. The challenge is to demonstrate how design makes strategy an everyday experience for all who come into contact with the business. A key point in this argument is that design is one of the critical business resources that can manifest a strategic idea. As such it can, if properly managed make strategy tangible.

There are very few resources that can make business strategy as visible and easy to understand, and do so in a practical way that is unique to a particular business, as design. Of course it is not the only one, but it is the one where its impact can be seen and experienced most clearly.

As the differences between competitors diminish, and competitive products and services become similar in what they do, it becomes increasingly more difficult to differentiate between one business and another. For example, there is only so much you can do with cost reduction as a point of difference. Someone once said to me, 'only one company can be the cheapest – the others have to use design' – a strategic point that is difficult to argue with! A good example of this working in practice is well illustrated by the following extracts from speech and interview material Sir John Egan used when he was Chief Executive of BAA, the world's largest privately owned airport company.

Case Example – Linking design and strategy

Sir John Egan has led many large companies including being Chief Executive of Jaguar Cars and BAA. When at BAA he believed design was key to being the best in the business. He believed that design helped shape customer experience, and the quality of experience that people have of any company is one of the most influencing factors in shaping their attitude towards it. It affected loyalty, repeat purchase and the way people talk about the company to colleagues and friends. Extracts from an interview he had with Peter Lawrence 1998, Chairman of Corporate Design Foundation, elaborates more.

'As an airport operator, we must be capable of moving millions of people efficiently, but we must do more than just move people. We must be experience managers. In others words, we must create the most appropriate experience for every individual using our airports. At the same time, we must ensure that our facilities are designed so they are easy to build, efficient to run and affordable to maintain.'

Design of an airport is about more than painting and decorating. It is about much more than visual things, although this matters more than you might first think. Creating the right customer experience is a function of the facility's size and shape, its ambiance, the quality of light, visual characteristics, the behaviour of the staff, how we communicate with people – the message, the medium, and perhaps most important, the tone of voice. Design is a primary means by which we give customers what they want and what they need.'

'BAA customers want quality facilities that provide them with a continuity of quality experiences as they journey through our airports. In an industry like ours that has a project culture, it is too easy to forget that any one project is only one element of a customer's experience of that company. Projects must be seen in the context of the customer. What is it like for them to pass from one space, or experience, to another? Is the experience they have in one space appropriate to that point in their journey? Does it provide the necessary continuity to the next step on their journey?'

'At an airport, there are a variety of steps that you go through – from where you leave your motorcar, or get off the train, to when you board the airplane. It is critical that customers have the experience most appropriate to where they are on their journey. While waiting for a flight, retail shops and entertainment that excite and surprise maybe-welcome. But at the baggage drop or check-in, that's the last thing you want. There, you probably want a sense of order and calm and a feeling that someone is in control. Defining the experience that customers want becomes a criterion by which you can judge the design work you commission.'

Another good example is that of the Body Shop initiative described below. It shows well the connection between a challenging strategic aim and a successful design response. Although it could be seen as an advertising campaign rather than a design programme, in this case the differences are academic. Without a clear engaging design idea, implemented with courage and commitment, it is likely this would never have been so successful.

Case Example – Stop sex trafficking of children

The Body Shop's groundbreaking campaigns for change are legendary but in recent years other companies have been moving into this area. 2009 saw the launch of Stop Sex Trafficking of Children and Young Children, a three-year global programme in partnership with NGO ECPAT, the international network of children's rights organizations. The campaign aims to put an end to the trafficking of children and young people and guarantee their rights to be protected from exploitation.

A strong brand, visual identity and ideas were devised by the creative agency 300million to fund the project, drive petition signatures and help The Body Shop regain its campaigning authority, see Figure 2.1.

After two years the results speak for themselves. Donations to ECPAT to fund the campaign exceeded the objective by 200 per cent, and with 6.6 million signatures on petitions worldwide it is the biggest campaign ever for The Body Shop. It is already inspiring governments in eight countries to create change and former United States president Bill Clinton hailed the campaign, 'an exemplary approach to addressing a specific global challenge.'

Figure 2.1 *Stop Sex Trafficking of Children, a clear demonstration of support for the programme outside the National Gallery, London*

So, what do you do?

The idea that design can have a critical role in manifesting corporate strategy is one that would be readily accepted by designers although many prefer the comfort zone of being involved in the designing of things rather than the directing of what should be designed and why. However, this link between business strategy and design is not one that is readily accepted by business leaders.

In response to this the Design Management Institute in Boston, USA, was founded in 1975 to improve organizations worldwide through the effective integration and management of design and design principles for economic, social and environmental benefit. It does this by bringing together design practitioners, design academics and business people from all over the world to share their experiences of using design to manifest corporate strategy. Its focus has always been the management of design. Now it is becoming more active in the equally challenging field of design leadership.

The *Design Management Journal* and *DMI Review*, both publications of the Design Management Institute, publish many papers and case studies about how companies and countries are beginning to address the potential of design as a key practical resource. Many of these demonstrate the link between the strategic discussions of the boardroom and the cabinet table with the day-to-day activities of government and business. It is a good place to look for examples of how design works for strategic purpose.

Show how design can deliver corporate strategy, mission, vision or values and, in doing so, you provide a key link to design briefing, development and implementation.

Chapter 3
Demonstrate added value

The third issue is about demonstrating and measuring design's value-added impact on business. Henry Ford is reputed to have once said that it is the product not the business that pays the wages. At the heart of this profound statement was the realization that the product, and in today's world we would add the word 'service', generated the means to survive and succeed. It would seem that Henry Ford did not need to be persuaded about the role of design in his business. He could see that it needed to be the business engine, not money. He unashamedly put his product on a podium, and he knew his product could not exist without design.

These alleged words of Henry Ford are even more poignant today than when he may first have said them, particularly in the context of increased competition, consumer awareness and expectations for change. Despite this it is still very common for businesses to equate money spent on design with a line item of cost on the profit and loss account. Part of preparing the ground for design in business is to change this view to one where it is seen as adding value and, more particularly, being a worthwhile investment.

The fundamental challenge facing all businesses, irrespective of size or sector, is how to increase return on investment whilst at the same time reducing the cost of making that investment. A corresponding challenge facing design consultancies is to ensure the client sees their commitment to design as an investment with a measurable return and not a cost. There is plenty of evidence to show that design can increase brand value, reduce costs and time to market. But it is not sufficient to say it, there needs to be demonstrable evidence as well.

'design can increase brand value, reduce development costs and time to market'

Design and business measures

To get support within a business, or organization, for increasing investment in design, that investment must be seen to have a positive impact on the key business measures that the business uses to judge its own success. Designers and design managers can always get business executives' attention if they start using the language they use themselves. Let them see that design can contribute to gross and net margin, return on investment or capital employed, operating costs or the value of less tangible assets like brands.

It is hard to find a resource in business that has a more comprehensive impact on these measures than design. Yet, despite the ease with which it can be demonstrated, this opportunity is often ignored in the battle to put design onto the transformation agenda and consequently it so often fails to register.

'design is a business tool that can be measured'

Five of the most often used measures in business are listed below together with an outline of how design contributes to each of them. Definitions vary a little from one source to another but good references include the *Oxford Dictionary of Business and Management* 2009 and Graham Mott's *Accounting for Non-Accountants* 2008. For the purposes here I have kept my definitions very simple.

Gross margin

In its most basic form Gross Margin (also referred to as gross profit or gross profit margin) is the difference between the value and cost of sales. It does not include costs related to borrowings, the administration of the business or product lines, or distributing the final goods to sales outlets or wholesalers. It is invariably expressed as a percentage and is often used as a critical measure of trading performance, particularly by retailers. In their case the only way they can improve profits is by reducing the costs of purchase or production, or increasing the value of sales. See Diagram 3.1.

$$\textbf{1}\quad \textbf{GROSS MARGIN} = \frac{\text{SALES REVENUE} - \text{COST OF GOODS SOLD}}{\text{SALES REVENUE}}$$

Diagram 3.1 *Gross margin, the difference between the value and the cost of sales and often expressed as a percentage of sales*

It is generally expected that the gross profit margin generated by different companies in the same sector will be similar, although these same margins could vary enormously from sector to sector.

Being aware of these differences is very important to the designer because even small improvements in design's contribution to margin can be very significant to high turnover businesses.

Design has an impact on both parts that make up gross margin. For example, it can help reduce costs of goods sold by reducing costs of production. This is often achieved by rationalizing the number of components used, or by lowering distribution costs by making them more compact and lighter to ship. Equally, it can create additional sales revenue by giving a product wider market appeal. Gross margin is the territory that product and industrial designers work in. Sometimes design impacts one part of this ratio, sometimes on both parts at the same time.

A good example of design's impact on gross margin is the development of a new steam iron for Calor Aquaspeed that won a DBA Design Effectiveness Award.

Case Example – Calor Aquaspeed iron

Figure 3.1 Aquaspeed steam iron with a range of new innovations

When French company Calor approached Seymourpowell to develop a new version of its mid-price steam iron range Avantis, it was against the backdrop of a declining market. In the key territories of France, Germany and the UK. The overall market value of this sector had fallen by 6 per cent in 2003 and 7 per cent in 2004. Calor needed to deliver demonstrable product innovation to lead a reinvigoration of the market.

Steam irons present a complex industrial design challenge; their internal workings are inseparable from the external form, itself partly determined by ergonomic and functional considerations. Additionally, any new product design proposals had to facilitate easy manufacture at low cost and with reasonable investment. The challenge was that all this had to be achieved in a saturated market exhibiting falling sales. To demonstrate product innovation and create differentiation, the new concept also had to address some typical complaints about steam irons. In particular they are slow and messy to fill, heavy and hard to handle and have a dangerous tendency to topple off the ironing board.

Seymourpowell Foresight, the consultancy's research division, mapped out a visual history of the Calor range (known as Tefal in the UK), as well as national market analyses of key irons, charted against price and visual sophistication, and an assessment of the relative successes of brand languages used by Tefal/Calor and its competitors. This product research included the involvement of an external panel of design experts and an analysis of general, social and product trends.

From this a concept for the new product was developed and presented to Calor's engineers. See Figure 3.1. The resulting technical solutions involved rethinking the iron's basic configuration, assembly and functionality, providing Calor with a series of defendable patents. The lightweight and stable design included a completely open heel and a large trapdoor through which water could be quickly and conveniently poured.

The new model, called Aquaspeed, was launched across Europe in 2004 and achieved incredible sales. In the UK and France it was a number one best seller; in Germany it reached number four in the market, where its predecessor ranked at number 33. Share in the mid-price segment rose by 9.9 per cent year on year in Germany and by 13.3 per cent in France. Global success followed and production volumes rose by more than 25 per cent. Three national independent consumer associations voted the iron a 'Best buy'.

Another good example of designs impact on gross margin is the development of a pen injector for delivering medication.

Case Example – Solostar disposable pen injector

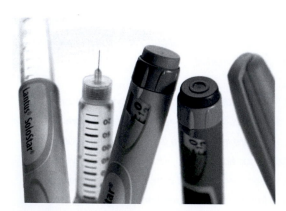

Figure 3.2 *Solostar disposable pen injector is discrete and convenient to use*

Pen injectors were introduced over 20 years ago to deliver liquid medication. They allow users to select a medication and inject this via a needle connected to a small reservoir within the pen.

In Europe, Japan and the USA pen injectors are commonly used to deliver insulin for the treatment of diabetes mellitus. In many countries injectors have largely replaced the traditional vial and syringe because they are easy and discrete to use while ensuring an accurate dose is delivered every time.

Lantus®, a new once-a-day basal insulin, was originally offered in a licensed injector device but to sustain the development of the new insulin, Sanofi, Aventis decided to begin developing its own pen in 2003. The new device, see Figure 3.2, had to offer significant improvements over all other disposable insulin devices on the market.

The design brief was suitably ambitious. To satisfy the needs of patients requiring high-dose volumes of insulin, the new pen injector had to be capable of delivering a single dose of 80 insulin units (over 30 per cent larger than all comparable devices on the market) with no penalty for comfort or convenience. Along with being extremely robust, the device also had to satisfy the very high accuracy standards outlined in ISO-11608 dealing with pen injectors for medical use.

The response to this challenge was the creation of a new product called SoloSTAR®. SoloSTAR® meets all of these requirements and exhibits significant advantages over previous devices in terms of comfort, safety and ease of use.

Since its launch in 2007, SoloSTAR® has rapidly established itself as a leading disposable pen injector for insulin, accounting for 41 per cent of all growth in the global injectable insulin market in 2008.

Net margin

The second business measure is net margin (also referred to as net profit or net profit margin). Net margin is what you are left with when the costs of administration, sales, advertising and promotion are removed and is expressed as a ratio, or percentage. It shows how much of every pound earned is turned into profits. See Diagram 3.2 where net profit is equal to sales revenue minus cost of goods sold, operating expenses, interest and tax. The rate of net margin can vary from company to company as well as from industry to industry. This is important for designers to understand. For example, very small net margins may be made by supermarkets, say less than 5 per cent annually, while some high technology companies can develop much greater margins of 15 per cent – 20 per cent or more. Over time, if net margins increase then often so does share price.

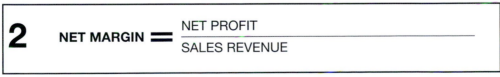

$$\textbf{2} \quad \textbf{NET MARGIN} = \frac{\text{NET PROFIT}}{\text{SALES REVENUE}}$$

Diagram 3.2 *Net margin, what you are left with when the costs of administration, sales, advertising and promotion are removed*

Design can have a significant impact on net margin. If the exercise has not been undertaken recently a significant contribution can be expected from an analysis of design's potential impact on net margin. Any such contribution goes straight to the bottom line and often comes from work in the area of communications. This is the field of graphic and digital designers, together with all the specialist support activities including photography, copywriting, programming and preparation of artwork. Savings can be made in cost of print by more prudent use of colour, increasingly by using digital communications methods and so eliminating print material altogether. Making changes to the design of operational documentation or administrative forms can also make savings in processing time and costs because errors in the information provided are eliminated. This is illustrated in a small project undertaken for An Post, the Irish Post Office.

Case Example – Irish Post Office

When An Post, see Figure 3.3, the national postal service in Ireland redesigned a number of key forms in a way that errors in completing them were virtually eliminated, the subsequent operational, behind the scenes, costs of processing those forms were drastically reduced. The return on design investment on these few items was achieved in less than one month. Although this is not strictly speaking an example of net margin working in its fullest sense it does show how elements of the net

Figure 3.3 *An Post, Irish Post Office*

margin ratio, like administration, advertising and promotion can be positively influenced by design even when its primary contribution is not aimed at sales.

Another example of designs impact on net margin is that of the UK's Department for Education and Skills 'Parent Know How' programme.

Case Example – Parent Know How

The Department for Education and Skills (DfES) needed to inform parents in the C2DE socio-economic groups about changes in policy regarding their children's education, as well as new choices and services.

Figure 3.4 *Part of the Parent Know How campaign undertaken by Department for Education and ASDA supermarkets*

These social groups are traditionally hard to reach. Often they are time-poor, low-income single parent families with no web access and have great difficulty accessing information broadcast through conventional. The traditional approach to such a campaign, above-the-line advertising which encourages people to call a free phone number and then be sent a booklet, can be expensive, slow, complex and inefficient.

The Team, a design and communications consultancy, developed a new approach to customer engagement by placing education policy on supermarket shelves. An unstaffed Parent Advice Centre called Parent Know How was created near the school clothes department in 14 ASDA stores inside the M25 ring road around London. Parents self-selected the information relevant to them, choosing from 32 booklets on topics defined according to audience segments and key stages of child development. The branding ensured clear ownership by the DfES but was complementary to the ASDA brand image, balancing authority and accessibility with a direct, inclusive and non-selling tone. In-store communications, including trolley media and point of sale, drew shoppers' attention to the centre.

The results exceeded expectations and the print run of the booklets was doubled during the ten week campaign. In total 583,780 booklets were self-selected by 145,000 parents. On average four booklets were picked up at any one time, and 85 per cent of people kept hold of the material. Follow up interviews found that parents were keeping the material for future reference. The cost per booklet was 31p, while in a comparable orthodox media campaign the cost per response was £177.99 per booklet. This makes Parent Know How over 500 times cheaper on a cost per response basis or 54,000 per cent more effective. It proved to be an inventive and effective use of public funding.

Return on investment

The third measure is Return on Investment (ROI) or Return on Capital Employed (ROCE). It is all about getting the most from the capital spend on plant, premises and people. See Diagram 3.3.

3 **RETURN ON INVESTMENT** $= \dfrac{\text{GAIN FROM INVESTMENT}}{\text{COST OF INVESTMENT}}$

Diagram 3.3 *Return on investment, getting the most out of the capital spend on plant, premises and people*

To calculate ROI, the gain (return) of an investment is divided by the cost of the investment; the result is expressed as a percentage or a ratio. It is one of the most frequently used ratios for assessing the performance of organizations.

As there are so many types of investment and related costs this ratio can be interpreted in many different ways. For example, a marketing manager may compare two different products by dividing the gross profit that each has generated by it's respective marketing expenses. A financial analyst, however, may compare the same two products using an entirely different ROI calculation, perhaps by dividing the net income of an investment by the total value of all resources that have been employed to make and sell the product.

This flexibility has a real benefit to design because it can be used in different ways by the business. For general managers ROI, or ROCE, highlights the benefits obtained by reducing investments in current or fixed assets.

Keep in mind that the calculation for ROI and, therefore its definition, can be modified to suit the situation – it all depends on what you include as returns and costs. The definition of the term in the broadest sense just attempts to measure the profitability of an investment and, as such, there is no one 'right' calculation.

The key point is that irrespective of the ROI variation that is adopted, carefully targeted design activity can have a positive impact on both sides of the dividing line. It can help to deliver a step-change in efficiency and so deliver a better return.

For example, interior and process design can be used to layout a factory for higher efficiency and throughput. Environmental design can make the factory or office a more pleasant place to work, or reduce the incidence of absenteeism from what is called 'sick building syndrome', and so improve productivity levels. Twenty per cent improvement can be expected, and is often achieved, but it does require close collaboration between designer and finance director. ROI is an area that is particularly relevant to the work of environmental and interior designers, architects and space planners. Although their work is often measured for effectiveness by using ROI calculations there are other measures that are not so financially orientated but can have a radical impact on reputation and attitude. For example appropriately designed environments improve the experience for everyone involved – from visitors and passengers to employees. A redesign of the reception area in a large London office block, for instance, led to a dramatic effect on everyone visiting the building. The problem was that the main automatic sliding doors let in cold blasts of air every time they were opened in the winter. The receptionists were very uncomfortable, hot one minute from the heating system, and cold the next because someone had entered the building. They gained a reputation for grumpy behaviour, which gradually affected the atmosphere until it became an unwelcoming environment all year round.

The redesign was relatively simple – using a revolving door in place of the automatic sliding ones. The prevailing winds could no longer affect the reception area, and behaviour changed overnight.

Two other examples are those of Waterside, British Airways's headquarters near Heathrow Airport and Oskar, one of the three largest mobile phone operators in the Czech Republic.

Case Example – Waterside, British Airways's headquarters

Figure 3.5 *Main atrium at Waterside, British Airways's headquarters, set a new benchmark for working environments and resulting productivity*

Waterside, at Heathrow Airport, is British Airways's headquarters designed by Niels Torp Architects. See Figure 3.5. According to Francis Duffy 1998, an internationally recognized authority on office design strategy, it represents in business terms nothing less than a revolution. It also happens to be an excellent example of a rapidly developing, international movement towards rethinking workplaces at the same time as reinventing work. What all such new ways of working projects have in common are two objectives: first creating greater efficiency through driving down operating costs and, second, generating more effectiveness through stimulating already razor sharp office workers to even higher feats of creativity. The intention is change – as much change as you can manage. In this case information technology was a principal agent in this process. The social method used to affect change is called change management.

From the overall shape of the office building, to the shape of meeting tables, to the use of mobile telephones – every detail of the physical and technological environment of work changed too. At Waterside design meant nothing less than determining the future of British Airways by changing the culture of the entire airline. Symbolically, not one of the 2,800 people employed there, not even the chief executive, had been allowed to work in the new building without a 'passport' indicating the achievement of certain retraining targets – new skills in the use of information technology, in organizing the use of time and space, in communication.

Case Example – Oskar mobile phone

Oskar is one of the three largest mobile phone operators in the Czech Republic. It has a strong local personality and was voted Most Dynamic Czech Company in 2004.

However, the high street experience was not living up to Oskar's brand values. The company wanted retail spaces that would create a unique and memorable environment, deliver the ideal Oskar experience and improve the transactional nature of its stores. And with the Czech market for mobile phones at near saturation (90 per cent of the population have a mobile phone) the stores also needed to attract new, high-value, younger consumers.

Enterprise IG (now renamed as The Brand Union) created a store that felt playful, distinctive and surprising. Unexpected elements, for example each store contains a real tree, embody the brand's ethos of vitality and growth. Customers can explore the interfaces of live phones on purpose-built seating and a new queuing system using characters rather than numbers, leaving people free to browse at their leisure. All-in-one pods combine cash desks with interactive self-help tools to help break down boundaries between staff and customers.

Sales in renovated stores have increased by 10 per cent and new stores hit sales targets. 98 per cent of visitors left the store with positive or very positive feelings, compared to a benchmark of 81 per cent in the old stores. 78 per cent rated the queuing system as good or very good; 58 per cent used it straight away without any help from staff. 80 per cent are using the all-in-one pod spontaneously; 76 per cent said the pod helped them find information without having to ask a member of staff. Nine out of ten customers found what they were looking for – a 27 per cent increase on the previous benchmark. The new stores have resulted in more spontaneous visits (57 per cent of visits are now unplanned) and customers are browsing for longer – with twice as many staying more than 30 minutes in the store.

Operating costs

The fourth business measure is operating costs or overheads. These are the costs associated with administering a business on a day-to-day basis. Operating costs include both fixed costs and variable costs such as manufacturing overheads, administration, selling, distribution, research and development. Fixed costs remain the same regardless of the number of products produced, whereas variable costs, such as materials, can vary according to the volume of production. Operating costs can mean different things to different companies and as a consequence the design interventions can also vary. For example they can include:

- Efficiencies in production. For example, within the factory, by designing one component to do two jobs where two were needed before. Or utilizing the design of digital communications to reach either a wider audience or to tailor messages to specific target groups.

- Cost to buy verses cost to own. For example, the purchase of low-cost school furniture may have a lower impact on revenue budgets in any one year than that which is 50 per cent dearer. But, the latter lasts four times longer because of how it is designed, it may be much cheaper to own in the long run. The same argument can be applied to equipment that is procured for use in the production process or the design of buildings and infrastructure systems.

- Human resource utilization. This aspect of business is often ignored by designers and design leaders but can be a rich source of positive design impact. For example, by reducing walking distances for staff on retail selling floors, or creating more efficient hospital ward layouts where nursing staff have clearer lines of sight to a higher number of patients at any one time.

- Space planning and rationalization. For example at an airport departures security screening or when laying out queuing lines at post office counters.

Most aspects of operational costs are an opportunity for positive design contributions and for demonstrating design value. A good example of this is Unilever's colour harmonization programme.

Case Example – Unilever colour harmonization

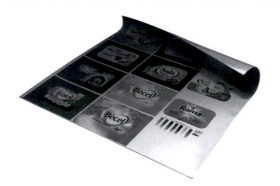

To help Unilever effectively compete in the Spreads & Cooking Category (SCC), designers had traditionally erred towards the selection of different spot inks when redesigning and extending the brand range. This meant that the number of inks used to print the entire SCC range had increased to over 100, a technical complexity that resulted in huge production costs.

Figure 3.6 *Unilever color harmonization programme had a significant impact on the operating costs of printing packaging material*

In 2005 a decision was taken to reduce those print costs without detriment to the 'look and feel' of the brands. Working with Unilever's in-house technical team their design consultants, LHF Design, found a way to faithfully reproduce 150 different SCC brands using a fixed and constant set of just six inks, see Figure 3.6.

The result was lower print fixed cost allocations leading to lower print costs. 'Project Rainbow' was a commercial success with brand value actually enhanced. Approximately 10 per cent of the annual print spend on tubs was saved and over five years 250 working days were saved. As the print quality was guaranteed by the design consultants there was no need for the traditional visit to the presses by a member of the marketing team for the purpose of quality control.

Brand asset

The fifth business measure is brand asset, or brand equity, and is the most intangible of
the measures.

In marketing terms brand assets are often described as a quality that goes beyond a product's basic
functional purpose. The value of this asset is often based on loyalty to the brand or brand name,
the level of recognition it has or its perceived value. Market share can change, sometimes up and
sometimes down depending on the goodwill associated with the brand. But it must be managed
very carefully because of its potential to have an immediate affect on business, both positively
and negatively.

For example, Gerald Ratner wiped approximately £500 million from the value of Ratners Jewellers
with one speech at the Institute of Directors in 1991. He said, 'We also do cut-glass sherry decanters
complete with six glasses on a silver-plated tray that your butler can serve you drinks on, all for
£4.95. People asked me how can we sell this for such a low price? I say, because it's total crap.'

Conversely, once Apple announced it was to produce a new version of the iPhone there were queues
stretching around the block leading to every shop that was to stock them. Both examples serve to
illustrate the critical nature of brand asset.

One simple way of thinking about brand asset is to consider it in terms of being a living business
asset. Another is to consider it in terms of the value of customer experience. Increasingly a value is
being placed on this. Sometimes like Tesco and Marriot Hotel Group they feature its importance in
leading parts of their annual reports, sometimes independent analysts like those at Interbrand try to
put a value on them, often measured in the billions of dollars.

Putting a value on brand asset is, however, a very controversial subject. Some commentators say
that measuring an invisible asset like brand is twaddle, some say that you can take a scientific
approach to it and measure it against a number of criteria. I am of the view that valuing brand assets
is all about gauging corporate reputation. Understanding how confident stakeholders are in what
the company does and how it does it. This may be largely anecdotal, although there are always
research companies that will tell you even anecdotes can be turned into scientific or statistical data.
There seems little doubt that if confidence is rising, then investment in design is doing the right
things. Conversely, if confidence is falling then examine the customer experience to see where the
weaknesses are and redesign accordingly.

'when design investment is strategically focused and coherently managed then the value of the business and its brands increases'

An innovative and efficient branding strategy will be able to reduce risk and spread the product's name across the market, increasing the brand value. This holds true for domestic and global markets alike. A company must first determine its branding strategy and establish its position or it will not be able to build a strong brand identity.

While intangible assets don't have the obvious physical value of a factory or it's equipment, they can prove very valuable for a firm and can be critical to its long-term success or failure. For example, a company such as Coca-Cola wouldn't be nearly as successful were it not for the high value obtained through its brand name recognition. Although brand recognition is not a physical asset that you can see or touch, its positive affects on bottom-line profits can prove extremely valuable to firms whose brand strength drives global sales year after year.

At a less esoteric level, the spend normally associated with brand management also offers opportunities of cost saving and strengthening differentiation. For example, it is critical that all the money spent on design works to build the brand, what it stands for, the nature and quality of customer experience associated with it, the values and reputation of the business.

So, what do you do?

Design effectiveness can be measured in many ways – impact on gross margin, net margin and ROCE; increase in market share, share price and market penetration; the creation of new markets and new products, improved recruitment and increased loyalty; the speed of product development and time to market. All positive impacts and easily identified.

There is also considerable potential to save significant sums of money through the strategic management of design development of products, facilities and communications. The greater the size and complexity of the projects, and the more multidisciplinary the team structure, the greater the potential for savings or losses. Design managers and design leaders must learn how to do this, and it is of equal relevance to those working within an organization as well as in consultancies.

Internally, if design managers demonstrate these benefits then the business case for greater design investment becomes a lot easier to make. They must, however, emphasize that design spend, when managed properly, is not a cost to the business, but rather an investment and its impact can be measured in the same way as most other investments the business makes.

Externally, it is the most important challenge to address for the successful marketing of design consultancy services. This will happen with much less effort if consultancies understand better how their work can positively affect these critical business measures. External people usually have an advantage over their 'internal' design management colleagues because they can usually draw on a greater variety of case studies to make and substantiate their argument.

Creating value through design is a multiskilled task where designer and client work as a fully integrated team. To be effective they must be clear what it is they are trying to achieve and have a belief in the potential impact of their collaboration. However it is only by understanding what to expect from the investment in design that confidence will build to continue with that collaboration.

Whether working within an organization, or in a consultancy providing design services, design managers have the responsibility to ensure their clients fully understand the potential of the design investment they plan to make. There is no option, design managers are required to do this. If they don't it should not be assumed that business leaders will be inspired to know how to.

Chapter 4
Build reputation

The fourth issue to confront when preparing the ground for effective use of design concerns the role it plays in building corporate reputation. The responsibility for this rarely rests with one person or department. Often it is assumed by Public Relations, sometimes by Marketing, rarely by Design. It is, of course, the collective responsibility of many people ultimately led by the chief executive.

The point often not appreciated is that design can make a profound contribution to corporate reputation through the development and management of customer experience at every point of contact they have with the business. These encounters are numerous and can come from using the products or services the company offers, through the way the company explains what it does and how it does it, through the facilities it uses to provide the services or make the products available, and through the behaviour of the people the company employs in what it does.

Reputation is also built or damaged by the company interface with all other stakeholders, including staff. Designing clear and easily understood financial reports for investors, or comfortable and pleasant work and rest places for employees, are all opportunities for building reputation. In fact, getting the reputation right for internal stakeholders is a powerful way of getting it right for external ones. Not forgetting that many individuals are both!

The client, whether they are an internal colleague or manager commissioning work from an external design consultant, may always be looking at the product, service, communications or operational environments in isolation from the other areas of design influence. If so, there is a real opportunity to build a better, sustainable, reputation through a comprehensive, systematic and co-coordinated approach to the use of design.

Increasingly company success is less dependent on how well its products work. Customers presume they will! This is simply the price for being a player in the selected industry or marketplace. What is much more important to the user is the experience they have when using the product or service. Design is an extremely effective resource that can be used to shape these customer experiences, in general and specific ways.

A detailed analysis of customer experience is critical if the company is serious in using every opportunity to ensure their values are consistently delivered. This analysis also represents a powerful opportunity for using design as a tool to deliver these values in a relevant, meaningful, way.

It is not too much of an assumption to make that once the customer experience is well managed then the reputation of the business is enhanced and so is its potential profitability. Of course the reverse is also true! And the process of designing is critical in shaping every point of contact between company and customer. In this way design resources can make a very useful contribution to enhancing an organization's reputation. Reputation is something that can, to a large extent, be controlled and design is a useful tool in this process. It is worth emphasizing the point that if reputation is not overtly managed using all appropriate resources, including focused design effort, then it will be out of control, it will be left to chance and almost certainly suffer badly as a result.

Managing reputation is something that has already entered the digital world. Tools for managing information about a company on social media channels, and managing search results for its name, are well established. The presentation of that information, the tone of voice adopted by it and clarity of the message are all within the designer's remit. New skills are being developed all the time to enable designer's work in this field and help organizations take control of not only what they say about themselves but what others are saying too.

This technology will become an increasingly important aspect of reputation management and so the need to utilize its full potential will be key. Not only is it an outward facing tool but also a tool that can be used to measure changes in reputation over time. For example by:

- tracking of the success of marketing, communication or brand campaigns both in terms of volume of conversation and the overall impact on reputation;
- tracking the success of the brand's reputation over time;
- helping to understand the relationship between volume of conversation and brand reputation;
- allowing for the comparison of the success of various campaigns in increasing awareness and improving the brand perception.

Of course design is not the only resource available to a business in the effort to build reputation but it is significant. After all it does contribute in a major way to how products and buildings work, how information is conveyed and the behaviour of front-line staff in how well they deliver services. The two short case examples below show different aspects of design's influence on reputation management.

Case Example – King's College London recruitment

The Florence Nightingale School of Nursing & Midwifery at King's College London was looking to increase recruitment of quality students and communicate its position as the best university for nursing and midwifery programmes. They wanted to cut through the noise of increasing competition with a design of communication programme that was radically different to their previous ad hoc and disjointed campaigns.

Figure 4.1 *The Kings College recruitment campaign aimed at increasing the level of quality students to the Florence Nightingale School of Nursing and Midwifery*

999Design's solution drew upon the strong emotions associated with the nursing profession, bringing them to life through a mix of strong typography, bold colours and dynamic imagery. The design concept was adaptable to the various audiences and true to the values of both the school and the profession. 999Design created a compelling suite of communication collateral that had real resonance and set King's apart from the crowd.

Undergraduate applications increased by 18 per cent for the 2010/11 academic year, and postgraduate applications by an unprecedented 1,195 per cent. The increase in applications by international postgraduates was particularly important for revenue generation. In July of that year, for the first time ever, it looked likely that the school would not need to go through the student clearing process. This meant a saving of £11,800 in design and advertising costs, and 300 man-hours, see Figure 4.1.

Case Example – Culture and Sport Glasgow

Culture & Sport Glasgow (CSG) was formed in 2007 as a charitable division of Glasgow City Council. Its remit was to deliver cultural and sporting services to Scotland's largest and most diverse city. However, research showed that although there was affinity with many of the services run by CSG, such as museums and libraries, there was little public awareness of the overall organization and what it did.

Figure 4.2 *Culture and Sport Glasgow*

Tayburn, the Scottish design consultancy retained to address this challenge, was to take this anonymous and undervalued public sector service and reinvent it as a modern, relevant and customer-focused leisure brand, see Figure 4.2. They started by assessing the current brand structure (with over 50 brands), created a new parent brand with eight categories and developed a clear and coherent communications system. One year after the brand was launched, Glasgow Life delivered 14.4 million customer occasions, 800,000 more than the year prior to launch and 400 per cent more than they were expecting. The number of visits to the website was up 830 per cent in one year, with over three million users, up 750 per cent on previous web presences. In 2010/11 Glasgow Life, under the new corporate brand, raised £480K in corporate sponsorship; a 60 per cent increase against the levels in 2008/9.

So, what do you do?

Those people responsible for design activity in the business need to demonstrate the opportunities for using it to manage reputation through delivering the most appropriate customer experience in line with corporate strategic intent. This experience can be physical, as in the interaction with a product or building, or it can be virtual via the use of social media or targeted demographic messaging. Whichever, this puts design in the firing line of helping build reputation. To do this, adopt an attitude of standing in the shoes of the customer – it is a good place to start, understanding every small step, every interaction, so that it can be crafted to be a potential contributor to raising the standard of an organization's overall reputation.

Chapter 5
Design spend

This last chapter in the section concerned with 'preparing the ground' is less to do with a prejudice and more to do with an ignorance regarding design spend. If nothing else has worked so far in establishing a better understanding of how design can be made to work harder in an organization then this is likely to engage managers, if for no other reason than because we are talking about the money side of business.

Why do I say this? Because if you ask the management team, 'Do you know how much you spend on design, do you know who is spending it, where is it being spent and what is it being spent on?' most will not be able to answer with any certainty or accuracy. Persuade the finance director that this is worth looking into and they could well become one of design's greatest advocates. In my experience it is true to say that the money spent on design is usually the largest single sum the board of most companies knows the least about.

'the money spent on design is usually the largest single sum that the board of most companies knows the least about'

This may seem an extraordinary statement to make but it is invariably true. Never be afraid to ask this question, 'Does anyone in the business have an overview of what is classed as design spend?' Most companies don't! The chances are that many people are spending money on design, many not even realizing that is what they are doing:

- whether manufacturing new products and using industrial designers;
- or service companies using the skills of a communications designer to get their message across to a geographically widespread marketplace;
- or retailers dependent on interior designers to differentiate their particular proposition on the high street;
- or research and development organizations using the creative skills of development designers to explore ideas beyond the normal environment in which the company works;

- or government departments wanting to use creative resources to develop briefs for more versatile classrooms;
- or architects helping to create more space in confined public environments;
- or imagination laboratories trying to better understand changes we can expect in the future;
- or the CEO's office preparing for presentations at an annual general meeting;
- or information designers disseminating data in order to make public transport timetabling easier to understand;
- or the finance director preparing data for the annual report.

All of which leads to the inevitable conclusion – someone in the business must be made responsible for the collective effect of design investment. If this is ignored then the opportunity of maximizing return on assets will be missed which, in turn, will deprive shareholders of corporate wealth.

Although the responsibility for design must remain with the senior management team, design mangers and design leaders are in a uniquely informed position to raise the issue, to illustrate its potential and then develop the argument for addressing the lack of information to decide what to do about it.

Problems arise when design investment is uncoordinated, often because responsibility for it is so diverse. This means that design spend is invariably underestimated in business simply because the responsibility for it lies with so many people, in different departments and down through all layers of the management hierarchy. If each person commissioning design does so with no reference to how the rest of the business is doing so, then customers will get mixed messages, become confused about a company's offer and end up going somewhere else.

As a consequence of this lack of coordination, huge sums of money are wasted. This is not only because the effort lacks strategic focus, but also because money is spent on redesigning things that have already been designed, simply because no one knew it had been done before. Equally, uncoordinated communications design can lead to one part of the company saying one thing about itself and another part saying something quite different. Sometimes these messages are so contradictory that it would seem they were talking about a completely different business.

Always remember that every pound spent on design says something about the company spending it. Some companies spend a lot on design, which means they say a lot about themselves. The real issue then becomes, 'Are they saying the right thing, and is anyone managing or directing the investment in design so that it makes clear what they want to say and what the company stands for?'

However, if every pound spent on design is focused on delivering those things that provide differentiation, and doing so in a way that is coherent with all the rest of the company's investment in it, then the consumer's understanding and confidence in the company increases, and with that so does the value of the company brand.

Slowly, more and more organizations are realizing design impacts on more and more of their day-to-day activities. Whether it is a physical product that is made or purchased to resell, a service package that is provided, an environment in which products are made or sold, or a piece of communication that tells people about what a company does, it needs to be designed by someone.

How effectively this is done depends on the skill of the team creating it and the skill of the client in defining what is needed in the first place. For a design solution to work in the marketplace depends also on whether or not it is seen in isolation, or as part of a co-coordinated activity, every piece of which is directed at manifesting a company's basic proposition in that marketplace.

Here are two examples of how a focused approach to design can make a real difference.

Case Example – Legal & General brand and culture change

Figure 5.1 Legal & General strategic repositioning took employees through a two-year engagement journey, from awareness and understanding to commitment, action and advocacy

In 2009, Legal & General launched Every Day Matters, the strategy and visual identity around which the business planned to deliver its objectives. The following year, Legal & General's Chief Executive outlined plans for them to become a single, unified brand. For an organization of such size and complexity, this was never going to be an easy task.

Smith & Milton were appointed to align all employees behind Every Day Matters, and to ensure all communications were consistent, compelling and clear. Smith & Milton conducted a rigorous brand audit and created a new flexible identity, part of which can be seen in Figure 5.1. They then took Legal & General's employees through a two-year engagement journey, from awareness and understanding to commitment, action and advocacy.

As a result of this work, Legal & General have seen a 24 per cent rise in brand value, a 16 per cent increase in advocacy and brand attraction, and best-ever employee engagement and consumer brand performance scores. Legal & General's share price has also risen 465 per cent faster than the rest of the market.

Case Example – McDonald's global packaging

Figure 5.2 *McDonald's global packaging design management system helped deliver unique solutions in 39 cultural versions in 24 language variants*

McDonald's were keen to change consumer perceptions by delivering a 'food quality' story in a consistent and effective way, a story that would connect with 60 million customers a day in 118 countries. Boxer Creative design agency was appointed to meet this challenging brief. They began by creating a 'brand bloodline' to define McDonald's global packaging equities. To connect with customers at a local level, Boxer Creative then devised a design management system that offered genuine flexibility. A movie was made to communicate the brand packaging strategy and food quality story to internal stakeholders. This led to the new packaging being embraced and endorsed by McDonald's Global Executive Leadership. Face-to-face and virtual workshops also helped to motivate, educate and inspire the global franchises on how to use the design guidelines. Boxer Creative's design management system helped to deliver 1,500 unique packaging design solutions in 39 cultural versions and 24 language variants, see Figure 5.2. It became the first McDonald's marketing initiative to achieve 100 per cent global acceptance.

So, what do you do?

An easy answer would be to undertake an internal audit to find out who is doing what with design and assess what relationship these, inevitably many, activities have with each other and with the wider corporate aims of the business. However, this is much easier said than done and the topic is expanded upon later in Chapter 8. Suffice to say that the most important thing to establish at this point is the opportunity to save money through the reduction of duplicated design effort. The next is to achieve greater impact and return on the investment in design through strategically focused direction of all design activities.

Once this has been achieved it is well worth referencing the study that Tom Lockwood 2007 undertook when President of the Design Management Institute. It is called Design Value: A Framework for Measurement, and identifies Ten categories in which design value and performance can be evaluated. They vary from time-to-market and cost savings to customer satisfaction and the ability to influence preferences. All of them should serve as useful ammunition for the designer, design manager and business executive.

Chapter 6
Summary of Part One – Preparing the ground

A design manager's first challenge is to demonstrate that design matters to the business. Equally challenging for these businesses is to recognize that this resource called 'design' is of critical value to them.

Invariably businesses do not:
- manage design as an investment, rather it is usually considered and treated as a cost;
- recognize the link between the management of design activity and its relevance to reputation management;
- know how much they spend on design – it is often the largest sum of money the company's board knows the least about;
- have anyone accountable for the overall spend on design or its affect on stakeholder perception,
- recognize the role design can play in delivering strategic intent;
- appreciate the full context for design in their business and so fail to understand what needs managing;
- have clear management systems for design that fit with how other investment issues are handled;
- understand how they can use non-design staff to make effective design investment decisions;
- use the spend on design in one area to lever benefit in another.

This chapter has outlined a number of key arguments that can be used to prepare the ground for design to be managed effectively – at least to open the eyes of some managers who can facilitate change. As a result, the business or organization will have taken the first critical step in making design work, in leading through design. The second part of this book goes into some detail as to how you can build on this awareness and deliver design-driven-change in line with corporate aims.

Part Two – The how and what of delivery

Part Two of this book is concerned with the practical issues of making design effective and working to advantage. It deals with the different roles of design managers and design leaders in this process; how to assess the state of design in a business or organization; some processes for managing and leading design; and the behavioural styles needed for effective design management, functional design leadership and being a better design client.

Once some managers – even one will do – have seen that design could become a relevant and wealth-creating resource within an organization, what should be done to clearly demonstrate this ability and how should it be carried out? Although this will vary from one business or organization to another, two things are very important at this stage.

First, any action needs to be taken quickly to capitalize on the support already gained. The idea is to create a snowball effect with one successful design intervention leading to another.

Second, this action needs to be appropriate. In other words, whatever is done first should be in response to a perceived and acknowledged business need, no matter how small that is. The important thing is to build confidence that this design resource should be taken seriously by the business investing in it. Also, and this is really important for the longevity of design's influence in the business, it should be something that can be owned by the manager who is sponsoring the action. After all, the design manager knows the value of what he or she can bring. The critical issue is for this realization to be owned by the general managers in the business. Persuade one manager that design is of value and the others will, in time, follow.

The role that design can play in any organization varies from one place within that organization to another. For example, you may well find that it plays a very active part in the product development and manufacturing process but quite a superficial one in the communication and marketing departments. The reverse can be equally true. It may be that design is not seen as a key tool at all, that it is still suffering, by and large, from the sceptical attitudes described earlier.

As we have seen in Part One, the potential of design is enormous. It will, of course vary depending on the history of the business, previous experiences the managers in the business have with design and the willingness of these managers to embrace challenges and change. You can be sure that managing and leading design will always result in challenge and change!

There is no point in trying to superimpose any preconceived idea of a standardized approach to making design work, or design management structure, on to a business. You can't. It doesn't work like that. It must be made to fit the culture and current practices of the business. Equally, using design as a business leadership resource (sometimes it is called 'leading through design'), or using design to help achieve strategic intent, can only work once the organization has an understanding of what design can do. They also need to understand how it can work to achieve short and longer-term tactical and strategic advantage.

The processes for managing design and leading through design should be developed to fit in with all the other processes of the business. In this way you are likely to eliminate one of the commonly held views about design – that it needs special people with special knowledge who somehow make it all happen as if by magic. It may well need the first and the second, but definitely not the third!

None of this is easy, neither is it something that happens over night. However, if you are seen to be trying to understand how:

- the business works;
- decisions get made;
- those decisions are implemented;
- it assesses investment;
- it measures return on that investment;
- it looks at the future of the business;
- it behaves when managing change;

and relate that to the way design might be made to work within the organization, then you stand a chance of being given a fair hearing.

Your argument becomes even stronger if it is done without pleading any special case for design to be treated differently to any other resource, or process, the company may employ.

Chapter 7
Managing and leading

This chapter is divided into two parts. The first looks at the roles and
responsibilities of design managers and the second, similarly, at those of
design leaders. It provides guidance on how best to integrate these roles
into an organization's DNA. It will act as an important precursor to Chapter
8, which examines different ways of assessing the current and potential
role design can play in developing a successful business, organization
or enterprise.

In the same way as there are fundamental differences between leadership and management in
general business administration, so there are similarly fundamental, clear and important differences
between design management and design leadership. These differences were initially outlined at
the Design Leadership Forum when I addressed their inaugural session, London 2002 and were
subsequently issued as a paper recording the event. The key point to establish here is that design
leadership is not a new buzzword for an older subject, design management. It is an important
business resource and activity in its own right.

In summary, design management is essentially reactive while design leadership is essentially
proactive. The difference between reactive management and proactive leadership generally lies in
asking the right questions. Peter Ellyard, at the Preferred Futures Institute in Australia and former
advisor to the United Nations, sums up the fundamental differences between the two by asking us to
consider not what the future will be like, but what it should be like?

This provides some useful insights.

There is a fundamental difference between the skills needed to address both issues. Ellyard goes on
to say that management is essentially about responding to a given business situation. The basic skill
required is about facilitating a change process. This is at the core of what design managers do.

On the other hand leadership is about describing what the future will, or needs to be like, and then
choosing the direction to take to get there. This is at the core of what design leaders do.

'design leadership helps define the future, design management provides the tools for getting there'

The critical point is this – each area of expertise depends on the other for its relevance and effectiveness to business. Without design leadership, you don't know where you are going; without design management, you don't know how you are going to get there. One is a stepping-stone to the other. Both are critically important to business and both are necessary in order to maximize value from design activity and investment.

Roles and responsibilities of design managers

Fundamentally, design management is about delivering successful design solutions in an efficient, cost-effective way. As the problems they address are often very complex, design managers need to have a deep understanding of how their particular organization works, administratively and culturally, and have mastered a wide range of skills for them to be effective.

When a new design manager is appointed to a business, or when a business asks, 'How well are we managing design?' it is necessary to look at the business with a critical eye before this can be answered with any authority. This is not supposed to represent a design management audit, nor will the answers to the questions below represent the totality of the work to be done in this area. They will however give some useful insights.

- How is design currently managed; who does it, at what cost, to what end, what organizational systems are in place for assessing design work, how are decisions made about it?
- What design content is being managed?
- What is currently being designed and what is planned for the future?
- What disciplines are being used, which design consultancies are retained by the company and how are they selected?
- What is the relationship between any internal designers and those design consultancies engaged from outside?
- What, if any, is the relationship between design project activity and the strategic aims of the business?
- How do managers within the business view design and what experience do they have of using design?
- What reward mechanisms are in place for the effective use of design?
- How does design work get commissioned, who writes and approves the briefs, what return is the company getting from its design spend?

If the business cannot easily answer these questions satisfactorily then the chances are design is not being managed at all. Partial answers are not enough if the business wants to capitalize on the potential of its design investment. In these circumstances the business should appoint someone with specific design management responsibilities.

But, what are these responsibilities? What does a design manager have to do to make the investment in them, and the wider investment in design projects, worthwhile? In broad terms the fundamental roles and responsibilities at the core of what design managers do can be summed up under five headings. These are described in outline below. They are in no particular order of importance. They can be used as the content basis of a job description, or as a brief for a design management consultancy to act in this role while the organization finds someone, either from within its own staff or as a new recruit. However, a word of caution about the task. Although at first glance the role of a design manager may seem to suggest it would be of part-time status, with all but the smallest businesses it will almost certainly be a full-time activity. It is difficult to share this work with the responsibilities of being, for example, a marketing manager or part of an advertising and media department, or a member of research and development. I have seen this attempted but with little effectiveness.

The responsibilities described below can apply to either a 'corporate', centrally placed, design manager, or to one located in an 'operating' division of a business. In some companies both types of design managers are employed – hopefully, working in unison with each other!

Design management responsibility 1: Design people

The first responsibility is concerned with managing design people, and there are usually many more of these than you might think. By design people I mean everyone involved in the design activity in some way or another whether they are design trained or not.

Here is a generic list that might help in identifying who these people are in any particular industry, company or organization:

End-users and customers

This is the obvious place to start. I distinguish between end-users and customers because their needs are often very different. I also distinguish between domestic customers, as in the world of retail, and business-to-business customers where the most common showcase is likely to be a trade fair or showroom. Those customers who buy things to resell will have design-related issues to do with storage, handling and displaying for example. On the other hand the end-users will have the more obvious requirements of functionality, fitness for purpose, style, tactility and, where appropriate, that special wow factor. The requirements of each of these groups need to be well understood.

Stakeholders

These people have an interest in the final result of the design work but are not directly involved in its production or, sometimes, in its use. These people can provide real additional insights into what is needed to be incorporated into the final design solution, for example in the case of incorporating advances in technical solutions relevant to the service or product. Other times stakeholders can present real obstacles to progressing the design work, for example when specialist pressure groups are involved in planning for new public facilities like airports or motorways. The issue is not so much which stakeholders are right and which are wrong, it is more to do with giving proper consideration to their particular points of view.

Clients

This is a very special group of 'design people' that design managers need to interface with. They may be internal colleagues or managers who commission the design management work from external consultants. They are the people with the business issue that needs addressing and who may have drafted the initial brief for the design work. Not forgetting that, for the consultant, they may also be the person who authorizes payment of their invoices. Whatever the contractual relationship might be the design manager has a special responsibility to the client and therefore the management of that relationship is critical to the success of the work. In every case, but especially when the client and the design manager both work for the same company, it pays great dividends for these relationships to be built on trust and understanding. An easy thing to say but not always easy to achieve!

Consultants

They often represent the primary source for the design work and to get the best from them requires a carefully managed relationship. Long gone are the days when the client's design manager simply says, 'This is what I want and this is how you do it.' Getting the best from the design consultant requires a well-developed relationship with both parties respecting each other and working together to produce the best response to the business problem. On large projects, especially ones involving high levels of capital expenditure, it is likely that there will be many different consultants. For example, when designing transport infrastructures there may be architects, interior designers, civil and structural engineering designers, space planners, lighting designers and landscape designers.

A similar number of different designers might also be involved with the introduction of a new manufactured product which may require industrial designers, electrical and mechanical engineering design, packaging designers, graphic and digital design specialists and advertising agencies. This represents a very significant task for the design manager in human relations management, in co-coordinating effort, design interface management and consolidating a final design solution.

Staff designers

These people are permanent employees of the company. They are sometimes grouped together into a design department, but not always. When assembled as an internal resource, located in one part of the business but supplying services to all parts, it presents very particular challenges. For example, ensuring that the level of resource is sufficiently high to respond quickly to demands from internal stakeholders but not so high that productivity levels for the department as a whole are low. In some cases the management task is made more complex when the designers are spread out across the business in different departments. For example, in some companies I have worked with there have been staff designers working in public relations, advertising and publicity, architecture and planning, marketing and product development departments. Each with their own reporting lines, briefs and budgets. In these circumstances a centrally placed design manager begins to understand the difference between management and leadership. But more of that later.

Technical specialists

Thes are people who have industry-specific expertise like research and development staff in pharmaceutical companies, or programmers for computer manufacturers, or material technologists for packaging or specialist clothing. They are similar to the consultants group described above except that they tend to be internal experts rather than external ones. Their input into design projects is critical and must be integrated at the right time to get the best from the collective effort of the whole team. This invariably means their early involvement in a project as their input can often mean a new approach to solving the problem not always possible if introduced later in the process.

Opinion formers

These people outside the organization have a wider view about what is happening in the industry. They are often editors of technical journals or representatives of special interest groups. These can include historical societies who have an interest in the protection of ancient buildings that might be affected by plans for modernization of a rail station. They may be residential pressure groups concerned about a new high-rise apartment block, representatives of disadvantaged groups like those with sight impairment and the design of signing systems in public transport or printed instructions on food packaging. They could be representatives of elderly people concerned with the design of controls for a television or the use of kitchen appliances. The design manager needs to identify these opinion formers and develop a relationship with them to understand their views, interests and, sometimes, concerns. I have met these people in every organization I have worked with. When approached in the right way they can be very helpful in developing a comprehensive understanding of any issues that need to be addressed during the design work. When approached in the wrong way they can be confrontational and counter-productive, sometimes raising objections to the extent that causes very costly delays. All because they were not consulted earlier enough in the design process.

Suppliers

They provide the materials and components used in the development of a new product or aspects of it. Understanding the characteristics of what is being supplied, or finding alternative suppliers who can offer better solutions, is often left in the hands of the design manager. Certainly developing a good working relationship with suppliers such that their expertise can be incorporated into the design proposals is often key to creating a new product with differentiating characteristics.

Specialist outsiders

These people have expertise in a business, market or industry that, on the face of it, may have nothing to do with your own organization or project. These people can reveal an insight into their world, where changes they expect to occur could have a bearing on your future design plans. It is often a good idea to step outside your own industry and explore others that could have a bearing on how your own may need to develop or change more significantly. The design manager needs to be alert to these opportunities or requirements and introduce these 'specialist outsiders' when pertinent.

Engaging with these design people is a specialist skill and it does not fall to everyone to be a good manager. I have often met excellent designers, highly creative and insightful, who have little sensitivity as to how people can be motivated, led and encouraged to contribute to a project or a team. A good operator does not automatically make a good manager, and a good manager does not necessarily make a good leader.

There is one set of skills to learn when managing designers if you are a design-trained person yourself. Particularly being impartial when it comes to critiquing work or successfully representing the business perspective when guiding the work of designers.

There is another set of skills to learn if you are not design trained, particularly coming to terms with the way designers work, especially the iterative process that they are often engaged in. The fact is that good design managers can come from either side of the design/management divide.

What is important for all practitioners is to develop the skill of being comfortable in straddling both the design and business disciplines and being able to represent both sets of interests at the same time.

Design management responsibility 2: Design budgets

At the highest level this means securing the necessary budgets for design work and ensuring the maximum value is derived from such expenditure. Securing the budget in the first place is often a major challenge. Sometimes the money can come from one department; sometimes it comes from a combination of revenue budgets from different departments. Unless the sums required are small it is usually the case that approval from a management board or executive committee is needed to spend the money. This approval is dependent on the submission of a business case which outlines the cost/ benefit argument for the project. This in turn requires a good understanding of the likely design costs before the work is commissioned and so a close relationship with the industry, how it works and how it charges for that work, is essential.

In some situations the design manager will have their own annual budget for design work. Even in this situation it is usually the case that approval for drawing down against that budget will still be required. However, unless an annual budget is prepared in the first place for anticipated work then there will be no money available when the time comes. It is the responsibility of the design manager to ensure that appropriate levels of funding are available either centrally, to be apportioned as needed across the business, or within each of its operational divisions. Either way it requires the design manager to be on the pulse of the business. A close working relationship with other managers who may have a requirement for any design work is a prerequiste for sucess.

Design management responsibility 3: Design timetables

Anyone who has tried, for example, to manage the design activity involved in developing and launching a new product knows how difficult managing to a timetable can be. In most cases, getting the timetable wrong, or letting it slip, can be very costly.

For instance, I have seen companies commission rapid prototyping of new product concepts from suppliers in the Far East. This is a common practice. However, if that work is not delivered in time for presentation at a predetermined board meeting then a new product launch can be delayed for months before another slot in its agenda can be found. This can mean either a significant loss of potential revenue from that product in the marketplace or a complete cancellation of the project because the market opportunity will have been missed. Another example concerns the cost of delay in opening a new retail complex in a town centre or airport as a result of poor project or design management. Such delays can result in the loss of massive revenue streams, sometimes measured in millions of pounds. Such is the pressure on design managers.

An early challenge in preparing design timetables is assessing how long the 'creative' part of the project will take to complete. Even the most experienced designers sometimes find that resolving a problem takes longer than anyone could have reasonably anticipated. When faced with a blank piece of paper or, more likely, a blank computer screen, knowing how long it will take for a design solution to be developed is a real challenge. But it must be done, and success depends on much that we have already discussed – in particular the relationships with potential design suppliers and the early preparation of anticipated design budgets for future work.

A real help in preparing design project timetables is to be sure exactly what it is you are expecting from the designers. Of course this should be in the brief but so often is not. Designers and clients can be extremely sloppy when it comes to this! Be specific about how many 'deliverables', in terms of design concepts, how much development and application work you are expecting, prototypes and so on. Also, be clear about what is not part of the commission. It is easy to overrun on budgets and timetable if these points are omitted in the first place. And then plan into the programme the preparation of a business case for the work, design review dates, presentation dates, and build in enough time for the client to do their own internal reviews. And then map it out, task by task, week by week, deliverable by deliverable. Already it can be seen that none of these design management responsibilities exist in isolation.

Design management responsibility 4: Design work

This is all about ensuring that appropriate design projects are set up to address identified business issues; that adequate briefs are written, understood and accepted by all concerned; that appropriate design teams are identified and commissioned, and that the design solutions generated represent effective responses to the business issues that caused them to be prepared in the first place. Most design managers will confirm that this responsibility alone demands an inordinate amount of their time.

Clearly the brief is critical. Design work cannot be managed successfully unless a clear brief is prepared in the first place. A number of books concern themselves with the preparation of design briefs including those by Topalian mentioned earlier, Philips 2004, Best 2010, and Cooper and Press 1994. Each of these is excellent and requires no elaboration here.

I would only add this emphasis that my experience suggests – no matter what else may be in it, the brief must cover three basic issues:
- strategic context;
- stakeholders;
- success criteria.

Strategic context

A design brief with no strategic context limits, from the beginning, the impact the design response can have. By existing in isolation it cannot build on other design work being, or having been, commissioned elsewhere in the business. It cannot help aggregate towards a better reputation, brand recognition, continuity of customer experience, differentiation or growth. Give the design brief some strategic focus and the design response has a chance of doing more for the company than just solving the specifics of the problem that gave rise to it in the first place.

Stakeholders

Although the context and content of the brief is clearly important, equally important is the way the brief is put together. By this I mean the collaborative effort by all concerned with creating it. This approach requires time, the ability to listen, and uses one of the fundamental skills that designers are taught to cultivate – the ability to iterate and reiterate until a solution (in this case a brief) is forthcoming. I have seen this work very effectively, particularly with large infrastructure projects like the brief for an airport terminal, but also with much smaller projects like the development of new signing systems and banking services. Each needed the inputs from all the stakeholders and users to get to a point where the nature of the design response could be more easily described. Note that I say all stakeholders. It is critical that all those people who may have an interest in the final solution are identified and their views taken into account during the design work. It is important that they all agree with the objectives of the brief – without their support you may well find that another stakeholder will sabotage a good piece of work for the commissioning manager. When at BAA we had a simple device called a Briefing Charter that all stakeholders signed thereby indicating they were in agreement with the requirements of the project and that their interests had been properly defined. There may well have been battles about interpretation after that but at least everyone was in agreement at the start.

Success criteria

The means by which the design work will be measured must also be an integral part of the brief. And this is a key point – without a clear indication of what is expected from the design work, and the impact it should have on the business, how can the consultant or internal design team know when they have a solution that is worth presenting back to the client? 'What good looks like' at the end of the design work must be part of the brief at the beginning. The brief must contain the criteria by which the design work will be evaluated. This assessment criteria might include the extent to which the project:

- is delivering against vision and mission;
- is addressing improvements to customer experience;
- utilizes established design standards and learning from other projects;
- is using existing benchmarking material to achieve 'international best practice';
- is intending to set a new benchmark that can be used elsewhere in the future.

This is often a difficult thing to do, but it is critically important to final success.

Design management responsibility 5: Design infrastructure

By 'design infrastructure' I mean the organizational systems that specific companies need for handling design within their 'way of working'. At the very least this system needs to accommodate the need for:

- allocation of sensible design budgets and other resources to address business needs,
- formal mechanisms to approve design briefs;
- procurement routes to commission design work;
- review process that monitors design implementation and approves final proposals;
- feedback loop to build on the experience gained for the benefit of subsequent design work.

There are no standard ways of doing this. Some companies include the review of design work as part of the regular presentation of business activities at executive meetings. Some have specially formed 'design boards' which review design work. Some have consultants attending any of these options as non-executive advisors. Some companies rely on design guidelines as the principle means of conveying design intent to all parts of the business and to all designers involved in working for them, see Figure 7.1. I have seen them all work.

Figure 7.1 *Design project guidelines as part of wider processes for capital projects*

London Transport, for example, had a design policy committee, chaired by the chairman which met three times a year. Attending were the managing directors of each of the main businesses, the corporate design director, two external design advisors and one non-executive director of the main board. Their job was not to review design implementation on specific projects, as this was undertaken within each of the businesses commissioning the work, but rather to discuss wider strategic policies that would give direction to all the design work of the company. In support of this they had a suite of design guidelines covering most aspects of design in the group.

At BAA the chief executive chaired a design board that did review major design projects as well as give direction on key issues of policy. This group met every second month and reviewed all major projects. Although this was time consuming it did have the clear benefit of involving all key executives in all major design decisions. It became part of the process of inculcating design into the DNA of the business.

In the late 1980s I was, for a while, an external member of the IBM UK Design Advisory Group. This met irregularly but with an agenda largely to do with identity issues.

The important point is that these groups were created, met and helped to make design part of the way they did business. There is no formula for agenda, meeting regularity or even membership. These have to be decided on a company by company basis, depending how the business goes about its normal work.

The benefit of having these high-profile committees is that they provide the opportunity to discuss design and its implications to the business at a high executive level. They can then give clear steer to overall strategic design direction. However there is a downside to this. Unless carefully managed, they can delay major projects whilst waiting for decisions from their next sitting. To avoid this is it is critical that groups such as these are supported by a senior design executive who can provide appropriate design leadership in light of those strategic decisions.

I have seen other companies use more informal methods to provide design direction such as clinics shared by an external design advisor. They all had one thing in common – a commitment from the top of the organization that design needs the attention of senior executives. No matter which organizational system is in place it becomes the design manager's responsibility to interact with those systems to ensure individual projects manifest the wider design aims of the business. And if those systems are not in place it becomes a responsibility of the design manager to recommend what design infrastructure is needed in their particular circumstances

A brief for design management

Design management is complex. Being a design manager is difficult. It involves getting close to the workings of the business and to the people who wield power in it. Their role is made even more challenging by the fact that some design managers fulfill design leadership roles as well. For the purposes of this book I have defined their roles separately but, like many other things, life is never that simple!

In essence the key requirement for a design manager is someone who has the expertise and knowledge of making design work in a business and who has the interpersonal skills to work with others to deliver practical end results. In particular they will be able to:

* analyze the state of design in the enterprise;
* measure what is being spent on design and where;
* understand and demonstrate the effect design spend is having on reputation;
* map the context, or opportunity, for design – where design does, can or should touch the business;
* put in place a design management organization that fits with their way the business does things;
* prioritize design spend and prepare a design plan;
* win hearts and minds, especially the sceptics.

Roles and responsibilities of design leaders

The essence of design leadership involves helping organizations envision the future; generating tangible, business scenarios, considering that future; utilizing design-related skills to clarify the implications of those scenarios for the company and its customers; and ensuring the most appropriate design direction is selected to realize the company's wider strategic intentions.

Once that direction has been set, design leaders formulate design strategies and programmes to turn those visions of the future into reality. Design leadership is all about looking beyond the immediate issues of design management. It is about ensuring the company or organization utilizes design resources to benefit all its stakeholders for the long term. Before they can start to be effective, design leaders need to understand how design is currently used in the business. This has been well covered in Part One, but in summary this should have led to an understanding of:

- design roles and responsibilities of the current management and leadership teams and identification of changes required, including the ongoing training for design leadership;
- how corporate culture is developed and the challenges for how design can become an integral part of the company's DNA;
- level of funding and design expertise needed to help deliver business objectives;
- strategic purpose, if any, of current design activity or investments;
- key design-related drivers for change that will make design effective;
- key elements of a prioritized design plan that will ensure design has a role in the long-term development of the organization;
- strategic relevance of design to short and long-term goals, and the plans for design's future role;
- behavioural styles being used by the business when managing design.

Assuming that all this is understood, what actually are design leaders responsible for and what do they do on a day-to-day basis? Understanding this can be difficult because many organizations close their doors to these advances, so doing the job can be even more difficult – but nonetheless worthwhile!

I have found that the following six headings capture the fundamental roles and responsibilities at the core of what design leaders do. Of course they do not do this work alone, they are always part of a wider business team. The important thing is to ensure that this wider leadership team understands the potential of design's contribution and that it is given the chance to make it.

Design leadership responsibility 1:
Envisioning

Organizations need to understand what their future business could, or should, be like and design leaders have an important role to play in this process. One of their core responsibilities is to work with the business or organization to understand what their strategic options are, and what these might 'look' and 'feel' like. Encapsulating a company's vision is a fundamental role of design leadership. Envisioning enables everyone in the company, and everyone else with whom it deals, to relate to it.

The scope of a company's vision may be demonstrated by presenting a range of real scenarios covering the spectrum from simple and cheap to complex and resource-intensive. These scenarios can be made tangible through vivid imagery and descriptions of the experiences you want people to have when dealing with the company, or when using its products or services.

It is noteworthy that other design leaders recognize the imperative of envisioning. For example, Clive Grinyer, the Director of Customer Experience at Cisco Internet Business Solutions says, 'Design leadership's ability to marshal the design process to deliver customer focused, usable futures will make the difference between success and failure for many companies.'

An example of envisioning at work is how it was used to provide focus for the creation of a new organization, New West End Company. Its brief was to create a much-improved future for the West End of London together with how that vision could be realized.

Case Example – Envisioning London's Future

NEW **WEST END** COMPANY

Bond Street | Oxford Street | Regent Street

Figure 7.2 *Envisioning in practice at the heart of all that New West End Company does*

London's West End is the world's top shopping destination. Its unique and huge mix of shops, restaurants and theatres is unrivaled in the UK and throughout the world. However, the West End can never stand still. It faces increasing and evolving competition from abroad, at home and through new technology. It must respond to new opportunities presented by major infrastructure changes like Crossrail, the major new rail link being built under London. It also needs to help deal with the barriers to success, such as by reducing traffic levels, improving the environment and encouraging a flexible approach to new developments.

To maintain the West End's predominance needs constant innovation, significant investment, effective management and continual promotion, but this needs to be done in a sensitive way to ensure a healthy balance between business, visitors and residents. This case example looks at the role of design leadership in creating a new focus for the West End of London, and shows what can be achieved as a result of a preoccupation with giving the streets back to the pedestrians.

The New West End Company was created in 2000 to provide the focus and drive to promote and consolidate the West End of London retail and metropolitan experiences around Bond Street, Oxford Street and Regent Street. It is a leading partner in a major regeneration programme to the area which will ensure London's West End continues to be unsurpassed as a leading destination around the globe. It has developed a range of innovative marketing initiatives and campaigns to improve the quality of shopping, living and visiting experiences. These have all been driven by a vision of 'giving the streets back to the pedestrian'. A simple visionary idea was used to drive an exploratory look at what the area could be like in the future and how changes might be achieved.

There were three basic 'imagine' concepts:
- *Imagine the three streets, clearly branded, clean, litter free and crime free. Imagine a sense of entrance to the area, a comprehensive wayfinding system, state-of-the-art lighting and coordinated street furniture demonstrating the best of contemporary design.*
- *Imagine a surface transport system that is environmentally sound; streets that are; oases of calm with seating and greenery; themed markets; planned street trading; entertainment, promotions and celebrations.*
- *Imagine this pre-eminent centre with character and style where everybody wants to be – to live, work, shop, eat and enjoy themselves. It will be a mix of the best of the old with the best of the new.*

This was envisioning work of the most practical kind. It moved the stakeholders to take action and create an organization that could spearhead the plan.

The early vision is still alive in what the company has achieved so far and is at the heart of its action plan for the coming years. New West End Company's declared next steps, all based on the early envisioning work and all with a pedestrian and visitor focus, are to:
- *reduce levels of traffic to make pedestrian movements easier;*
- *create wider pavements for better circulation;*
- *install new street lighting;*
- *improve wayfinding and signage;*
- *install new street furniture;*
- *develop 'break-out' oasis spaces for rest and relaxation.*

Envisioning a new future, even with a supporting masterplan, is never an easy task, but implementing that new future is far harder still. It takes a long time, sometimes many years, and a lot of work to bring every stakeholder along with you. But without a vision of what might be in the first place there is no real hope of moving forward at all. New West End Company has already made a very significant improvement to the pedestrian experience and looks set to continue in the same way.

Design leadership responsibility 2:
Manifesting strategic intent

This is essentially about using design thinking to help align the corporate aims of a business with the process of manifesting the delivery of those aims. It is about linking decisions emanating from the boardroom with the organization's day-to-day activities. These could be factories manufacturing goods, showrooms selling products, offices delivering services, operators providing passenger transport, technology developers creating greater access to knowledge and sharing it. No matter what the business size or industry sector, design has proven to be one of the few resources that can demonstrate this strategic intent. One of its most useful characteristics is that it is easy to see, touch and experience. It can be related to in so many ways and so has the potential of clearly manifesting the strategic direction of a company.

'design is one of the few resources that can provide a clear and practical link between decisions of the board room and the day-to-day activities of the business'

It is the design leaders who are responsible for establishing these links, making them clear and tangible, ensuring the links are maintained and that the standard of design response is appropriate and rigorously maintained.

Case Example – Heathrow Express

Figure 7.3 *Heathrow Express service between London Paddington and Heathrow set a new benchmark for short distance, fast, rail travel*

Heathrow Express, the train service between Heathrow Airport and London's Paddington Station, provides an example of these connections in practice. Heathrow is one of the world's busiest international airports, used by over 50 million people a year. Until the creation of the Heathrow Express it was the only major international airport in Europe without a dedicated rail link. As such this project was vital for the airport's future. Its aim was to establish itself as 'the only way to travel' between Heathrow and London.

BAA and the British Railways Board formed a joint venture to build and operate this high-speed rail link. It was one of the largest transportation projects at the time to be financed through the UK's Private Finance Initiative and went into service in June 1998. To draw passengers away from cars or the underground, Heathrow Express had to be perceived as the most desirable and trouble-free means to travel between Heathrow and London.

The Managing Director expressed his strategic intent for creating a rail service that customers wanted, at a price they could afford, all delivered for £350 million. However, he recognized that this statement did not provide enough of a steer for the design team to develop their design response. Therefore, an early need was to identify what this strategic intent meant in terms that the design team would find meaningful and so help him achieve his business objectives. Eventually the essence of the proposed rail service was captured in the vision statement, 'Bringing Heathrow Airport to London in 15 minutes.'

Of course there was much more to the subsequent design brief than that, but it did provide direction for everything that followed. It was not enough to tell designers how much money was available and how fast the service should be. Without a tangible grasp of the service aspiration and the offer to customers, designers were unlikely to generate the right solutions to deliver it.

For example, they needed to know whether the business proposition of a rail journey lasting only 15 minutes was for a low-cost commuter-like service with a ticket price of, say, £5, or was it to be a luxurious intercity service priced at, say, £15? Or perhaps something completely different was needed.

The design team presented alternatives showing the design implications for a range of business scenarios and ticket price options. These were then taken to the marketplace for testing. Customer responses pointed to a service more like a plane than a train; something that was based on quality, not a pack-em-high-move-em-cheap kind of service. Significantly, potential customers said they were prepared to pay for that. This was the steer the design team was looking for to develop the product that is currently in service.

The project took five years to complete and involved the collaboration of six design consultancies, coordinated by a design manager, to fulfill the scope of design disciplines required. The concept design work was undertaken by Wolff Olins whose role was to develop a clear service offer that met the demands of the market and was communicated consistently. Design Triangle joined the team when the design of the train was being developed. The branding and design responses needed to attract customers and give the service a distinctive identity. The concept was developed as a 'no-frills plus' service, offering as features high speed, high capacity for passengers and luggage, high levels of information, special ticketing and check-in facilities, and comfort in travel. Absolutely everything had to be designed, all informed by the same strategic idea – the train exterior and interior, staff uniforms, ticket machines, communication material, sign-posting, platform design at Heathrow, check-in office for the airport at Paddington terminus.

The Heathrow Express has been a remarkable success delivering a service to about 15,000 people every day, and that service is still in line with the original vision and strategic intent of the business. Some of the less obvious benefits from the introduction of this service are its environmental impact. It is estimated that it removes over 2 million cars from the region's roads each year and saves the British economy about £100 million, when compared to the use of other forms of transport like the tube, taxi or bus.

Design has the capability of interpreting the implications of strategic business intent in an easily understood way. It can imply a particular service standard, product quality, communication and tone of voice. When these are all aligned to the aims of the business it can add real value.

The process for manifesting strategic intent is concerned with showing how corporate aims, the vision for itself in the marketplace, the values by which it operates, key drivers for change, projects and day-to-day activities are all linked.

Diagram 7.1 illustrates these connections and is fully explained in Section 8.

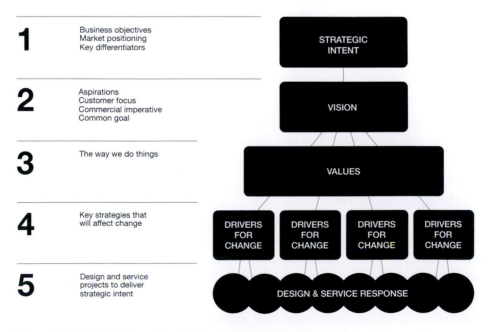

1 Business objectives
Market positioning
Key differentiators

2 Aspirations
Customer focus
Commercial imperative
Common goal

3 The way we do things

4 Key strategies that
will affect change

5 Design and service
projects to deliver
strategic intent

STRATEGIC INTENT

VISION

VALUES

DRIVERS FOR CHANGE

DRIVERS FOR CHANGE

DRIVERS FOR CHANGE

DRIVERS FOR CHANGE

DESIGN & SERVICE RESPONSE

Diagram 7.1 *The basic links between strategic intent and design/service response*

It is an associated role of design leaders to ensure that the strategic intent, vision and values of a company are defined in such a way that it becomes possible to inform every design decision and ensure they deliver, or exceed, consumer expectations and business ambitions. The short case example that follows about Babington's English Tea Rooms illustrates this well.

Case Example – Babington's English Team Rooms

Figure 7.4 *The strategic repositioning of Babington's English Tea Rooms helped the business to survive and grow in a very competitive environment*

Babington's English Tea Rooms is a simple example of a strategic intent being manifest through a carefully thought out design programme which has driven business development and growth. Babington's English Tea Rooms, in the heart of Rome, is the place to meet for locals and tourists alike. In 2010, Babington's commissioned a programme to reposition the business and emphasize its English heritage in order to heighten awareness of the tea rooms, increase branded merchandise sales and create an attractive concept for potential franchisees.

Minale Tattersfield, an international identity and branding consultancy, developed a personality that could be owned by Babington's. The focus was English eccentricity – that in England, everything stops for tea. Advertisements, menu covers, point of sale material, packaging and merchandise all communicated the vision, using imagery of bizarre Victorian inventions. The brand's visual identity was also given a stylish makeover. Despite declining market conditions, sales in all parts of the business increased as a result of Minale Tattersfield's work. Total footfall in 2010 increased by 40 per cent, alongside the same increase in sales value, a 60 per cent increase in gift shop sales and a 10 per cent increase in online merchandise sales.

Design management responsibility 3: Directing design investment

Vast sums are spent on design, although only a small proportion is formally acknowledged as design expenditure. It is the responsibility of a design leader to determine exactly what the total sum is from across the whole company, securing responsibility for that expenditure, ensuring it is invested in the right way and then maximizing the return on that investment.

Effective investment in design requires an enlightened understanding of the context for design within an organization – where design touches it, or is used by it. For example, retailers will have different design requirements to, say, train operators, car manufacturers, research institutions, dance acadamies or insurance companies. So, understanding 'design context' is a key route to determining who within an organization is investing in design, and the extent to which responsibility for that design investment is divested. Without that knowledge executives cannot determine whether the level of expenditure is appropriate for the achievement of corporate objectives or not. Without that knowledge they cannot determine how best to direct that investment. Nevertheless, information on the wider context for design is not always forthcoming.

In reality, wherever one looks, some kind of design activity is likely to be taking place involving all levels of staff – in finance, production, research and development, marketing, personnel and so on – although much of this activity is not acknowledged to be design related.

In the 1980s Peter Gorb and Angela Dumas, at the London Business School, identified 'silent designers' across organizations. Typically they were individuals with no design training who, often unknowingly, influence or make design decisions, without consultation or guidance.

This phenomenon still exists today. Relatively junior people rather than those at board, or senior management, level make the majority of design decisions. It is clearly not sensible to allow such influence and discretion on design expenditure without a wider strategic view and awareness of the implications. A simple matrix can help to clarify how much is at stake, showing 'Management Hierarchy' along one axis and 'Operational Activities' on the other, with a plot of how much is being spent on which design activity, by whom, and who sanctions the allocation of resources, see Diagram 7.2.

This can be very illuminating. I have found that, invariably, the amount spent on design is the largest single sum of money the board knows least about!

When I ask where money is being spent on design the answer is usually something like "advertising and marketing deal with that". People can rarely cite all the places where design is being used, or who is commissioning it. Areas like retail and office interiors, factory and workshop layouts, staff and customer communications, construction manuals and wayfinding systems, products and other manufactured goods. In most cases, when the total spend is added up the reaction is one of shock.

It is critical that design leaders address this blindness. Typically, well-informed executives spend three to four times more on design than they realize. Less-informed executives often underestimate their expenditure on design by a factor of 5 to 10. And, or course, in companies where executives are completely unfamiliar and inexperienced with design, it could be even more. In a presentation to the UK's Design Leadership Forum a few years ago Harry Rawlinson, then Managing Director of Aqualisa Products, maintained that design is one of the most effective ways to increase value, and yet top

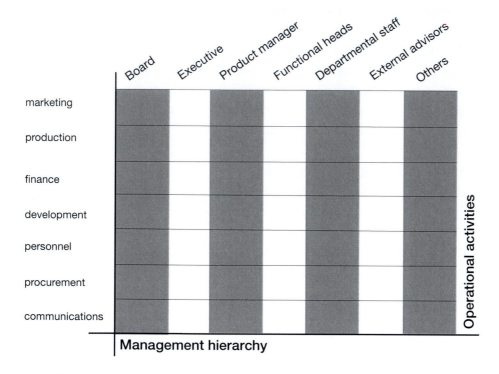

Diagram 7.2 *Basic design spend/activity matrix is one way to assess current commitment to design activity and associated costs*

executives are rarely aware of its true nature and reach within their enterprise. As a consequence they grossly underestimate the level of expenditure on design. His view is far from unique.

Many large companies, especially those undertaking capital investment projects – whether they be, for example, information technology related, construction, mining or transportation – will focus a great deal of management attention on a £200 million project, not least how the design budget is spent just because of its shear size. On the other hand a portfolio of, say, 200 £0.5 million projects, presents a considerably greater challenge.

Relatively speaking, each project represents a much smaller amount of expenditure and therefore can attract much less senior management time; however, when put together, those projects could have a far greater affect on their individual customer's experience than the £200 million project. It is critically important, therefore, that someone in the organization is responsible for the collective effect of this design investment on everyone that comes into contact with the organization. That includes customers, staff, employees, suppliers, stakeholders, business partners and investors.

The inevitable conclusion from this is that directing design investment is a key responsibility of design leadership because it is crucial to the way an organization operates as well as providing a focus for otherwise – dispersed design activity and expenditure across the business.

Design management responsibility 4:
Managing corporate reputation

Design can help an organization manage relationships with all its stakeholders, and so affect its corporate reputation. A fundamental challenge for design leaders is to ensure that design is used to deliver the most appropriate experience at every point of contact between company and stakeholder. These points of contact were, very aptly, called the 'moments of truth' by Jan Carlzon, in the 1980s, when he was Managing Director of Scandinavian Airlines.

Customer experience is fundamentally a function of two things:
- People: the behaviour of those you interact with.
- Product: the nature of what the company is offering, including services of all kinds.

There is an irrefutable link between company reputation and the experience customers have of that organization. Design can be used to create those experiences for every one who encounters them.

Good experiences with a company normally lead to an enhanced reputation in the minds of those involved. Conversely, bad experiences tend to diminish reputations. In shaping those experiences design has, therefore, a powerful influence on image and reputation. This, in turn, has a direct affect on the profitability of the business. Yet executives rarely acknowledge that the reputations of their

Managing

1

Customer
Experience

Leads to

2

Enhanced
Reputation

Leads to

3

Improved Business
Performance

Diagram 7.3 *The link between customer experience, reputation and business performance*

organizations are a function of the way they direct design budgets. The logic of the relationship between design, experience and reputation is simple and is shown in Diagram 7.3.

'corporate reputation is built on customer experiences and design helps create them'

Case Example – London Bus

To a great degree design can shape the experiences that people have of a company's products or services. A case in point was the design study commissioned by London Bus and undertaken by Ogle Design regarding the redesign of the entrance to its buses. The work was based round a careful study of exactly how the flows of people moved when boarding, moving through and alighting from the bus. The objective was to see if the boarding time could be shortened to facilitate a more efficient process. The entrance was reconfigured allowing for smoother flows for passengers and shorter boarding times of several seconds. This meant that the bus stopping time at each bus stop was less. When extrapolated over all buses, all routes and all stops the bus services had the potential of being more efficient, more people could be carried in a day and so generate more income.

Figure 7.5 *Getting passengers on and off buses has always been a key factor in operational efficiency*

Not much money was involved in the design study but the business case for doing the work was easily made, as was the argument for its contribution to an improved customer experience.

Design intervention such as this is not a curer of all ills, but it can have a significant bearing on people, product and service. When reputation goes up as a result of personal experience, business objectives are more easily achieved. In this way, bottom-line improvement, design and reputation are all linked.

Understanding customer experiences, and how to manage them, has become a critical concern in business and, as such, this understanding should be high on business development agendas. You have only to read the writings of Pine and Gilmore 1999 and Lindstrom 2005 to really understand the commercial imperative of the point.

However, again quoting Clive Grinyer when speaking about end-to-end experiences he says, 'Very few companies have managers who are responsible for the customer journey.' Design leaders should grasp that responsibility, but it means working across vertical corporate divisions whilst holding a single customer vision for the whole business.

Tom Lockwood, Director of Lockwood Resource and President Emeritus of the Design Management Institute based in Boston, USA, holds a related view. He maintains that one of the big issues for the future is to, 'Find ways of working together to create not only integration, but synergy, between design and business, to achieve relevancy for customers.'

It is interesting to see that Dublin Airport Authority (DAA) have adopted customer journey mapping as one mechanism to evaluate customer experience. They have produced sophisticated diagrams of people on 'outward bound' and 'inward bound' journeys through Dublin airport. See Diagram 7.4. The case example DAA Design Integration, found in Part Four, illustrates this more fully.

If you drill down behind each step in the diagram, you will find a complete description of the experience people have, or need to have, at that point. Understanding the difference between

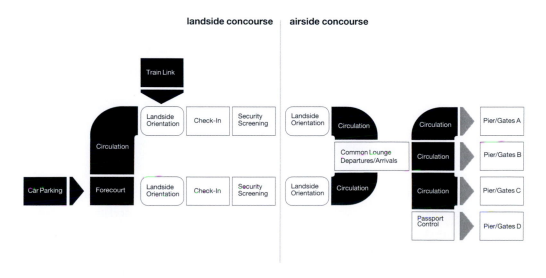

Diagram 7.4 *Customer experience mapping, as used by DAA to evaluate opportunities for improving quality of delivery*

the two is a key issue for corporate management. The direction given through design is crucial to distilling and addressing those differences.

The Lexus motorcar company is another organization that has, in the past, explored in considerable detail the experiences their customers have of the organization and how design might help to improve the quality of those experiences, see Diagram 7.5. BT, the communications, information and technology company puts managing the customer interface at the heart of their operation. A number of national rail companies are looking at the value of customer experience mapping in developing its services.

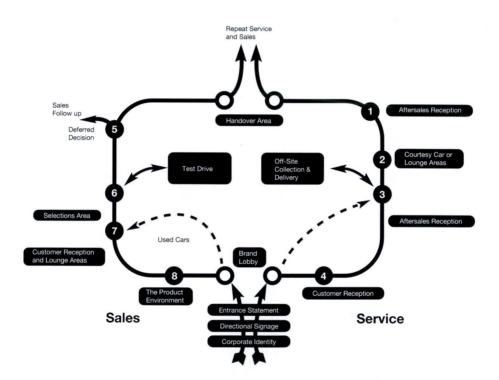

Diagram 7. 5 *Key steps in the customer journey for sales and service at Lexus*

It is only when you get to this level of detail that design leaders can be confident they have sufficient information to direct design resources effectively for the business and its customers. Ultimately, these diagrams indicate that leading through design is about creating total experiences for everyone encountering the organization. Without such focus, customer experiences will not be optimized and neither will reputation. Designers alone cannot make design effective. This can only happen when they work closely with their clients, internal or external, and together can realize business objectives.

A word of warning

Design leadership is key to creating those customer experiences on which corporate reputations thrive. This in turn is heavily dependent on how the identity of the company is conceived, developed and managed, and how the design work the company commissions relates to this. The responsibility for corporate identity is often in the hands of a part of the business, like corporate affairs or marketing. This is usually separate from where the main thrust of design management activity takes place, for instance in product development or environmental design. The net result is that many opportunities for using design to create and manage customer experience and corporate reputation are lost. Situations can arise where the company's identity presents the business in one way and other design activity presents the same business in quite a different way. The case example, Eurotunnel: design in a service industry, found in Part Four explores this point more fully.

Design leadership responsibility 5: Creating an innovation environment

Continuous and radical innovation is often critical to business success. Though not well understood in society (or the design professions for that matter), design leaders have to harness and sustain innovation by creating environments in which innovation flourishes.

Innovation is home territory for the design professions – most believe they are in the business of innovation – which of course many are. But innovation is not the exclusive domain of designers. Many other specialist disciplines, such as accountancy and law, are often equally as innovative as designers if not more so.

James Berry, Design Director of Woods Bagot, maintains that creative capital is not just a collection of individual ideas, but a product of interaction. This captures the point well.

David Kester, the Chief Executive of UK's Design Council, makes a similar point in conversation with him. He maintains, 'We now live in an era where innovation and creativity frequently happens as the product of many hands in many places.' He sites the fact that Linux, the open software programme, is the work of a distributed collective of perhaps 120,000 registered developers. Innovation is one of the most effective routes, and sometimes the only way, to gain advantage and deliver value.

There is always an element of risk with innovation, taking people out of their comfort zone, and organizations tend to resist being made vulnerable in this way. However, new channels, such as those pioneered by Ryanair, the low cost airline, or GloHealth, the specialist health insurer, show the real value of innovation. Once such an initiative has proved successful, people wonder why no one else had thought of it, and a whole range of clones appear, applying the same principle. However, in getting it right the innovator creates an entirely new area of high ground, which, if it is wise, can then dominate the industry, at least for a while.

The key to innovation is taking a fresh look at how an organization operates. To challenge the status quo and ask searching questions. The answers are not necessarily what you would expect. The process encourages people to move further than if they had not looked. In this way a company can find an alternative world that offers a much wider range of options than they thought possible.

Innovation ranges from the radical to the evolutionary. The success of innovation depends on having a strong brand, or the ability to create a strong brand. Good examples of this are Virgin and Apple. The combination of exclusive high ground and strong brand means added value.

But how is strategic context provided for innovation? There is no point in innovating for the sake of innovation. Some organizations set up special innovation centres, and their work is assessed and filtered through a strategic relevance process. The strategic intent map described earlier can be used to test the relevance of all innovative thinking undertaken in a business.

Kester maintains, 'It is the responsibility of design leaders to engage users of innovation in the business development process.' A sentiment shared by Berry who says, 'Successful and innovative projects depend on a cooperative collaboration between users, designers, managers and operators.' This is a long way from the attitude of leaving it to the design experts to come up with the answer that so many companies adopted in the past.

It is the responsibility of design leaders to create environments that nurture and sustain innovation, because without this the future of many businesses is left to chance and almost certain failure.

When thinking of innovation, it is all too easy to focus on advances in consumer technology such as the iPod, robot lawn mowers, or even feather-light materials like Polartec, that we take it completely for granted. However there are less conspicuous forms of innovation that affect our everyday lives, yet rarely get acknowledged. Examples of this include odorless paint; multi-modal travel tickets; light, virtually unbreakable, plastics; knives that stay sharp; or cars that only need servicing every five years.

Two particular favourites of mine in this category of unsung 'heroes of innovation' are the simple but brilliant knife block designed by Priestman Goode, see Figure 7.6, and the flexible plastic holder for a six-pack of soda cans designed by BIB, see Figure 7.7. Both are product design companies with reputations for product innovation.

Figure 7.6 *Knife block that comes apart for easy cleaning the insides*

The knife block consists of two identically shaped blocks of wood held together by magnets.The interface between the blocks is shaped in such a way that a series of narrow gaps are created, providing ideal spaces for storing sharp kitchen knives. The blocks keep the knives safe and secure but are easily separated for cleaning, something not possible with the conventional knife block. Lateral innovative thinking produced a design solution that solved many problems associated with traditional knife holders.

Figure 7.7 *Six-pack holder made from scrap material*

The six-pack holder, see Figure 7.7, according to BIB's ex-chairman Nick Butler, was conceived as a way of using waste material from the production of another, unrelated, product. And look how clever it is. A flat sheet of thin, flexible plastic, pierced with large holes, sized to go over the top of the drink cans and held in place by their rims. Once in position the six cans are easily carried, and the material cost is negligible considering the plastic was originally scrap from another process and destined to be thrown away. Considering its weight, the plastic can holder supports a staggering level of load. Now that is an example of simple innovation, if ever there was one!

These innovation heroes have at least two features in common. The first is a response to simple human needs. Cleaning, in the case of the knife block, and carrying, in the case of the six-pack holder. The second is that design is the source of each. Design is fundamental to the process of innovation, whether the focus is a new product or service, a built environment, a corporate proposition, or even a vision of the future. It is fundamental, not because we like to think it is, but because history shows that at the heart of all innovation is the rigorous challenge, lateral thinking and practical approach of the designer.

Innovation, brand development and partnerships

Particularly good routes to innovation include brand development and partnerships. In order to encourage innovation it is important to demonstrate tangible benefits. Organizations are often unaware of their own condition. By benchmarking themselves against world standards you can see the scale of the problem. This helps understand how far you have to move. The braver you can be, the more value you can potentially add. Innovation can lead to significant business benefits, financial benefits and psychological benefits.

For example, like railway operators, many retailers are caught in a low-inflation climate where there is very little scope to increase margins. By innovating, they can work smarter, and by developing their brand they can increase perceived value.

Bringing innovation and brand development together is also the most obvious route out of the price war experienced by low-cost-airlines. Retailers are ahead in this game. An excellent example of how to transform an inexpensive product range into an experience that customers value is IKEA. There are real lessons to be applied here, for example, to airports designed for low-cost-travel.

Low-cost-airlines can benefit from looking at what is happening, for example, in the retail electrical sector. Here, Argos, Currys and Dixons are all fighting hard on the same territory. When products become so commoditized, it is only brand perception that will drive the propensity to purchase. Sony is a good example. Seen against manufacturers like Sanyo and retailers' own-label products, Sony quality is seen as superior. The really clever thing is that Sony prices are not that much greater than its apparently lesser rivals, which makes an easy decision for the customer. By aligning your brand to the right market you increase the likelihood of people actually using your service or buying your product.

Brand partnerships are being used by organizations to strengthen their perception in the markets where they operate. Depending on their business objectives, partnerships may be strategic, such as between Dell and Intel, or promotional, as with McDonald's and Disney.

There is much written about the process of innovation. In my experience, however, business as usual is not the way to release innovative thinking. If the mindset does not change, neither will the solution! Creating an environment where challenging the status quo is actively encouraged is at the heart of the innovation process. This process needs clear, firm leadership, and it is the design leader's responsibility to do just that, to make innovation part of the business's DNA. It is then the job of the design manager to help realize the innovative thinking. Designers can be the source of innovative thinking, but not the exclusive source – in fact, professionals from all parts of business can be innovative. After all a good idea doesn't care who has it.

'a good idea doesn't care who has it'

Michael Schrage of MIT Sloan School of Management, when speaking at a recent Design Management Institute European Annual Conference, argued that designers should be bolder. More specifically he argued, 'Innovation is not what designers do, it's what customers adopt'

Design leadership responsibility 6:
Training for design leadership

Little is known about training for design leadership, or about grooming successors to positions of design leadership. Yet to maximize the full potential of design in business, it is crucial that those gaps in knowledge, skills and experience are addressed. It is one thing to say that design leadership is important, but quite another to put in place appropriate mechanisms to develop design leaders. We are far from understanding how to do that, it is virtually virgin territory. However, we are required to investigate the issues involved and develop some responses to them. The Cultural Leadership Programme, an initiative of the Arts Council England, Creative and Cultural Skills and the Museums, promotes excellence in leadership across the creative and cultural industries and the British Standards Institute have produced the BS series relating to the management of innovation and design, and there may be more. However this represents very little in the context of what needs to be addressed.

Training and organizing for design leadership is about putting design into the DNA of organizations. It means getting to the position where design becomes a normal mainstream activity in business, where it is second nature to all involved – just like quality control or financial management.

The Latin maxim seems very appropriate here 'abeunt studia in mores' or 'practices zealously pursued become habits'.

'abeunt studia in mores' – 'practices zealously pursued become habits'

Unless this is achieved, the long-term benefits and value from all that design offers as a rigorous business discipline will not be realized.

Design leaders need to facilitate the use of design in business and encourage other executives to embrace it as a core discipline in their companies. Though designers will always have a pivotal role, many others have a valid creative contribution to make as well. That is why design needs to become part of the DNA of companies and should not be left exclusively to, so called, 'specialists'.

David Hancock, ex Director of Consulting at Halcrow Group and now Head of Projects Risk at Transport for London, says, 'There is a clear move away from experts as 'guardians of great design' to responsibility being held more widely within the business.'

Reward systems need to be reoriented towards providing incentives for staff to use design more effectively and sharpen-up their design decision-making. Systems already exist for rewarding success in other disciplines, so there is no reason why similar upgrades are not possible for design. In support of this point, David Griffiths, Change Management Trainer with extensive design management experience of working in India and the UK says, 'The paradox of design's success is that design will not always be led by designers.' Alan Topalian, from Alto Design Management in the UK, says that design leaders can be prepared for their role and outlines some early thinking on the subject in his paper entitled 'Promoting Design Leadership through skills development programmes' published in the *DMI Journal*.

A brief for design leadership

So, if design leaders are hard to find what should we be looking for in a brief for them? I suppose the easy answer is 'all of the above'. However, an outline set of objectives would help a potential employer to spot the right sort of person, or brief a recruitment specialist to do so. There are a small number of organizations worldwide that focus on finding experienced design managers and design leaders for their clients. Amongst them are Lockwood Resources, already mentioned, and RitaSue Siegel is another, both based in the United States of America.

In essence the key requirement is for people who can engage with senior management to:

- create differentiation, sustain competitive advantage, enable world-class performance that is sustainable into the future;
- help envision the future; generate tangible, design related, business scenarios considering that future; clarifying the implications of these scenarios for the company; and ensuring the most appropriate design direction is selected to realize the company's wider strategic intentions, formulate design strategies and programmes to turn those visions of the future into reality;
- provide clear direction regarding the levels of design investment required for helping manifest the aims of the business;
- establish an innovation culture and training managers for design leadership roles;
- improving organizational performance by:
  - maximizing value from design investment;
  - delivering enhanced customer experience through design, communications and behavioural change;
  - developing design awareness in business leaders and managers.

Summary of Chapter 7

There are fundamental differences between design management and design leadership. Each area of expertise is dependent on the other for its relevance in business. Without design leadership, executives don't know where they are going; without design management, they don't have the means of getting there. One is a stepping stone to the other.

Design managers and leaders are charged with a mixture of responsibilities that require them to be at the heart of what the business does. In some cases they contribute to corporate thinking, in others they help direct it. They can make a significant contribution to envisioning the company's future and manifesting the strategies for getting there. In addition, design leaders are responsible for directing design investment in line with those strategies in such a way that the full value of that investment is realized.

Joe Ferry, Senior Vice President of Global Guest Experience and Design at InterContinental Hotels Group, endorses this point. He believes, 'One of the greatest future challenges for design leaders is to clearly demonstrate that design creates a positive return on investment, measured in terms to which the business can relate.'

A key role of design leaders is to use design to create and maintain customer experiences and, through that, build and enhance corporate reputation. They are also directly responsible for creating an environment for innovation and for organizing and training for design and innovation within business.

Michael Wolff, of Michael Wolff and Company, once partner at Wolff Olins, is rather more extreme in his view of this point. He says, 'Design management is irrelevant without design leadership.' He goes on to say, 'Most public companies are still led by people with an exclusively short term focus, but that will change because business without vision and design leadership will perish.'

Business executives must acknowledge their ultimate responsibility for rigour and professionalism when handling design is not only to generate quality solutions, but also to retain their integrity through exemplary implementation over time. That responsibility should never be abrogated and design leaders must ensure it is not.

All of which is why I am certain that, ultimately, design leadership is a commercial imperative – not because it is just a 'nice thing to do', but because it enables a company to differentiate itself from others, create and sustain competitive advantage, and evolve into a world-class performer.

Chapter 8 outlines some of the tools and processes that have proven to be useful in carrying out this work.

Part Four contains a number of detailed case examples. Three in particular illustrate, more fully than was possible in the text above, some of the issues and principles discussed here.

The first is called 'BAA selecting designers'. It looks at the role of design leadership in establishing a framework of design partners in a regulated environment. Although the case concerns a large multinational company, the process and learning from it could be of real value to many other sized businesses.

The second is called 'Eurotunnel: design in a service industry' and focuses on Eurotunnel, the rail link between England and France. The management of design work is sometimes made particularly complicated when a new business, especially a new service business, is being created. Under these circumstances not only do you have the need to develop a new identity for the business that fully represents its strategic aims and values but also to manage a range of individual design projects that enable the business to become tangible – together with the added complication of managing the complex interface between these two disciplines. A good example of this relationship can be seen in the creation of the Eurotunnel service. Although this was a very big project, and is now about 20 years old, the challenges of using corporate identity and design management to create a new service are still relevant today and are similar to those found in smaller projects and in other industries. Among the outcomes of this work are valuable lessons concerning distinctions between corporate identity and design management and their respective positions in an organizational structure.

The third is called 'Design for future needs – Heathrow Terminal 5'. It examines the role of design leadership in helping with the requirement to understand future needs (referred to as Foresight in this case example) when making significant investment in infrastructure development. It also illustrates how a clear vision can help shape that investment and the design responses that they depend on. It shows how by putting received wisdom to one side a new attitude of mind can be created in the whole team, not just the designers, and how this enabled a new benchmark in airport terminal design to be developed.

Chapter 8
Understanding opportunity

Understanding the potential, or scoping the opportunity, for design in an organization involves getting close to all key management functions. It means going to places where design people often don't go, and if they do are not always welcome. However, no one said this would be easy! Managing and leading through design is a very serious matter if stakeholder value is to be maximized – and this is something not to be afraid of.

To a very large extent the degree to which a company capitalizes on the potential benefits of design are dependent on the degree to which it is open to being influenced by it. In turn this is dependent on how well the design manager or design leader exposes the current shortcomings in its use and the potential opportunity that exists if used in a more strategically focused way.

There are no easy formulas or processes to follow for doing this. However, when faced with the problem of 'where do I start?' it does help to have some sort of structure by which you can examine the business or organization and assess its potential for improvement through design.

Four of the mechanisms I have seen work effectively are described in this chapter. They are not mutually exclusive. Each one has a slightly different primary focus and they can be used in combination. Collectively they can provide a comprehensive design view of the whole business.

By their nature the steps described in each are sequential but it is not always possible to undertake an 'opportunity analysis' in this rational way. You have to start where there is an opening rather than wait until the ideal time arrives to start at the beginning of the process – you may be waiting forever. Someone once said to me that there are times when 'the best is the enemy of the good' – how true this is when managing and leading design!

Process for design management

Before we get into the 'how' of design management we should briefly remind ourselves of the 'what' of it. As has been described earlier, the term design management is used in many ways, often to describe managing design projects, managing design groups, and managing design investment. It is about all of these things – and much more.

What design management means in any particular instance depends on the relationship between design and business. This relationship varies considerably in its complexity from company to company and from division to division in the same company.

The degree to which design can be a positive contributor to business success depends on how well developed the relationship is between the two. That relationship becomes more effective the more integrated one part becomes with the other. The journey to full integration of design and business is usually long, arduous and marked by a number of significant milestones. This section sets out to define and understand those milestones and to highlight some of the risks and benefits that can be expected when managing design.

It is often the case that in large organizations the level of design integration varies from department to department. It may be that Marketing are using design very effectively but Manufacturing are not, or Research and Development are practising the most recent developments in innovation design but retail are in the relative dark ages.

Even with this 'spotty' use of design there is still much to be done to make it fully effective and there is certainly a risk that mixed, incoherent, messages about what the business is all about will be confusing or alienating customers until this is sorted out.

Milestones in design management – an overview

This process is largely concerned with understanding how design works currently in a business; understanding where it is being used, where it might be used, who is doing it, who is commissioning it and how, if at all, it is being managed. This is more of an audit process rather than a doing process. It is about painting a current picture of how design works, or doesn't, and mapping what might be done to maximize its potential.

Diagram 8.1 illustrates this process and an overview of it is described below and is followed by a more detailed description with examples. The process consists of four basic steps, Design in Crisis, Design in Context, Design in Place and Design in Management.

Design in crisis

The first milestone in this analysis is for the business to reach an understanding of the degree to which design is in a state of crisis or not. In other words to understand whether it is being managed, is under control or is happening at all. It should also be clear at this point whether design is serving a corporate purpose. This first milestone is reached when the business acknowledges it has a design issue to address and resolves to do something about it. At this stage it usually becomes apparent that money is being wasted and opportunities are being lost.

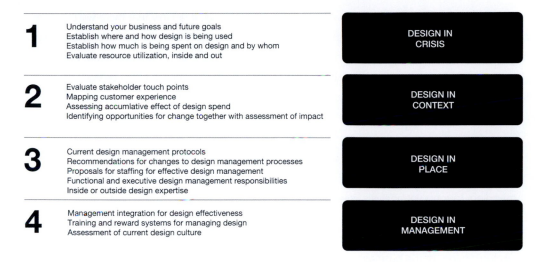

1
Understand your business and future goals
Establish where and how design is being used
Establish how much is being spent on design and by whom
Evaluate resource utilization, inside and out

DESIGN IN
CRISIS

2
Evaluate stakeholder touch points
Mapping customer experience
Assessing accumlative effect of design spend
Identifying opportunities for change together with assessment of impact

DESIGN IN
CONTEXT

3
Current design management protocols
Recommendations for changes to design management processes
Proposals for staffing for effective design management
Functional and executive design management responsibilities
Inside or outside design expertise

DESIGN IN
PLACE

4
Management integration for design effectiveness
Training and reward systems for managing design
Assessment of current design culture

DESIGN IN
MANAGEMENT

Diagram 8.1 *Milestones in Design Management is a basic audit process that explores the current state of design, where it could be used managed and integrated into the business DNA*

The work to be undertaken includes understanding and analyzing the:

- current status of design, where it is used or ignored, how many projects are being undertaken, who is commissioning them, what are the success criteria for each;
- visual language of the company as depicted by its products, communications materials, places where it does business and in relation to insiders and outsiders;
- extent to which design is used to convey relevant, consistent or conflicting messages;
- design management processes currently being employed, how they work, where the gaps and blockages are;
- degree to which established design standards and other protocols are being used, and quality levels are being achieved;
- appropriateness of design skills being employed, whether from inside or outside the business;
- level of design spend, which budgets are being used, how much is being spent, who is responsible for it;
- connections between the design work that is being undertaken and the expressed aims of the business.

This list is not exhaustive, but it is a start. There could well be industry-specific issues to explore. By the time the work described above in this first phase of the audit has been completed a view of whether or not design is in a state of crisis will begin to emerge.

Design in context

The second milestone is all about reaching an understanding about where design could be used rather than where it is currently being used. It is about understanding the context for design in the business, or put another way, understanding where design touches or impacts on business activities and the people it comes into contact with – internal and external. It is likely that there will be more opportunity uncovered for using design during this phase than can be capitalized on immediately. That is not the important bit. What is important is knowing where design could be used, particularly in helping achieve corporate purpose. It is not about preparing a prioritized list of design activities, this will come later, once the audit is complete, in the form of a structured and accountable design investment programme.

This step should include, at least, the following activities:

- mapping the spectrum of design opportunity through a process of customer experience mapping, touchpoint analysis, investment plan analysis, short/medium/long-term development plans;
- exploring fully the connection, or potential connection, between design investment and the strategic intent of the business and indicating the key issues to be addressed;
- identifying the spectrum of projects that could be used to manifest strategic intent, together with assessments of their potential business impacts;
- articulating the strategic intent of the business in such a way that will inform design work.

Design in place

The third milestone is to reach an understanding regarding the sort of design organization that needs to be put in place in order to manage design effectively. Criteria for managing and judging design investment often result from this phase, replacing ignorance and adhocism.

The work during this phase includes addressing issues about:

- whether to centralize design management or devolve it to key operating parts of the business;
- design management structures, including roles and responsibilities;
- appropriate approval procedures for design briefs and design solutions;
- line and functional relationships and responsibilities;
- the role of design standards and principles,
- pros and cons of having an internal design department or relying on external consultants, or both;
- designer selection processes;
- organizing for design implementation;
- how key design projects are to be managed;
- providing design advice.

The output of this part of the audit will be either clear recommendations about how design should be managed and the administrative systems needed to support that management requirement, or, more likely, a number of scenarios to be discussed with key members of the senior management team. Design management processes and the people involved in those processes are always very sensitive issues. This is why it usually makes sense to share the options with the people they will most likely affect. It is perfectly normal for a period of negotiation to take place about who does what, and how, before final agreement is reached as to the best workable solution for managing design.

Design in management

The fourth milestone is all about evaluating opportunities for putting design into the DNA of the business such that all managers are better equipped to make informed design investment decisions. This is the condition when design is fully integrated into the way a company works, when it has become part of the management ethic, when it has become an accountable activity for all managers.

This step is about assessing:
- the current level of design awareness amongst managers,
- what training mechanisms are, or should be, in place for the management of design projects and what are the associated reward mechanisms for success;
- assessing the behavioural styles of staff and what implications these may have for how design is used in the business;
- what design policies need developing to support the delivery of strategic intent.

An audit of this kind will give a very good picture of how design works in the business and the opportunities for making it work more effectively. It will provide managers with the basic facts on which to build an action plan for change.

Milestones in design management – a closer look

Although the outline given above is short there is a lot of work in undertaking this design audit. It does, I hope, give a sense that it is a worthwhile exercise. If more information is needed as to what is involved a more detailed description of the process follows together with some real case examples.

Design in crisis – a closer look

The first significant point in the integration of design and business is reached when a company recognizes that design is out of control and particularly is considered to be a cost rather than an investment. This first milestone is called 'design in crisis'.

The best way of illustrating this condition is to look at a real example. I have chosen London Transport during a very particular part of its history. Despite its fame for being associated with the use of design to create the most well-known public transport system in the world, London Transport, for a period in its history, did go through a crisis of design.

Frank Pick, its Chief Executive from 1933, had a vision to use design in a coordinated way as a means of 'harnessing commercial methods to the achievement of large social objectives'. And he used the best designers of the day to this end. London Transport became famous for this and ran successfully in this way for many years. This coordinated design approach culminated in two discrete projects, the development of the Victoria and Bakerloo lines between 1969 and 1979.

As a result of many complex factors there followed a degeneration of design throughout the organization. Underground platform designers became preoccupied with superficial decoration, particularly in overemphasizing the geographical sense-of-place of each location. Passenger information on both trains and buses became sloppy, unclear and uncoordinated. Much of the hardware in use became treated as though it had nothing to contribute to the public perception of the company. And there was even gross disrespect for the one thing that the company had developed and established as representing all that was good in public transport, and in London, the symbol. It was redrawn in a variety of comic ways, often degenerating into advertising gimmicks for such things as the London Transport health plan or annual carol service. See Figure 8.1.

It would be over simplifying the situation to say that all this happened as the result of one incident. During the 1970s plans were made to move the control of London Transport away from local government to central government. Perhaps these political issues diverted everyone's attention away from their integrated design policy, it is difficult to be sure. However, long before this, and despite the early commitment to a coordinated design approach, and similarly later regarding the two newer underground lines, design had lost its way both in terms of purpose and focus.

Figure 8.1 *Is this suggesting a 'sticking plaster' solution to design in crisis?*

London Transport had experienced a major crisis. Design was no longer coordinated, nor was it fulfilling a strategic purpose – worse, design was out of control. Almost without noticing that anything had happened it had reached the first milestone in the relationship of design and business. Design was in crisis. A more expanded version of this case can be found in Appendix.

Design in crisis is a phenomenon that afflicts many companies. It is also not the prerogative of the large and the mighty. Small businesses can as easily fall into the same trap. The important thing is to recognize this first milestone and be prepared to do something about it.

London Transport's design crisis can teach some valuable lessons about identifying where design makes an impact on a business and the implications of not managing that impact properly. In their case there was lack of investment and possibly complacency. There was certainly a failure to manage design. There was also a failure to understand where design could be used, a failure to understand the context for design, and so a failure in knowing what to manage and how to do it. That failure was made manifest in two, seemingly contradictory, ways.

The first was inevitable, and the results were easily predictable. So what happened? Design investment ceased, post war prosperity had not made it to the world of public transport. This led to a degradation of both service and infrastructure. Consequently passenger numbers diminished which in turn led to further loss of revenue, no investment and more decay.

The second manifestation of design management failure soon followed on from the first, that of an active programme of uncoordinated design reinvestment. The theory was that if enough design money was available for infrastructure and service development then all would be OK again. Unfortunately one of the consequences was the steady creation of the good, the bad and the ugly. In short, design anarchy.

During the early years, London Transport had developed a design strategy where each aspect of design activity, product design, environmental design and information design – supported the same business idea. In later years the company either had no design policy or they had three, all different, one for each area of design. In any event, whatever there was did not work. And to make things worse there was no overall design management or even design coordination.

The design of their products should have been integrated with their environments and information, but they were not. Consequently the London Transport message was hollow. The London Transport idea had become lost, particularly on the customers. That is why they didn't use the system. In fact the message they did get was so horrible that they left in large numbers. Fortunately the error of this strategy was spotted in time and a properly modulated design programme was put in place and has been implemented in part since then.

Design in context – a closer look

So what is there to learn from the London Transport experience? Acknowledging when design is in a state of crisis is often the first step in managing it. The next step is to understand where design has an impact on a business to determine what needs managing. This milestone I have called 'design in context'.

There are many things that need to be done in response to the anarchic situation design finds itself in so many businesses. The first is deceptively simple; know where design operates in your business. Understand the context for design and it will help you to manage it, and to do this, you must start with understanding your company's business or central idea.

Central business idea

And here the principle is quite simple. All successful companies are driven by an idea, something that makes them unique in their business sector or industry. We have already seen this in the short case example about the Heathrow Express. Their central idea was to 'bring the airport to London – with a train that was more like a plane'. In London Transport's case, in the early years it was to 'harness commercial methods to the achievement of large social objectives', in the case of Lego, for example, it is 'developing children's creativity through playing and learning'. But by itself a central idea cannot exist in isolation. It is only as good as its manifestations. And a central idea is made manifest in four, closely related and totally interdependent ways. Each, by varying degrees, determined by design. The original thinking behind this principle and the diagrammatic way of illustrating it was first developed by Wolff Olins, the international branding company based in London.

The first is concerned with what you do. Clearly the product you make, or the service you offer, is of prime importance to you and your customer. Managing the design of these so they reinforce the ideas and ambitions of the company are clearly vital.

Designing products involves many disciplines like research, technology, engineering, production; all of which have a major input from such people as product designers, industrial designers and design engineers. When the product is a service such as those provided by police forces, banks, insurance companies or recruitment agencies, it is less tangible. In these cases there will be other specialists involved in creating the service like psychologists, behavioural scientists or futurologists, who then need the skills of the designer to make their inputs accessible and understandable.

The second is concerned with where you do it. The environments in which you make the things you sell, or provide your services, can be made to work efficiently for staff or engender the right ambience for customers to buy. All by carefully focused use of design.

There are often more critical environments than you may at first think, and they exist in the physical and virtual worlds. They include your buildings, showrooms, offices, factories, reception areas, canteens, shops, social clubs, your web sites and digitally-based social sites. These environments are primarily the concern of space planners, architects, interior designers and, increasingly, those working in the digital arena.

The third way a central idea is made manifest concerns what you say about yourself. The information systems you use to tell people about your business have a profound affect on your success in the market place. It is not just the image projected by these systems that is important, but also their efficiency in conveying information. This is the particular concern of graphic and digital designers and typographers, PR and investor relations specialists, exhibition and promotion organizers, advertising agencies, events producers, copywriters and editors.

The fourth manifestation of a central idea is concerned with how you act. What your organization is like to deal with. What sort of corporate behaviour does it have? No amount of clever product design or communications will be of any use if you treat your staff badly and are rude to your customers.

You must take a view about the behaviour of your people and the corporate language they use. Although this is not an obvious design issue, it certainly influences behaviour in a very direct way. How would you feel about, and then react to, working in an environment that was dirty, disorganized, did not allow for easy or appropriate communications, and was inadequate for its task? Yet many people do, and consequently their contribution to the business is the poorer for it.

Manifestations vary in importance

Naturally these four areas for manifestation in central business idea vary in relative importance to each other from one company to the next.

For the company making a car the product is all important, although the web site or brochure that will tempt the customer, and the showroom where they first see the car are also important. But if the car performs less well than expected, is more costly to run than promised, the company will have lost a customer, and probably their friends as well.

In a bank the product is intangible. You cannot touch an overdraft, feel it or walk around it. So in a bank the environment in which financial transactions take place play a critical part in the success of the business. Again these environments are becoming increasingly digital based, and as such are one step away from the face-to-face contact that banking services have traditionally relied on.

For companies like travel agents, online bookstores or private health insurers, it is the information about the organization that is of prime importance. That is how, initially, a potential customer makes a judgment about the business.

For those organizations looking after the welfare and security of the public, like our nurses and police forces, it is the behaviour of the individuals, and their attitudes to the public, that shape our perceptions of the services as a whole.

In virtually every business there is a combination of product and environmental design, communication and behavioural issues. These are the manifestations of the central idea of the business and design can make a significant contribution to each of them, ensuring they work to maximum advantage. To make things more complex the design skills needed to manage the manifestations of the central idea are becoming increasingly interchangeable with the critically important role the digital world plays in people's lives. For example, affecting a banking transaction, buying a rail or airline ticket, or watching a movie, all no longer require the skills of an interior designer or architect. But they do need dedicated environments to do business. The big difference now is that these environments are all created digitally by specialist designers and are all accessible from anywhere in the world.

If all these manifestations of the central idea do not work in a coherent, effective and synchronized way, you create contradictions, and undermine the idea. Get the balance of design right across these key areas of business and you will be on the road to success. Manage design badly and you will end up going the wrong way back to design in crisis.

Small things as well

Just in case I have given the impression that the context of design in a business is only about managing the broad issues, it must be said that it is also about managing many smaller things as well.

In the same way that a large wall is only a collection of small bricks, so a company's attitude towards design is often exposed through ordinary detail; detail upon which a central idea is often built, or founders.

For example, look at that critical early association a potential customer may have with your organization. That string of initial contacts has been aptly described by Wally Olins as The Journey. Those points of contact can start in the most remote of ways, for example via the internet or a complex recorded answering system when you try to call to fix an appointment. And when you do manage to connect directly with the potential customer, or employee, it really does matter how they answer the phone, or what condition the reception and offices (or showrooms or shops) are in when you eventually meet and try to do business. All of this is before you experience the service or product.

The context of design in any organization is broad and this is the canvas of design management. It is critical to managing the manifestation of a central idea. It is as much about managing small things as it is about managing big things. Recognize this and you have reached the second milestone, and are well on the way to passing it. Given that the context for design is well understood, what must organizations do to control, manage and make it effective?

Design in place – a closer look

The next milestone in the integration of design into business is to establish an organizational structure, appropriate to the business, which allows design to be managed. This milestone I have called 'design in place'. However, before we consider what place is given to design in organizations I have a word of warning. Because design operates at both the macro and micro levels, and is so pervasive, you must make a considerable effort to control and manage it, or it will, in a sense, control you. Creating a formal place for design in business is a major step in this process.

In my experience of working as a consultant to, and a staff member of, very large companies there are a number of customary measures that are often taken to bring this issue of design to the organizational heel.

Centralize

The first is to give it a central position in the organization, in just the same way as other corporate resources are, like Finance, Personnel, Research and Development.

Commitment

The second is to get commitment from the top, often from the chief executive, that design should be given full and proper consideration in all parts of the business.

Leader

The third is to appoint a centrally-based design manager or leader, thereby ensuring it does not become a subset of Marketing, or Advertising, or Public Relations, or Engineering. After all, it contributes to them all. It provides the vital glue that helps other functions work towards realizing the central idea for the company.

Budgets

The fourth, which invariably (although not always) follows from the third, is the creation of discrete budgets to pay for special projects, and for employing designers. These special projects I refer to are invariably cross-functional in nature, like the development and management of corporate identity or communications, or the setting up of envisioning work that will help in strategic decision-making. Sometimes it is necessary to use a central budget to demonstrate the advantage of a new way of design thinking to the operational divisions of the business.

Policy

The fifth measure is to create design policies to guide managers on what is wanted from design investment across the business.

Approve

The sixth measure concerns the principle of go or no go. Depending on the nature of the business, it may also require its own independent approval procedures governing quality as well as content.

These six measures, or a combination of some of them, often represent the culmination of considerable effort to put design in place in a company. As commendable as each of them may be, and indeed I have been party to (and in some cases responsible for) establishing all of them in a number of companies, they do very little good in the long term, at least on their own. Even collectively they represent only one small step (albeit a very positive one). The start of something and not the finish. This is because these steps represent the mechanics a business employs to get things done. What they do not do is change culture, and this is what is needed for design to become a long-term effective resource.

Design in management – a closer look

Considering the journey we have made it is 'so far so good' but there is still further to go. Which brings us to the often most difficult to reach, milestone in the progress of design's relationship with business. The management of design will only achieve lasting long-term success once it goes beyond the establishment of systems and procedures and is made to live in an organization. This is the next and most important milestone in the relationship between design and business which I have called 'design in management'.

Common practice

The measures taken to put design in place represent the commonly practiced art of design management. In my experience companies are often quite content to accept this as their goal. As good as this is it will not realize design's full potential. Unfortunately this does not go far enough. Design departments, bosses, budgets, policies or approval procedures are often necessary in making design respectable, and allowing it legitimate entry into an organization. However, they can have a constricting effect, often isolating those managers who are making design-related decisions every day of their lives.

For example, a design director can be an effective internal focus, or an external public symbol. Both are very useful. But if the director then becomes the exclusive channel for all design decisions then that guru runs the serious risk of becoming a barrier to progress, a retarding influence on timetables, a crutch for the organization, often becoming a bully or bureaucrat who insists on doing everything his or her own way. Or worse still, a stifler of initiative, interest or integrity for those who make design decisions all the time, whether they know it or not.

The positive side of creating a formal place for design is that chief executives wave flags, policy groups provide focus, approval groups give access to opinion and provide forums for limited understanding, and systems provide a framework for teams and budgets.

Even documented design policies have a place as long as they capitalize on the culture and commitment of the business and are written in such a way that does not alienate the people who are expected to use them.

Some potency but not enough

Each of these measures possesses some potency in the battle against design anarchy. The downside of all this is that by themselves they are of little long-term consequence. They cannot create a culture. That comes from an inherent belief about what is right.

No amount of legislation, rule writing, bureaucratic system building, or indeed the installation of someone with absolute authority will allow design to live in a company. The use of design in a company is always much bigger and more extensive than any simple mechanism for monitoring or control can ever handle. The flood is always bigger than the barrier can contain. Effectiveness comes from beliefs and attitudes, not laws and police officers. Design management is important; design IN management is imperative if the ultimate aim is to get the most from its potential and the investment in it. And this is the most critical, and often most difficult to reach, milestone in the marriage between design and business.

A new way of life

Design must become a way of life in the organization. Managers must learn to think of design as part of the way they do things, like safety, finance, quality or commercial astuteness. After all, it is they who are concerned with it, whether they recognize it or not. These people have been very aptly described as silent designers. Remember the point about design in context? There are many people, at many levels in an organization, making decisions about design.

Design must become part of the nervous system of an organization before it can be efficacious and so create long-term benefit. A quantum leap needs to be made whereby the guru image of the design boss must be replaced in favour of the responsibility lying with more people. Design must become part of the fabric of the business. It must be automatic, regularized, unexceptional in its use and second nature to all.

A facilitating mechanism

To realize this situation, where design IN management is invisible but all embracing, will require a facilitating mechanism. This may be the championing chief executive, or design director acting as their agent, working with others to help them recognize the design issues they deal with daily, and to help them manage their way through them.

It may be a question of a much more sophisticated type of management technique. That of providing firm direction, but with a light management touch.

It is necessary for the company to create a cultural climate in which design is considered normal. This may be achieved through internal promotional and educational projects.

It is also necessary to train managers in understanding the value of design and how to use it. They in turn will then become its ambassadors. This will lead to increased cooperation in the many complex design implementation tasks involved in most businesses. It is very important that managers become familiar with design so that when suitably advised, they can take future discretionary responsibility for design implementation. Let me emphasize the point about being 'suitably advised'. An important aspect of design in management is that managers know where to go for advice and feel able and free to seek it. This point comes out strongly in the Eurotunnel case example that can be found in Part Four.

The route I describe is informal and low key. It is however very effective because the number of design responsibilities within a company increases as the cascading process of involvement and ownership takes hold. Eventually, when design gets under the skin, is absorbed into the culture, becomes part of the furniture of the business, formally invisible but informally all embracing it will no longer remain on the shelf as a commercial accessory to be used tactically by companies looking for marginal improvements in business performance. Design IN management will be there to stay and make a long-term contribution to success.

Summary

This process of Milestones in Design Management is a form of design audit. Its purpose is to get a good understanding of design in the organization. I have described the milestones in the developing relationship between design, its management, and its place in business. These not only form the basis of developing the understanding, they also represent a good way of presenting the findings to others in the business.

The first milestone concerned design in crisis. Left to its own devices, design will not manage itself. Unfortunately in many companies design is not managed at all. It is not even recognized as a potential force for coherence. Different people from different backgrounds, with different interests to protect, end up being responsible for different aspects of design.

The second concerned design in context. The context for design is directly related to and determined by the central idea of a company, and that idea is made manifest in both big and small ways peculiar to that business. In most cases design contributes significantly to each manifestation, particularly in how that idea is made visible, how it is communicated, and finally how the company behaves both internally and externally. These manifestations must be coordinated, and be seen to be aspects of the same central idea, if they are going to generate maximum commercial benefit in the market place.

BMW for example have a very clear view of where design touches their business. They have a design attitude that is made manifest wherever you look – their cars and showrooms, workshops and manuals, web site, promotional events and advertising, factories and management material. The tragedy is that this simple idea seems to escape the corporate consciousness of most businesses today. Identifying the context for design in a particular business is a key milestone in managing it.

The third issue concerned design in place. Putting in place a design boss, a structure, a design department, a policy and a budget are often important and necessary, particularly in large organizations. They are invariably needed to give design legitimacy in a business. They are all fine and effective measures.

Royal Philips Electronics, for example, had, when under Robert Blaich's design leadership, developed a design management system that still stretches across and down right through the company. However, systems like this will only be partially successful. By themselves they are simply not enough. The job to be done is usually much bigger than these people or systems can handle alone.

The fourth, and most important issue concerned design in management – the degree to which design is fully integrated into the organization. For design to be truly effective and contribute real commercial advantage, it must become part of an organization's DNA, part of its make up. This level of integration becomes ever more critical as other differences between competitors diminish. As more companies develop similar products to each other as a result of conducting research with the same, or similar, groups of people, it becomes essential that every resource be used to the full to reflect the real differences between one company and the next. And because of its pervasive influence, this is particularly true of design.

'putting design into the DNA of the company is the only way to maximize shareholder value from the investment'

Even so, and despite all the promotion and hype it has had over recent years, we still have much to learn about design's contribution to management. Yes, some enlightened companies use design as a strategic business tool. Yes, some companies recognize design management as a critical process in the use of design. However, to make the resource totally effective, to make us better employers of thousands and better suppliers to millions, and that must be a worthwhile objective, we cannot be content with design management as usually described and practiced today.

London Transport, 75 years ago, demonstrated that design and business could be integrated. Apple, BT, Virgin and Lego today, are some of the companies where design IN management is a reality. The journey to total integration of design and business is difficult, and often long. Fortunately, it is marked by clear milestones. Although there is much to do to get there the potential benefits of reaching the end of the journey and putting design in management surely make it worthwhile.

Process for design leadership

As with design management, processes to help design leaders make a difference will differ from business to business, although at the heart of them will be a very similar objective – to deliver a better business, a better organization, a better social system, all by maximizing the contribution from design.

There are three different processes described here as ways of helping make this happen. They should be treated as a way into the subject or task rather than something where, once the boxes are ticked, the job is done. Each process has a slightly different focus, but not by much. Each has a proven track record in being useful in the process of design leadership.

The focus for the first is Business Connections – *an overview process*, the second is Manifesting Strategic Intent – *a how and why process*, and the third is Opportunities to Action, a combination of the other two.

Business Connections – an overview process

The focus for this process is Business Connections and the role design plays design as a business leadership tool to arrive at a strategic actions plan.

Design can be used to deliver a customer experience that is in line with strategic aims and so significantly enhance corporate reputation. To ensure that this happens across all aspects of a business the process described below ensures all design activities are aligned to realizing this objective. Diagram 8.2 illustrates this process that consists of four sequential steps. Some of these steps are often already in place within the company's statement of policy, often they are not.

Note that the word 'customer' is used in the text as a collective expression for direct and indirect customers, employees, business partners and other stakeholders. The first row shows the four steps. The second explains, essentially, what each step is about. The third gives an example of the step working in practice. The example illustrated is from the Heathrow Terminal 5 case, described fully in the Part Four.

Motivating proposition

The first step is to define the strategic proposition of your business. This sometimes already exists, more often it does not. Where it does exist there is the need to establish a clear understanding of what it means. Where it does not exist there is a critical need to establish it. Establishing a motivating proposition often involves a consultancy process, experts who can help businesses identify the real essence of what makes them different. It is a real skill to distil this into a statement that is usually concise and encapsulates the strategic intent of the business. It is often used to motivate staff, to give them a sense of what the business is all about. This is why businesses sometimes find it useful to call this statement 'our motivating proposition'. Another good example of a motivating proposition informing a new corporate direction is that of Roca, the world's largest manufacturer of bathroom ceramic ware. Details of this case can be found in Part Four.

Proposition drivers

The second step is to identify the key drivers that enable that proposition to be become a reality. These drivers are often areas of major focus or change. There are never many of them – four to six is usually the case. In the example illustrated in Diagram 8.2, from Heathrow's Terminal 5 project, there were four. They are big things; they are the things that, once addressed, create significant differentiation. They are sometimes called strategies but I prefer either 'proposition drivers' or 'drivers for change', both phrases being more expressive than 'strategies'.

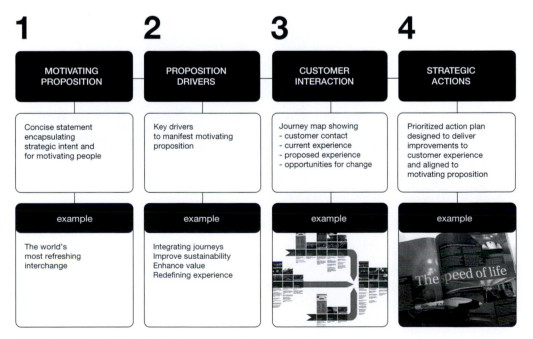

DELIVERING CUSTOMER EXPERIENCE – ENHANCING REPUTATION

Diagram 8.2 Design as a business leadership tool to arrive at a strategic actions plan

Customer interactions

The third step is to understand where the opportunities are for influencing the customer experience. A very effective way of doing this is to map where the customer comes into contact with the company, or with the products or services the company provides. These maps identify the points of contact, define the current experience customers have at those points of contact, propose changes to those experiences where necessary, and finally describe what design, communications, and sometimes behavioural, activity can manifest those changes. Figure 8.2 shows one of the many customer experience maps that are being used by a major international bank as one way to focus its design activity and brand investment.

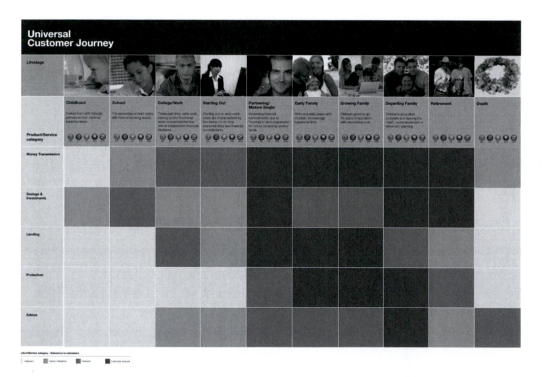

Figure 8.2 *Customer experience mapping for a major international bank*

Clive Grinyer advocates that a good way to alert company managers to the potential opportunity of influencing, what he calls Touchpoints, is to consider initially the interface between customer and company in a generic way. He maintains that research to purchase, first use and customer service, can all deliver customer delight or, conversely, dissatisfaction. His diagram illustrates the point well and is shown in Figure 8.3.

The customer experience journey is made of many touchpoints with the company, its services and products. It cuts horizontally across the different divisions or silos of a business. The designer increasingly has to operate across the whole journey – from the design of the proposition to the actual product or service that goes with it, and the users physical and virtual interfaces involved. Break this chain, or create discordant interfaces between the links, and you risk losing the customer and their long-term commitment to you.

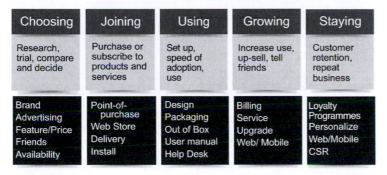

Seeing the Customer's Point of View

- Research to purchase, first use and customer service, each point can deliver customer delight or dissatisfaction.

Choosing	Joining	Using	Growing	Staying
Research, trial, compare and decide	Purchase or subscribe to products and services	Set up, speed of adoption, use	Increase use, up-sell, tell friends	Customer retention, repeat business
Brand Advertising Feature/Price Friends Availability	Point-of-purchase Web Store Delivery Install	Design Packaging Out of Box User manual Help Desk	Billing Service Upgrade Web/ Mobile	Loyalty Programmes Personalize Web/Mobile CSR

Figure 8.3 *Customer touchpoints start well before the purchase of a product or service, and can continue well beyond it*

Strategic actions

The fourth step is to draw up a strategic action plan based on the first three steps. This plan usually prioritizes the actions required for design to deliver changes, and often improvements, to the customer's experience such that they are aligned to the original motivating proposition.

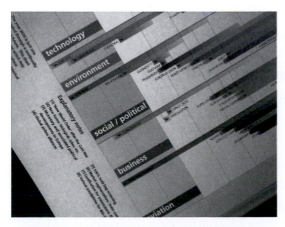

Figure 8.4 *Part of a chart mapping changes that had taken place prior to the development of Terminal 5 as well as the changes expected post its opening*

Figure 8.4 is part of a chart mapping changes that had taken place prior to the development of Heathrow's Terminal 5 as well as the changes expected post its opening. This helped to set the context for the Terminal 5 strategic design action plan. It was one of the enabling tools the design team used to develop a solution that was not based on 'business as usual'. Other prioritized plans can derive from customer experience mapping where they are used to focus design and capital investment to maximize impact in the shortest possible time, such as the one used for the development of Galway City centre, Ireland, see Figure 8.5.

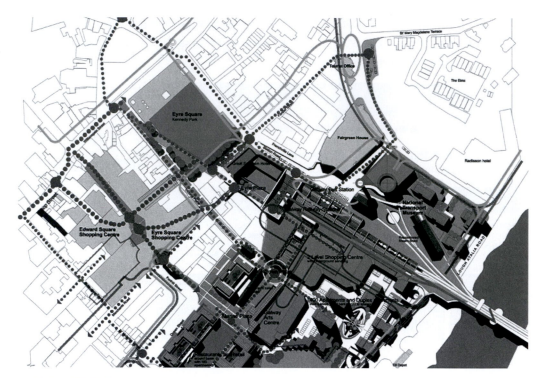

Figure 8.5 *Part of Galway City centre strategic design action plan*

Summary

This process looks simple; after all it has only four elements. However the process involved in developing each of the steps can be complex, involve many people and, for some organizations, be politically sensitive. However, it is its simplicity that makes it engaging for management boards and gives the design leader a sound starting point for a debate that is not based on esoteric, difficult to grasp language, but relates directly to the challenges that so many of them face.

Manifesting strategic intent – a how and why process

The focus for this process is manifesting strategic intent of the business and to do so in a way that can be understood whether you are looking at it from the boardroom or the factory floor through a series of clear connections between the two.

Diagram 8.3 sums up one way of showing these connections. If you are looking at the diagram from the top down you can see how the strategic intent is going to be realized through the design projects the company invests in. If, on the other hand, you are involved in working on one of those design projects you can look 'up' the diagram and see where it fits into the wider picture and reassure yourself why this work is necessary. This is why I call this a 'how/why' diagram. If there are any activities going on in the business that do not fit into this diagram then the question must be asked 'do they need them?'

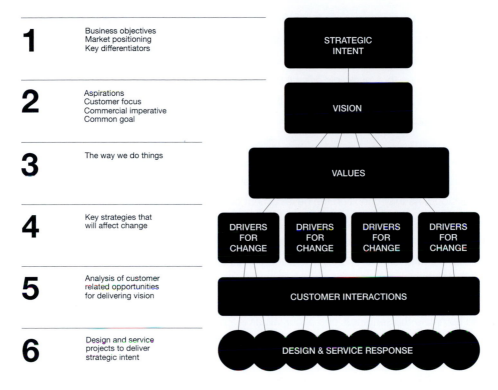

1 Business objectives
Market positioning
Key differentiators

2 Aspirations
Customer focus
Commercial imperative
Common goal

3 The way we do things

4 Key strategies that
will affect change

5 Analysis of customer
related opportunities
for delivering vision

6 Design and service
projects to deliver
strategic intent

STRATEGIC INTENT

VISION

VALUES

DRIVERS FOR CHANGE — DRIVERS FOR CHANGE — DRIVERS FOR CHANGE — DRIVERS FOR CHANGE

CUSTOMER INTERACTIONS

DESIGN & SERVICE RESPONSE

Diagram 8.3 A 'how/why' diagram with customer interactions added to provide the opportunities for deliver

Strategic intent

These take many guises. Sometimes they sum up business objectives or market aspirations. I have heard them expressed in many ways. For example at one marketing conference I remember attending they tripped off a presenter's tongue as sound bites: 'A Coke within arms reach' or, for the manufacturer of small Japanese engines, 'Three in every garage'. Neither of these was intended to be corporate aims but they do make the point that such statements can direct much effort.

As explained in the case example of 'Design for future needs', see Part Four, the strategic intent for Heathrow's Terminal 5 was 'to maintain the strategic position of BAA, the airport operator, and British Airways, the terminal's principal tenant, as industry leaders by creating appropriate additional capacity at Heathrow'.

Vision

However, strategic intent is not enough on its own; a vision is also needed to capture the potential of that intent. A vision should describe the high ground implicit in the statement of strategic intent. It should also provide the platform for developing design and operational strategies to realize that intent. In the Eurotunnel's case example 'Design in a service industry', described in Part Four, the vision was simple – a service where you could just 'turn up and go'. Previous to this booking was needed for a place on the ferry, which may not run anyway because of the vagaries of weather. BAA, on the other hand, say that their vision is to create an enjoyable experience for everyone visiting their airports. They expand on this vision by saying that their aim is to manage and enable world-class journeys and provide world-class experiences in environments that are safe and sustainable. Ambitious, but incredibly difficult to achieve. Nevertheless, without setting an audacious target how can you possibly hope to achieve the high ground that is appropriate to a company that wants to be an industry leader.

Values

Before strategies can be developed, the corporate values that steer everything a company does need to be understood, as they condition the development of those strategies and everything that flows from them. These values should be quite specific to the business. There is nothing more useless than a set of values that are so generic they could be referring to any company. Words like 'world class, efficient, user friendly, value for money', all fit into this category.

Values should always be written in a way that shows why each is important. You should always be able to complete the sentence 'one of our values is ???? because it enables us to ????', or something like it. Just fill in the gaps represented by the '????'.

GloHealth, a new entrant into the private health insurance business based in Ireland, believes its values summarize the way they work and behave. They believe these are critical to realizing their vision, are the basis of their differentiation and set them apart from competitors. They say they are key to winning new customers and retaining them. They have five values:

- Clarity, because it is important to make everything for our customers easy to understand and simple to use. When dealing with each other and with business partners, we will be clear, straightforward and direct. We don't use complex language; we always try to keep our way of talking simple and to the point.
- Smart, because we are always in-tune with our customers needs and respond accordingly. It means being innovative and forward thinking. It means giving customers the confidence that they were smart to join us and feel comfortable knowing we are the best fit for their health insurance needs.
- Courage, because we are prepared to be different when it is right for our customers. We will provide tailored services even though this approach may be at variance with what others in the industry do. We are always prepared to challenge the status quo, when it is in our customers' best interest.
- Integrity, because being true and honest to ourselves will reflect positively in all our relationships. It means we will be consistent and open in our dealings. It means being ambitiously engaged and dedicated, emotionally as well as intellectually, because this will ensure exceptional contributions in achieving our business objectives and delivering our vision.

BAA also have five values, in their case they were design values, which were quite specific to what they were trying to do through their investment programmes:

- Being Responsive, satisfying and exceeding the needs of customers and staff. This means listening to people, putting people first, meeting people's special needs, anticipating and adapting to changing market requirements and social attitudes.
- Being Simple, Clear and Coherent, making the experience predictable and trouble free. This means making the airport facilities easy to manage and maintain, achieving a sense of order through familiar processes and facilities, creating spaces that are logical to use and easy to understand.
- Being Responsible, by designing in a socially and environmentally conscious way. This means prioritizing safety and promoting integrity, being concerned with issues such as noise pollution and the use of non-replaceable resources, integrating new facilities with its airport setting and community context, not reinventing the wheel but building on experience and using tried and tested solutions.
- Being Appropriate in Style and Quality, by designing what is right for both stakeholders and customers. This means being sympathetic to established visual character, providing the best while being cost effective, using standardization to ensure specified levels of quality.
- Being Innovative and Exciting, by exploiting our creative opportunities. This means creating positively memorable environments, expressing our differentiated approach and market leadership, making the experience vivid and exciting.

Case Examples of both companies can be found in Part Four.

Strategies or drivers for change

It is only when these values are in place that a set of strategies can be developed that will be the key drivers for change. These strategies might be quite different in nature from each other, but all of them would be informed by the vision the business has created for itself. For example, you may have a group of strategies that include radical product innovation; increased investment in R&D; a new recruitment programme that attracts the latest bright minds; and a new way to raise market interest in the end product when it arrives.

Customer interactions

A clear understanding of the potential for manifesting these strategies or drivers for change can be found through a detailed analysis of customer interactions with the business. This is where such tools as customer experience mapping and touchpoint analysis can be of great help.

Design and service responses

Every strategy will have a number of design responses to deliver it, and they all link back through the corporate values to the vision and strategic intent of the organization. Without such alignment, shareholder value cannot be maximized from design investment, and no one can be sure that every design activity, and every pound spent on it, is contributing to the wider business ambitions. Tim Selders of PARK Advanced Design Management from the Netherlands points out from his research that many design leaders believe design is still seen as an operational benefit only. He maintains there is still much to be done before design is accepted as a core competency to help build business strategies. When DAA, the Dublin Airport Authority, wanted to review their brand and what it meant to customers, and to understand better how to improve their customers' experience of the airport, they used this process to guide the work. This is described in the case example 'Design integration' in Part Four. It very clearly demonstrates the power of design in making strategy a tangible experience.

'design is a business tool that makes strategy visible'

The case examples of New West End Company, outlined in Chapter 7, and GloHealth, described in Part Four, illustrate the connections between strategic intent and the day-to-day actions of the business. Each describes their clear strategic intent, vision, drivers for change and an outline plan of projects to deliver their strategic ambitions.

From opportunity to action

This is a cradle to grave process, see Diagram 8.4, and its focus is a series of simple steps that go from Opportunity to Action. I have found each process of value when managing and leading design. By themselves none of them are the automatic answer to how design should be managed or led. Different companies and organizations, and different people within them, require different responses to the situations they find themselves in.

This process contains aspects of the others described earlier in the chapter. It is similar to the first one but is not so intensive an audit process as that. It is proactive rather than reflective in nature. Ideally the audit should be completed before any other work in design leadership and management is considered. This process combines the analysis of corporate opportunity for design with that of stakeholders needs. It deals with the issues of ongoing design management as well as those concerned with devolving design responsibility into the wider management hierarchy.

It is a comprehensive approach to putting design into the DNA of the business and is one of the best ways of ensuring design brings ongoing and long-term benefits. There are five stages to this process.

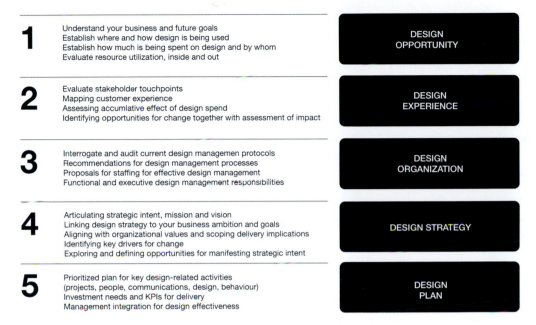

1
Understand your business and future goals
Establish where and how design is being used
Establish how much is being spent on design and by whom
Evaluate resource utilization, inside and out

DESIGN OPPORTUNITY

2
Evaluate stakeholder touchpoints
Mapping customer experience
Assessing accumlative effect of design spend
Identifying opportunities for change together with assessment of impact

DESIGN EXPERIENCE

3
Interrogate and audit current design managemen protocols
Recommendations for design management processes
Proposals for staffing for effective design management
Functional and executive design management responsibilities

DESIGN ORGANIZATION

4
Articulating strategic intent, mission and vision
Linking design strategy to your business ambition and goals
Aligning with organizational values and scoping delivery implications
Identifying key drivers for change
Exploring and defining opportunities for manifesting strategic intent

DESIGN STRATEGY

5
Prioritized plan for key design-related activities
(projects, people, communications, design, behaviour)
Investment needs and KPIs for delivery
Management integration for design effectiveness

DESIGN PLAN

Diagram 8.4 This is a Cradle to Grave process. It contains aspects of the others described earlier in the section

Design opportunity

This is about understanding how well the business is using design now. Key to making design work effectively for any organization is to determine where design touches the business and all those people with whom it deals. This step is about looking inside the business to determine where design decisions are being made. It means looking down through the management layers of the business as well as across its silos.

Some of the issues and questions that should be addressed by this study into design opportunity include:

- identifying where design is being used, where it touches the business, the degree to which it is being used to achieve corporate purpose;
- identifying how design is managed on a project level, personnel level, departmental level and a corporate level;
- how much is being spent on design;
- who is spending it;
- what authority and accountability do they have for its affect on the business and its customers;
- assessing the degree to which design is being managed or is 'in crisis';
- evaluate the skills and appropriateness of the designers employed, inside and outside the business.

Design experience

This part is about looking at how well design is shaping business reputation and the nature and quality of the customer and stakeholder interfaces with the business. It means:

- evaluating stakeholder touchpoints and mapping customer experience;
- critiquing how well the customer experience is being delivered at each point of contact, how it might be improved and the design activity involved in doing it;
- identifying additional opportunities for its effective use in the future.

Design organization

Design organizations are important in any business. They should fit in with the current organizational and management structures. They should not be seen to need special allowances just because it is design that is being managed. The work involved will include:

- assessing options for using the existing management systems in the organization to manage design and recommend how it might be integrated into them;
- establishing a management system and infrastructure for organizing design projects, budget allocations, reviews and approvals;
- identifying the amount of design resource, internal or external, needed either centrally in the business or within the operating divisions;
- putting in place functional and executive design management personnel.

Design strategy

Design works at strategic and tactical levels. This is about ensuring both are covered by the development and business plans of the organization. It will involve:

- defining design policy and strategy in line with the wider aims of the business;
- being specific about what corporate or design values mean in the implementation of design work;
- defining the change drivers that will improve business performance through design investment;
- defining implementation opportunities and specific design projects for manifesting strategic intent;
- providing the links between strategic intent and design activity.

Design plan

This is concerned with creating a prioritized plan of action to turn all that has been learnt from the other steps into something that makes design work in a tangible way. What this plan consists of, and what benefits it might deliver when implemented, will depend on the output from the first four steps of this process. It will almost certainly include issues to do with investment priority, training for design awareness and relating design briefs to manifest corporate strategy. The most critical output is an understanding of what needs to be addressed.

This is likely to include:

- creating strategically relevant design content and activities that will maximize investment in it;
- prioritizing the design actions needed to deliver the strategic objectives of the business and prepare a business plan for the investment;
- putting design into management training and awareness programmes so as to help develop a design centred culture within the organization;
- making design unexceptional in its use so that it becomes fully integrated into the way a company does business and has become part of its DNA, part of the management ethic, making it accountable activity for all managers.

Summary of Chapter 8

This chapter has outlined four different ways by which design management and leadership work can start in earnest. There is inevitably an overlap in what these processes cover, but there are also differences. Some situations demand one sort of approach rather than another. I have found that a combination of them is often needed. The important thing is to have some help in starting the work and these have proven to be useful in that regard.

No process, by itself, makes anything happen. No strategy by itself makes a business a better business. I believe Peter Drucker once said that plans are only good intentions unless they immediately degenerate into hard work. How right he was. And this work needs the right sort of people to do it and train others to continue it. All these processes set out to do is to suggest templates that could be useful in understanding what needs to be done, how to present that understanding to other people in order to solicit support, and to plan the subsequent action. The risk of outlining any process is to give the impression that processes are the answer. They are not. They are simply a way of starting.

Part Four contains three particular case examples that illustrate, more fully than was possible in the text above, some of the issues and principles discussed here.

The first is called Roca – what next? Roca is the world leader in the production of ceramic bathroom products and hardware. It is profitable, family owned, hugely successful, and based in Barcelona. This case example examines the role of design leadership and innovation in extending its business beyond the normal bounds of a production led organization to one that is focused on creating new, consumer-based, experiences.

The second is called DAA – design integration. The Dublin Airport Authority is an airport management company with 3,000 employees and a turnover in 2010 of €558 million. Headquartered at Dublin Airport, the DAA's principal activities include airport management, operation and development, domestic and international airport retail management, and airport investment. The company's domestic operations include the running of Dublin, Cork and Shannon airports. This case looks at the role of design leadership in putting in place the building blocks for integrating design into the organization in order to improve the quality of experience of everyone using their airports.

The third is called GloHealth – rethinking health insurance. This case example sets out the basic story behind the creation of a new business in a well-populated market but one where consumers were largely disillusioned with what was available. With respect to positioning, differentiation, values and identity, the executives of the new business commissioned Image Now to guide them through this challenging territory.

Chapter 9
Behavioural style

Much of the success of design managers and leaders depends on the behavioural styles they adopt within the business. In this section I have outlined the essence of those styles that have been seen to work and, equally important, are some notes on the attitude a company client should adopt towards their external consultants who may be retained to help with design management tasks. The better they are at being a client the better the results will be.

Design managers tend to be employed in one of two types of roles. The first are those with line responsibility. These managers are responsible for managing a design team producing design work. Sometimes this work is undertaken within the business, other times it is outsourced. Either way they have direct responsibility for the commissioning of design work and the appropriateness of its output. They invariably work for a profit centre in the business reporting into one of the operational divisions such as Marketing Communications, Development or Engineering. Sometimes, in very large companies, there are design managers with line responsibility in more than one division.

The second are design managers with functional responsibility. These are not usually directly responsible for the design work being produced by the company's designers, internal or external. They have a roving commission with broader responsibilities for the quality of design work across the business, and often its alignment with corporate objectives. These functional design managers tend to work for a corporate function, based centrally, and are part of the cost base of the business. If they do manage design projects they tend to be of a corporate nature.

These two types of design managers require different behavioural skills.

Line managers' behaviour

Those design managers with line responsibility are relatively easy to define, although not quite so easy to find. In essence they must be able to manage people, money and time, be able to deliver results and have the relevant technical knowledge. This was discussed fully in Chapter 7. They must be able to do these things in a way that gets the best out of people and money, through as much collaboration as possible. But never forgetting that they are required to get work done and have the management responsibility to deliver. They always have the ultimate power to instruct.

Functional managers' behaviour

The skills required by design managers with functional responsibility are rather more complex. They need a behavioural style that directs and guides rather than dictates, inspires not instructs, creates alliances not conflicts.

As with any functional manager, including design managers, it is important to understand the 'rights' that go with the role. There are three.

Right of access

The first is the 'right of access' to any meeting that is discussing the subject for which the functional manager is responsible. So, if a meeting is taking place in some part of the business that will include a design issue on the agenda, the functional manager for design has the right to attend – they cannot be excluded.

Right to advise

The second is the 'right to advise' at that meeting. The meeting may not like the advice being given, and they are certainly not required to take it, but the functional design manager has the right and responsibility to give it.

Right to appeal

The third right is the 'right of appeal' to a higher authority if that advice is not taken. It does not follow that this right is exercised every time there is a disagreement but it is an extremely powerful tool that has to be used with great caution. The hope always is that, because everyone knows the functional manager has this third right, it is rarely used. If it is over used the organization will find ways of working without the manager rather than willingly include them.

These three rights require the functional design manager to behave in a very particular way. For example, they must be able to provide firm design direction or advice, but to do so with a light, sometimes very light, management touch. After all they have been placed in a position where they must influence thinking over which they have no direct management control. This is something that needs to be cultivated – it does not always come easily, particularly when it can be seen that others in the business are making a mess of using design and the design manager is keen to wade in and try and correct matters.

An appropriate behavioural style

Both types of design management appointment require the people involved to adopt a behavioural style in a way that is appropriate to the culture of the business rather than expect the business to change to suit their style. This may seem an obvious thing to say but so often I have seen an appointment fail resulting from a design manager's inability to read how the business conducts itself.

And every company is different, some want 'dictatorial bandits' as design managers, some want 'collaborative diplomats'. The important thing is to choose the people to match the personality of the organization or, if you are the candidate, be able to read the organization well enough to adjust your style of behaviour accordingly if needed.

Design client behaviour

To repeat an earlier point, design is one of the few resources that can provide a clear and practical link between the strategic discussions of the boardroom and the day-to-day activities of the business. As such it is critical that any investment in design is focused on that link, and the success of this investment is dependent on one particularly critical issue – the relationship between client and staff designer or consultant.

For this relationship to be fully productive both client and designer must understand what a good relationship between them depends on. For the purposes of what follows I have assumed that the design services are being bought in from outside the business. However, most of my comments about the relationship between client and consultant also apply if the designer is a member of the same company.

Having made many mistakes over the years in managing this relationship (both as a consultant and a client) I can confidently say that a successful one depends, at least, on answering positively five simple questions:

- Am I sure what I want?
- Can I work with these people?
- Are we clear about money?
- Does it matter if they have done it before?
- How will I manage the relationship?

Am I sure what I want?

Invariably this is summarized in what most people call 'the brief'. Without a brief the design consultant has nowhere to start. But a brief is more than a starting point. Unless it also contains an explicit description of what is required as a result of the work you should not be surprised if the designer does not deliver – after all you cannot expect them to have second-sight!

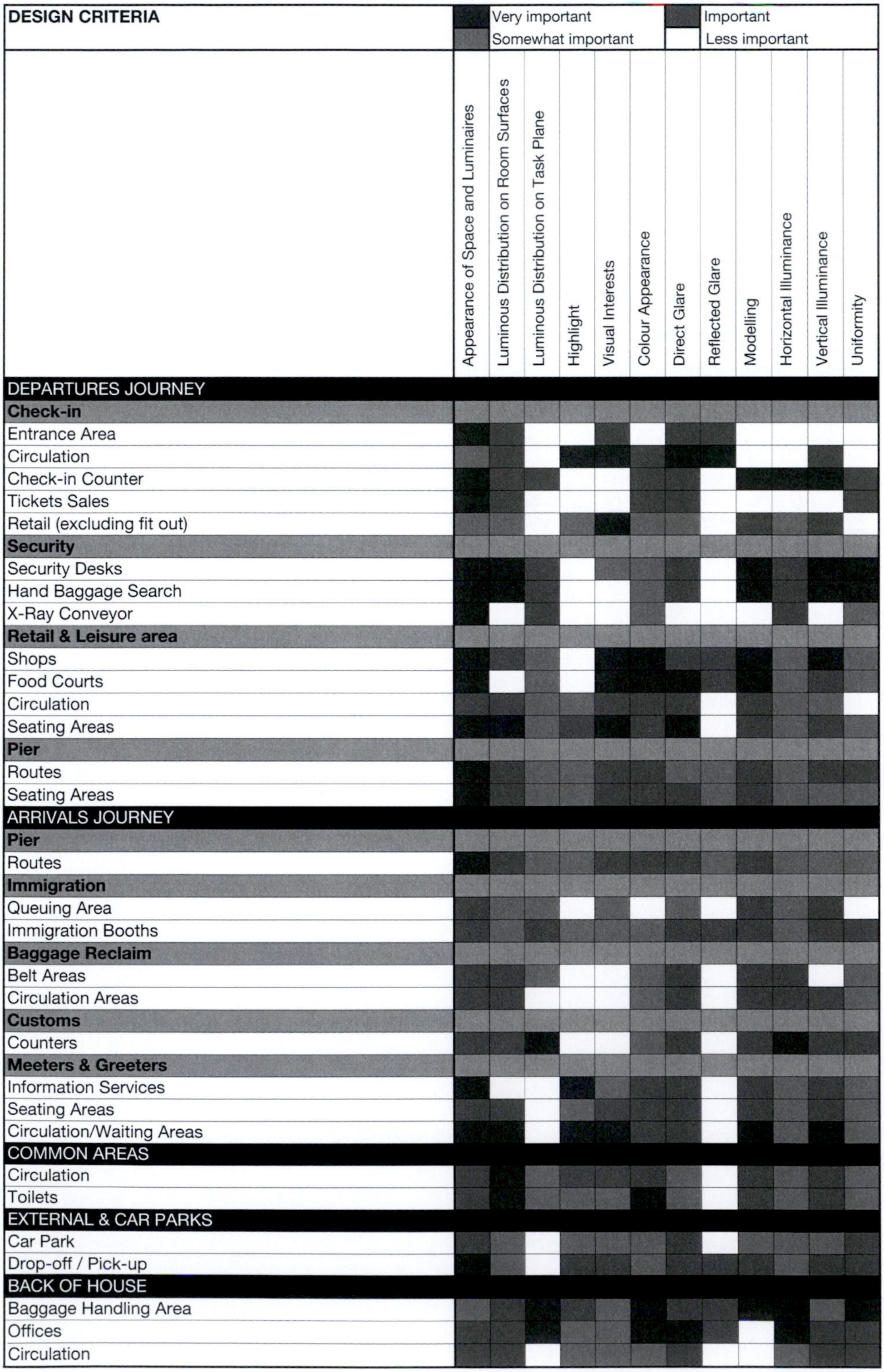

DESIGN CRITERIA

Legend:
- ■ Very important
- ■ Important
- ■ Somewhat important
- □ Less important

Column criteria (left to right):
- Appearance of Space and Luminaires
- Luminous Distribution on Room Surfaces
- Luminous Distribution on Task Plane
- Highlight
- Visual Interests
- Colour Appearance
- Direct Glare
- Reflected Glare
- Modelling
- Horizontal Illuminance
- Vertical Illuminance
- Uniformity

DEPARTURES JOURNEY

Check-in
- Entrance Area
- Circulation
- Check-in Counter
- Tickets Sales
- Retail (excluding fit out)

Security
- Security Desks
- Hand Baggage Search
- X-Ray Conveyor

Retail & Leisure area
- Shops
- Food Courts
- Circulation
- Seating Areas

Pier
- Routes
- Seating Areas

ARRIVALS JOURNEY

Pier
- Routes

Immigration
- Queuing Area
- Immigration Booths

Baggage Reclaim
- Belt Areas
- Circulation Areas

Customs
- Counters

Meeters & Greeters
- Information Services
- Seating Areas
- Circulation/Waiting Areas

COMMON AREAS
- Circulation
- Toilets

EXTERNAL & CAR PARKS
- Car Park
- Drop-off / Pick-up

BACK OF HOUSE
- Baggage Handling Area
- Offices
- Circulation

Diagram 9.1 A design criteria matrix used as part of the brief to improve customer experience when travelling through an airport

Many papers, university course modules, seminars and conferences have been run to explore and explain how to write the perfect brief. Suffice it to say that unless it describes, in some way, what success looks like, and how that success will be assessed or measured, then the rest of it counts for nothing. Sometimes these criteria are simply described – an improved return on investment, an increase in margin or sales, solving of particular technical problems. Other times the measurement criteria can be much more complex as shown in Diagram 9.1, a matrix of design criteria and their level of importance to customer experience.

No matter how simple or complex the success criteria might be, in all cases a successful brief is characterized by a clear statement of the strategic business intent that is intended as the focus of the subsequent design response from the consultant.

As a client it is well worth the effort to get the brief right first – even if it takes longer than you thought (and it nearly always does). It prevents grief later when abortive work has to be paid for, the implementation programme has slipped and the contribution to the bottom line of the business that is expected from the design work is less than it should be – all because not enough care was taken in being sure what you, and your client-colleagues, want from the relationship.

Can I work with these people?

It does not matter how expert the client is, or how creative the designer is, if the chemistry between the two is not right then neither will the product of that relationship. This is not to say that creative tension has no part to play in the way both sides work together, on the contrary. It is, however, only constructive when that tension exists between people who fundamentally respect each other and, ideally, like working together. Here are a few signals to look for when assessing whether you are working well with your designer:

- Are we being straightforward and honest with each other, do we have mutual trust?
- Do we have an attitude of partnership, with both sides sharing the thinking, contributing to, and owning, the final solution?
- Do I adopt an inspiring and motivating stance towards my designer?
- Are we both really engaged by the assignment?

If any one of these signals is not positive then you are not working as well together as you could be.

Are we clear about money?

It is said that money makes the world go round. This is no less true with the client and consultant relationship than it is with any other business-based issue. Of course both parties are often motivated by things other than monetary matters, but if you, as a client, are not clear about how much money you have to spend, what you expect for it, and when you expect to spend it, then do not engage the consultant. It will lead to disappointment!

Often the client is not clear about what budget to allocate for the design work simply because they are not experienced enough with managing design. This is quite common. In these circumstances have a frank and honest discussion with your potential consultant about what they will charge (including the 'so-called' hidden extras), and agree the limits before you start, then all will be well. And the same applies to what you are going to get for your money, and when you are going to get it. Get this discussion out of the way at the beginning and that is one cause of potential discontent dealt with.

Does it matter if they have done it before?

'Knowledge of my market, and experience in designing for it, is a good thing.' Often this is true; sometimes it is not. Either way the client must decide. Design consultants build expertise by working for many clients in the same sector. This is why you might employ them. You will not have to pay for the consultant to learn about the industry, or about the commonly used manufacturing or communication techniques. You will have a high level of the 'feel good factor' about such a consultant. The risks of them making a technical mistake are minimized.

On the other hand you may feel that a fresh eye from someone who is experienced in another industry, but where the learning is transferable, is more appropriate. This is often the case when you are trying to break the mould of tradition, when a lateral approach is the only way a breakthrough will occur, when a quantum leap, rather than an incremental improvement, is required. Sometimes you can find consultants who can do both things – this is good. If you, as a client, cannot make up your mind about which you want – this is bad! Sort this out and you are on the road to having a successful relationship.

How will I manage the relationship?

A conscious effort must be made to manage the interface of your design consultant with your organization, and this process must be fully understood by everyone involved in the work. In mapping out a management process a few, particularly key, issues must be addressed:

- How will the work be done?
- Who will be the key people from both organizations, and how will they collaborate with each other?
- How will decisions be made and who will make them?
- What time is being allocated for each stage of work?
- What will signal the completion of one stage of work and the start of another?
- What is the process for approving invoices?
- What will happen if the client does not like the first proposals?
- What happens if the client changes the scope of work?

For the sake of good logistical management, as well as for the encouragement of a good working relationship, being clear about the design management process is essential.

These five questions are simple to ask but surprisingly demanding to answer. However, time spent in addressing the issues underlying them will help to ensure that the client and consultant relationship is not only a successful one, but also a long-standing one.

Some other behavioural considerations

There are two other considerations when it comes to thinking about behaviour.

Collaborative design

'a good idea doesn't care who has it, the key thing is to have it in the first place'

This gives a clue to collaborative working. It is critical to maximizing success with design. Collaboration is key and works on many levels – on the development of the brief, developing ideas, critiquing possible solutions and signing up to the final proposal that, hopefully, has encapsulated most, if not all, the stakeholder requirements. In a collaborative environment it is important to encourage the development of ideas as a group rather than promote one of your own – although sometimes of course, a single idea from one person can change the direction of group thinking.

Guidance

'persuade by the authority of your argument, not by the argument of your authority'

Seems rather obvious, but it is often ignored in the panic not to lose the argument for design. Pleading the special case that design is such a different management issue from all others that it requires treating in a different way, with kid gloves, or with blind acceptance is not the way to succeed.

Summary of Chapter 9

Design can be made to work more effectively by the design manager employing a behavioural style appropriate to the way the employing company does things. Clues to this behaviour can often be seen in the declared values of the business. In particular the functional design manager needs a skill set that provides firm direction delivered with a light management touch. Equally important are the skills of the line manager in making design work within the company's management systems. They have complex duties that demand complex personalities to manage them. They must have the ability to balance many demands while being delivery oriented, being able to develop and run organizational systems.

Design leadership and design management go hand in hand. They are not the same thing but they are necessarily linked, and complementary. The manager's job is to plan, organize and coordinate. The leader's job is to inspire and motivate. Perhaps there was a time when the calling of the manager and that of the leader could be separated particularly when the focus was on efficiency. But in the new economy, where value comes increasingly from the knowledge of people, and where workers are no longer undifferentiated cogs in an industrial machine, management and leadership are not so easily separated. People look to their managers, not just to assign them a task, but also to define for them a purpose. And managers must organize staff, not just to maximize efficiency, but also to nurture skills, develop talent and inspire results.

The late management guru Peter Drucker (1909–2005) was one of the first to recognize this truth, as he was to recognize so many other management truths. He identified the emergence of the 'knowledge worker', and the profound differences that would cause in the way business was organized. With the rise of the knowledge worker, as cited in *Rise of the Knowledge Worker* by James Cortada 1998, 'One does not "manage" people,' Drucker wrote. 'The task is to lead people. And the goal is to make productive the specific strengths and knowledge of every individual.' Such are the skills and behavioural styles needed from of design managers and design leaders.

Chapter 10
Summary of Part Two –
The how and what of delivery

In this second part I have described some of the ways that design managers and design leaders go about their work. My observations come from direct experience of being on both sides of the client/consultant divide a couple of times. Although much of this section concentrated on processes I do not want to leave the impression that design management or design leadership is all about following one set of rules or another. The processes that have been described are intended more as a way or organizing thinking first and organizing work second. No one of them is a panacea for all situations but collectively they do cover many of the challenges that design managers and leaders will face. Equally important are the behaviours they adopt in carrying out their work. Success depends on getting the balance of the two right. This balance is not something that can be prescribed, it must come from a deep understanding of how a business works and the behavioural style and values it adopts.

The roles of design managers and design leaders are becoming increasingly more complex as the ways of doing business, and the technologies employed, continue to develop. People responsible for design in business, as well as in wider society, must continue to develop their skills to remain fully aware of the opportunities to make corporate and social life better for all concerned.

Part Three – Looking back to look forward

Part Three of this book is about understanding and learning from the past as a basis for understanding and preparing for the future. It sets out some of the challenges that these people will face based on the changing nature of our business and social worlds, including the issue of bridging the gap between what the design industry offers and what business, government and society need from it. It looks at the role of Innovation Thinking as an integral part of the design process and how collaborative working is impacting on design outputs.

Chapter 11
Challenges for design leaders

This chapter is concerned with the challenges that design managers and leaders will need to face in the future. I use the word 'future' advisedly because today's designers, design managers and design leaders are all involved in the process of creating our future, now!

There are four challenges:
- perspectives from around the world;
- design transformation and the mismatch between design pushers and pullers;
- innovation thinking and its relationship with design;
- collaborative design a way to make it all work.

Perspectives from around the world

The first of these challenges concerns the perspectives of other professionals from around the world. Design management is a little older as a profession than design leadership. Both still have much to learn from each other and from the environments in which they function. To do this it is interesting to hear what some of those people around the world, already working in these fields, believe will be the challenges for design managers and leaders in the future. In conversation with each of them they have made the comments below when they knew I was preparing this book or papers related to it. Although each comment is short, and as always from each of them 'to the point', they are packed with insights.

'*customer focused, useable futures will make the difference between success and failure*'
Clive Grinyer, Cisco Systems

'*there is still much to do before design becomes a core competency in building business strategies*'
Tim Selders, Park Advanced Design Management

'*design leaders must find ways of getting teams working together to create integration and synergy between design and business to achieve customer relevance*'
Tom Lockwood, Lockwood Resource and President Emeritus, DMI

'*the paradox of design's success is that it will not always be led by designers*'
David Griffiths, Design Management Consultant

'design management is irrelevant without design leadership, businesses without design leadership, and vision, will perish'
Michael Wolff, Michael Wolff & Company

'design leaders must demonstrate that design creates a positive return on investment, measured in terms to which the business relates'
Joe Ferry, InterContinental Hotels Group

'personal responsibility on all board directors for the quality of their products, services, processes and facilities is a key legislative requirement'
Alan Topalian, Alto Design Management

'we have failed to get across the message that design transforms, this is a key challenge for design leaders today and in the future'
Sean McNulty, Dolmen design and innovation consultancy

'design is the spine that supports industry, innovation and social wellbeing. It is time that Government acknowledged design education as vital to our future growth'
Sir John Sorrell

Each of these perspectives represents a powerful insight into the world of design leadership. In most cases these perspectives give us clues as to how design must change if it is to respond to those who need to use it. Getting behind these perspectives to the issues that they represent is critical to the long-term effectiveness of design in business and society. Much of this book has been devoted to shedding some light on how this may be done. Also key to this is creating the opportunities to exchange the views and experiences of these leaders and the Design Management Institute, based in Boston, run many conferences, seminars and webinars during each year to do just this.

I have had the privilege of working with, and having engaging debates with, many design managers and design leaders during my time at the coalface of design. The ones listed above are just a few of them. They have each taught me much that is reflected in my own learning.

Design transformation

The second challenge to consider is the issue of design transformation resulting from the missmatch between what I have called design pullers and pushers.

Throughout this book the case has been made that design has the power to transform businesses in a way that most organizations do not recognize or acknowledge. However, to realize its full potential for the future design must go through a transformation of its own. The following notes look at the nature of the transformation needed together with the tensions that will result as the change proceeds. There are two types of transformation to be considered.

The first is about the transforming potential of design – this is of primary concern to those people, usually within businesses, government bodies or public services, who need to pull design into their organizations to help attain or maintain the high ground of being a leader in product or service provision. They have the potential to use design to transform businesses, public services and our wider society. These people I have called Design Pullers.

Design Pullers are often able to use design to make strategy tangible, enhance reputation and business value, provide insights to the future for longer-term investment, uncover unmet and hidden customer needs and drive business innovation as a strategy to maintain differentiation.

The second is about the need to transform design. This is of primary concern to those people who belong to the design and related industries, and the educational system that produces them. Many are consultants and some 'in-house' design team members. These are highly trained experts in every aspect of their design disciplines. I have called them Design Pushers.

Design Pushers have the potential to radically change the way Design Pullers see and use design resources and, in particular, to create understanding of what is possible and demonstrate the value that design brings.

Currently there are major misalignments between the two groups. The challenge for the future is that for the full potential of design to be realized, a transformational synergy must be created between the Design Pushers and Design Pullers. To do this, both groups have to change how they work. It is only when this happens that we can expect design to maximize wealth creation for business, creating fully effective public services and totally inclusive social environments.

The proposition is this, when these two groups of people work with a common purpose it is possible to achieve the transformational synergy to bring about greater wealth creation for business, more effective public services, and improved social environments. Until then we cannot hope to make design's full potential become a reality.

Fork in the road

Everyone concerned with design is at a crucial fork in the road. At this fork are these two groups of people – Design Pullers and Design Pushers. The context in which these two groups find themselves is an unprecedented opportunity for design to contribute significantly to a world changing more quickly, and more comprehensively, than any human beings have ever encountered before. There are two issues with this situation.

The first is that Design Pullers often have transformational opportunities that can be addressed through design – its processes, techniques and methodologies. However, they may not know that design could be an invaluable way forward for them.

The second is that Design Pushers don't often find themselves in a position where they can influence the debate about the transformational potential of design.

Hence the 'fork in the road' analogy. Collectively these two groups must decide which direction to take. One way is to continue with what we do now, becoming better and better trained at designing the full gambit of products, communications and environments. The other way is to a new order where design becomes a major tool for transformation across all aspects of our lives. There are inherent problems in both ways.

The first is likely to lead to design becoming a tactical commodity supplied by very capable people with highly honed skills that have more to do with design's legacy than its future and who will have an ever narrowing opportunity of influence. The second is that it will be difficult to change perceptions about what design can do, the way we work, what we deliver, how we are educated.

Of course this is a polarization of the two options. I do this to clarify the issues although they are not mutually exclusive – but the more I think about it the more I believe there is no real choice. If design is to survive in our changing world it must take the more difficult way, it must be transformed to achieve its full potential as a transformer. If we are really serious about this we need to understand what each group must do to make design more effective.

Design pullers

So, starting with the Design Puller. For a long time we have been told that design can have the sort of profound impact I have been suggesting. Warren Berger 2009, in his book *Glimmer – How Design Can Transform Your Life And Maybe The World*, argues that 'design is no longer limited to design professionals'. Michael Wolff argued a similar point in a recent interview when he said, 'Don't think a design company is where a designer should necessarily be.'

Bruce Nussbaum, a Managing Editor of *BusinessWeek* magazine, recently asked, 'Is design too important to be left only to designers?' In asking this, he was restating the same question first posed about 30 years ago by Peter Gorb, a business leader turned design advocate at the London Business School.

This reflected the same sentiment as Bruce Archer, Professor of Design Research at the Royal College of Art in the 1960s and 70s, who said, 'Design is what you do, not what you've done.' Tom Peters talks about design as being, 'The soul of new enterprise – built into corporate thinking from the start – not add-ons and pretty stuff, but the Everest of intellectual capital.' Alan Jones, when at Toyota, was reported to have said that, 'Design was more than the product, it is the total business entity' – not much different to what Henry Ford believed 100 years earlier.

One important point emerges clearly from this – not one of these people would claim to be a designer. Global companies like Apple, Nokia, Roca, Virgin Atlantic and Lego are businesses, by varying degrees, using design to explore transformation as a route to competitive advantage, market differentiation, environmental acceptability or even survival. Although each of these companies employ very experienced designers as Design Pullers they also have others, working with design, who are not designers at all.

It was in the late 1980s that Peter Gorb, and his colleague Angela Dumas, coined the phrase 'silent designers' as a way of identifying those people who use design, or make design decisions, without necessarily appreciating that is what they are doing – what an amazing insight! However, whether they know it or not, these organizations are using design to explore other ways of doing business.

This is clear from the practical experience of companies like Hewlett Packard that believe intelligent design they can reduce the environmental impact of their products and those of their customers. And Philips, using design as a creative force for innovation. Or Roca, the global bathroom company, which has instigated a far reaching programme of innovation driven by Design Leadership and concerned with envisioning, defining and creating the bathroom space of the future – all led by a senior managing director who was trained as a lawyer.

Which brings me to a key point I want to make. People able to most directly shape our public services or business wealth – are not usually designers – but they do have a sense of what design might do and (and this is the important bit) are in a position to do it! These are the Design Pullers who can pull design into their businesses, government offices, transport systems, city planning departments, social networks – they can transform the things of real importance to us all.

For example, if you are a Design Puller in business you will want to use design to:
- make your strategic intent visible, clear and relevant;
- provide a practical link between the decisions of the board room and the day-to-day activities of the business;
- enhance reputation through a coherent customer and stakeholder experience;
- provide insights to the future for strategic planning;
- uncover hidden customer needs;
- drive innovation as a way of maintaining differentiation.

All of this is core to what designers can do – given the chance!

If you are a Design Puller in the public service sector you will have the opportunity to use design to create:

- hospitals that work better and are safer from infection;
- transport services that are seamless in their timetabling, interconnectivity, speed, comfort and reliability;
- government departments that are easy to deal with, and information systems that make sense and work well.

If you are a Design Puller working with social structures you could use design to help:

- reduce the levels of crime;
- create sustainability of natural resources and the reuse of man-made ones;
- educate creatively to encourage concern for the environment;
- make society safer and more secure.

Going back to Nussbaum, he has been making similar points in an interview with Peter Lawrence, Chairman of the Corporate Design Foundation, advocating that 'designers can tell you how to grow, how to innovate, how to change your culture' and that 'design, in the end, is about creating better things for people – along the way, it can generate better profits as well' – that's a good summary.

Of course I am not suggesting for a moment that Design Pullers only have design thinking and its processes available to them in their effort to transform their particular areas of interest. But what I am saying is – and this brings me to another key point – design can deliver what they are looking for; it can be critical to their success – if only they know where to look and what to ask for.

I am sure of this because of how design and designers work. First, design puts people at the centre of its process. It can help understand what they need to live a better life. Second, the design process has the capacity to be inclusive and holistic in how it is used. It tests and re-tests ideas, develops solutions, ultimately adding value and significance. Third, it can lead the way to transforming how Design Pullers think and what they do. Fourth, and most critical, is that, in the right hands, the design process can be expertly managed.

So, referring back to what Archer said all those years ago, I would say that Design Pullers, although concerned with what designers produce, will find the greater value in the way they produce it – that, I believe, is one key to unlocking design's transformational capability.

This sounds fine in theory, but what evidence is there for any of this transformation being possible? At a product level we only have to look at how Nokia, a technology leader, has reinvented itself as a service provider by redefining what the word 'product' means to them. With Ovi from Nokia, the product and the service have become one. And of course there are other examples from companies such as Philips, IBM, Cisco, Walmart, Walt Disney, all in *BusinessWeek's* 50 most innovative companies list.

At a social planning level New West End Company is rethinking how central London works. They are driven by a motivating proposition to transform the pedestrian experience by giving the streets back to the people. At the heart of this is the design leadership responsibility of envisioning 'what could be', and then using expert design management skills in the delivery of that vision. What they have done recently at Oxford Circus to reduce the hazards of crossing the road is a good example of lateral design thinking working in practice.

At an international level, Dolmen, a Dublin-based innovation consultancy practicing design thinking, is using hidden-need identification techniques as a tool to bring together Northern Ireland and the southern Republic of Ireland with a shared new business agenda.

None of these examples are very 'designerly' in the traditional sense, but they are examples of transformational design. Although it is easy to find the exceptional examples to illustrate the point, the real issue is, are we prepared to do what is necessary to achieve this on a much wider front?

Design pushers

So, if that is a look at the world of the Design Pullers, and the potential role that design can play in what they do, what about the Design Pushers and what they offer these Design Pullers?

Of course there are some consultants and educators who actively promote and use design as a transformational tool. However, in the order of things, they are rare. If you do a trawl of design consultant web sites, or design press analyses, or college courses in design, the clearest message is that most Design Pushers are pushing their basic design discipline – graphics, branding, web, product, interior, exhibition and so on. One reason they offer these services is because Design Pullers have been conditioned to look for them, largely by the design industry itself. Up to now these consultancies have been the backbone of a very successful design industry but they only represent part of what design thinking is capable of delivering.

We cannot expect Design Pullers to be inspired to know what transformational possibilities are available through design – it is the responsibility of the Design Pushers to do that. And if they can't, they must transform themselves so they can. This is beginning to happen but it will take quite some time to change as dramatically as is needed. There is a move to re-examine what the design industry is all about and asking itself who is designing the future? Only recently a large multidisciplinary group of creative thinkers met at a Design Festival in Cheltenham in the UK to debate and explore the future of design.

There are many things that Design Pushers could do to help reveal the wider potential of design thinking to the Design Puller's agenda. These ideas are not new and, as can be seen from my earlier comments, I am not a lone prophet in the wilderness. At a global level the Design Management Institute is already working in the space that I am talking about, so is the Design Business Association, especially with its Design Effectiveness Awards, and the Design Council here in the UK with its much wider Design in Business agenda.

To the Design Pushers I say if you're not working with the sort of Design Puller agendas I've described then it might be there are some basic barriers to overcome. In essence Design Pushers need to do two things.

First, create a much more comprehensive understanding of what is possible with design. Second, demonstrate the value that design can bring. I don't think anyone will argue with that, but it's difficult. Much of it is about stepping outside your comfort zone. There are a number of basic issues to address if design is to be taken seriously and contribute to the transformation agenda. These have been dealt with fully in Part One but are listed here for reference:
- the sceptics – bringing them on board;
- deliver strategy – the link with design;
- demonstrate added value – an unexpected persuader;
- build reputation – a controllable asset;
- design spend – the benefit of focus.

All of which leads to this inevitable conclusion – at the end of the day someone in the business must be made responsible for the collective effect of design investment. To ignore this is to rob shareholders of corporate wealth. The responsibility for design must remain with the business leaders but Design Pushers are in a uniquely informed position to make this point clear. Without business direction design will have no lasting effect, and business direction without design will fail to deliver its potential.

It could be argued that these five basic issues need to be addressed by the clients themselves, within their own businesses. Yes, of course, that would be ideal. But if that is not happening, Design Pushers have the responsibility to make the case to be treated as a business partner rather than a supplier of commodity services. They have the potential to radically change the way Design Pullers see and use design resources and, in particular, to create understanding of what is possible and demonstrate the value that design brings. Let me emphasize the broader point – releasing the transformational potential of design is only possible through close collaboration between Design Pushers and Design Pullers. Never forget that a good idea doesn't care who has it; the important thing is to have it in the first place! Do all of this and Design Pushers will be in a good position to work with, rather than for, the Design Pullers and so create the transformational synergies I am talking about.

Henry Ford (1863–1947), American industrialist and pioneer of the assembly-line production method, had real insight to human behaviour when he reputedly said that coming together was a beginning; keeping together was progress; working together was success. It is generally believed that Einstein said that it was impossible to solve a problem by using the same thinking that created it, and that's spot on.

Our challenge

Our challenge is to find more effective ways to secure the long-term survival of the business discipline we call design, so that it contributes to this ever more demanding and changing agenda of society at large. If we carry on with 'business as usual' then I fear we have already seen the best from design. We have it within our power to transform design and to use design to transform. If we do not grasp the opportunity to align both sides of the design push and pull we will have denied the benefit of designs possibilities not only to our own industry, but to our clients' businesses, governments and social communities.

Business as usual is simply not an acceptable option. There are signs that some of what I am talking about is happening already – design has been on the international Davros Economic Agenda for the past few years and the UK Design Council's 'Designing Demand' national programme is gaining real traction. So some people are clearly 'getting the message'. But in the order of things these exemplars are just that – 'exemplars', exceptional examples rather than common practice. It is still very unusual to find design as part of the 'DNA' of a business, something that is normal routine. For every encouraging example there are many more where Design Pullers are really struggling.

For example, recently, there was a large international conference in Brussels called Passenger Terminal 2010. They were trying to understand how to create the ideal 'customer experience' at airports. There were dozens of speakers and hundreds of delegates crying out for the sort of insights that designers and the design process can bring. This conference served to highlight two issues. First, there was a hunger to understand where design thinking can contribute to the subject. Second, the integration of Design Pushers and Design Pullers has not yet happened with something as basic as airport and airline experience.

They clearly are trying but success is slow – so why is that? Tom Lockwood says, 'For design to start fulfilling its full potential it needs capital "D" people that care about doing what is right, and have the influence to make it happen.' That is a clear message for the Design Pullers.

Clive Grinyer believes that, 'in many cases design is used as an experiment, once, and when not successful is not used again.' He goes on to say, 'Most reasons that design is not successful are because it is not understood.' Joe Ferry maintains that most of the mismatch occurs between designers with high views of what is required and design managers trying to integrate and resolve many more parameters. James Berry, a Director at Woods Bagot, a global leader in design and consulting, maintains that 'urgent change is needed to the way we train, organize and regulate those responsible for the design of our built environment.'

These are clear messages for the Design Pushers and their professional societies.

David Kester, the UK's Design Council's Chief Executive, makes two useful contributions to this debate. He first says that 'the supply and demand of design are out of sync with each other,' and, 'you don't need to be a designer to run a successful business, but you do need design to maximize your business success.' His two points very much summaries the argument I have been trying to make.

Key messages

So, what are the key messages to take from all this? How do we create this transformational synergy? There are three points to make.

The first concerns Design Pushers. Get your client to think differently about design. You could be the best thing that has ever happened to them. Do that while thinking differently about yourselves, not so much as pushers of discipline-based design skills but rather as people who can help the client unlock their own potential. And design education has a key role in this transformation. Design disciplines are important, but design as a tool for transformation is even more so. I know I'm pushing at an open door, but to fully open it Design Pushers must adopt the transformational agenda of business, government and society.

The second concerns Design Pullers. See design as a resource and a process – not a thing. See it as a tool to help look beyond the near horizon, not so much to consider what can be, but rather what might be. You have an almost unique opportunity to use design in a way that will change our norms of business, public services and social systems.

The third concerns all three groups. Come together with these aspirations and we will be a step closer to reaching the transformational synergy I have been arguing for. It is not enough to hope it will happen by it self – it won't. These issues must be kept in sharp focus if we are to provide the opportunity to consolidate a way forward.

It is much cited that Maurice Maeterlinck, the Belgium poet and philosopher, once said, 'On the paths that lead to the future, tradition has placed 10,000 men to guard the past.'

In the case of the design profession that barricade to the future is made up of many things including:

- an educational system that can, if allowed, condition and limit expectations;
- a large number of designers afraid of the risks involved in the new order, who do not see a clear way forward or are not sufficiently equipped to take it;
- business leaders with a misinformed prejudice about design.

My plea for the future is that we use every effort to be sure that, collectively, Design Pushers and Design Pullers have the commitment and courage to take the right direction at that fork in the road. We must overcome the legacy of the past and redefine our future. Our industry demands it of us and this is a serious challenge for design managers and design leaders.

Innovation Thinking and its relationship with design

The third challenge for the future concerns Innovation Thinking and its relationship with design. The fit is perfect in the sense that design led Innovation Thinking is all about placing end-users at the centre of how organizations develop new products, services and processes. It means discovering unmet needs and desires, generating the ideas to meet them, and rapidly developing those ideas into concepts that can be tested and validated for their viability. It means mapping a path for them to succeed commercially and then bringing those concepts to life.

Innovation and how it is fostered, managed, developed and capitalized on, is a core activity in business. The role of design in this process is fundamental. I am very much indebted to my colleague, Sean McNulty of Dolmen, who has helped me understand its scope and depth. Not only have design leaders the responsibility to foster an innovative environment as described earlier but also they must provide the leadership to ensure that innovation is practiced and rewarded. At the heart of Innovation Thinking is a consuming preoccupation with the user and so has a valuable contribution to:

- new business model innovation;
- product, experience and service innovation;
- platform innovation including engineered solutions and processes, and end-user experience platforms.

This Innovation Thinking is as relevant to the smallest company, the micro company, as it is to the biggest corporation. Small companies tend to be more agile than larger ones which usually means they can utilize Innovation Thinking techniques quickly and so generate growth in the short term as well as longer. However, every organization, no matter what size or industry, should be engaged in Innovation Thinking as a way of doing business today and preparing for the future. Like many aspects of what I have been trying to emphasis, Innovation Thinking can be directly linked to the strategic aims of the business. It can be directed and managed to deliver new opportunities to build on those aims. Diagram 11.1 shows how one company has used Innovation Thinking in platform and expertise development. It produced new engineering, experience and new business platforms as well as business model innovation. The outputs from this were then used as the basis for subsequent action. Note, all of this activity was linked directly back to corporate objectives.

In terms of using Innovation Thinking as part of business activity, it can be managed and directed like most design work. It is an iterative, repeatable approach that explores problems and opportunities in order to identify significantly better solutions and anticipate future needs. It is as much about making things better for today as it is about anticipating change in the future. This means it can be an invaluable tool in a continuous improvement environment, as well as being a way to scope opportunities for the long term. Key to it all is the challenge to create an innovative culture that involves every person in the business or organization.

To build this culture requires conviction and effort and relies on:
- encouraging a 'can-do' mindset in order to explore and seek out optimal solutions – in other words, inspirational new solutions over rational analysis;
- developing a set of core values for the company or team, for example embracing inclusive design or minimizing environmental impact, that when combined with the broader requirements of technical feasibility and market opportunity, get translated into practical responses and ultimately final solutions;
- a consuming preoccupation with the end-user and all other stakeholders in the process of delivery.

Figure 11.1 Business model innovation workshop

Innovation Thinking is derived from traditional design techniques. It begins with a series of explorative approaches undertaken by a cross-disciplinary team of people. This involves developing a deep understanding of the problem or opportunity by breaking it down into its core elements and understanding the different types of users involved with it. Then to overlay this understanding with identified user needs and use these insights to develop the final solutions within the constraints of available technologies and commercial realities. It can be used in the idea management process but it is equally the culture, values and behaviours that create an effective innovation management system in a company. It is a disciplined approach of understanding how to take data (ideas, problems, opportunities, market forces and trends) from multiple sources, external and internal to the business, bring it all together and reconfigure in new ways. This data is then transformed into usable information that can be reshaped, reorganized, linked in new ways and turned into knowledge that drives better solution hypotheses. This process can be applied to new business modelling as well as a means of scoping new products and services and is often explored through interactive workshops, see Figure 11.1.

Although process is clearly important in enabling Innovation Thinking, behaviours and attitudes are more so. The key ones are:

- observation and deep understanding of the issues;
- exploration, experimentation and iteration;
- conceptualization, user testing and gathered leanings.

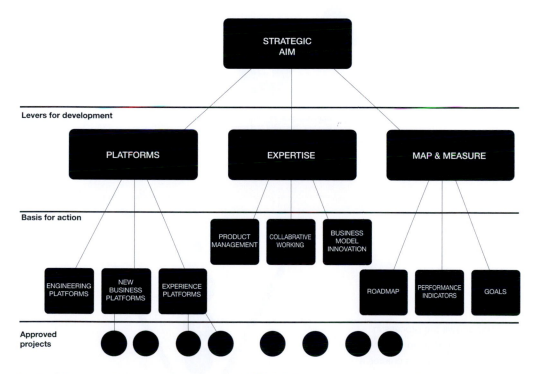

Diagram 11.1 *Innovation Thinking diagram showing the links between strategic aim, levers for development, basis for action and project activity*

For Innovation Thinking to be successful the business must prepare itself in very practical ways, in particular by:

- ensuring there is the capacity for investment and having a deep understanding of current and future market forces and trends;
- having available, either within the company or through a network of partners, the technical capability to deliver in a manner appropriate for the target users;
- creating alignment with real market needs and all user types.

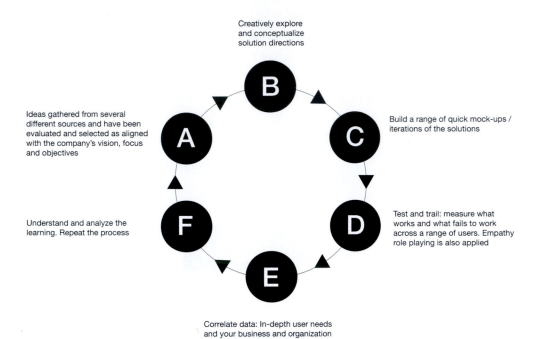

Creatively explore
and conceptualize
solution directions

Ideas gathered from several
different sources and have been
evaluated and selected as aligned
with the company's vision, focus
and objectives

Build a range of quick mock-ups /
iterations of the solutions

Understand and analyze the
learning. Repeat the process

Test and trail: measure what
works and what fails to work
across a range of users. Empathy
role playing is also applied

Correlate data: In-depth user needs
and your business and organization
needs (constraints and challenges)

Diagram 11.2a *Innovation Thinking processes*

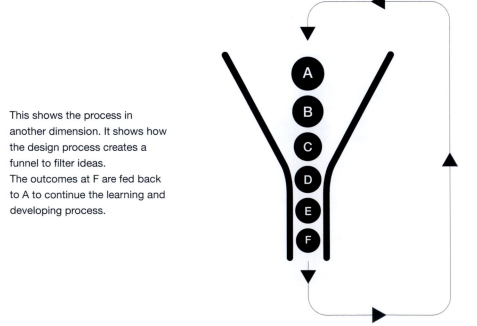

This shows the process in
another dimension. It shows how
the design process creates a
funnel to filter ideas.
The outcomes at F are fed back
to A to continue the learning and
developing process.

Diagram 11.2b *Innovation Thinking processes*

This Innovation Thinking process is illustrated in Diagrams 11.2a & 11.2b. First as a circular process where the learning from one step informs the next and ultimately redefines the starting point. The second is as a perpetually feeding funnel where the broad starting point gets gradually reduced to a point where there are working hypotheses to consider for testing.

The case example that follows is of Axiom, a small Irish technology manufacturing company. It describes a little of the work that they have undertaken to inculcate an innovation culture into what they do. This has resulted in a number of completely new business opportunities.

Case Example – Axiom

Axiom employ about 50 people and are based in Limerick, Ireland. Innovation Thinking was key in developing a new business model brought on by a serious crisis for the company.

Axiom is a subcontract manufacturer for large companies in high technology and DELL, the multinational computer technology corporation, was its key client. When DELL moved to central

Figure 11.2 The challenge of dependency on one large client can force the issue of innovation to the top of the business agenda

Europe, Axiom, which already had an operation in Hungary, set up a joint venture in Poland and Hungary to continue servicing DELL's requirement and to grow their business further.

Tony Treacy, Axiom's Managing Director announced, 'We are in a difficult situation right now in as much that DELL who are our largest customer are moving notebook production to Poland and this will mean a reduction on our workforce in Ireland unless we innovate and do something about it.'

Not all staff wanted to move which left the company with an urgent need to develop a new business for those who chose to remain in Ireland. A workshop was held involving Irish employees, external stakeholders, the overseas team and joint venture partners from Poland and Hungary. The objectives were to:

- identify the core skills, resources, capabilities and technical expertise within the business and describe them in broader and more open terms;
- systematically examine all elements of Axiom's current business model to identify those parts that could be developed and redefined;
- explore the extended network of their current clients, and other potential client groups, in order to identify potential new business;
- apply LEAN manufacturing principles to identifying and exploring new markets and services. These were to be based around, but not limited by, Axiom's defined core skills, resources,

*capabilities and technical expertise. They were also to be focused on where there was
an identified international growth trend. (LEAN is a production practice that considers the
expenditure of resources for any goal other than the creation of value for the end customer to be
wasteful, and thus a target for elimination.)*

*Several new business opportunities emerged as being worthy of further exploration. A development
team was established and briefed for each one, and champions appointed to drive the process
forward, reporting back to an executive team within an agreed timeframe. Each of these ideas was
evaluated against criteria set by the original team and four were selected for pilot testing to validate
the demand and prove the business case. Three business opportunities emerged worthy of further
testing:*

- *custom-built hearing aids for direct supply to customers and in cooperation with a network of
  ear nose and throat specialists;*
- *medical device manufacturing in cooperation with a new market partner;*
- *partnership in the repair, recertification and selling of branded products that fail during warrantee.*

Conclusions

Axiom saw innovation as a way for them to develop their business and to expand their horizons.
The first step of this process was developing a deep understanding of the unique expertise and
skill base the people in Axiom had developed through working in partnership with DELL over many
years. These skills were not all technical. They included knowing how to deliver a quality customer
experience and customized products to volume markets. This made Axiom more than just another
group of technical specialists.

Axiom's preparedness to be flexible and deliver a quick turnaround service within a culture that was
determined to succeed were all critical to creating a new business model. In this case the innovative
step was in the process, particularly in recognizing where the potential difficulties would be if they
were to enter an unfamiliar industry sector. They knew, however, that by doing this they could create
completely new opportunities that in turn had the potential of delivering significant, measurable
benefits and value over how other companies in those sectors traditionally operated.

Innovation does include a lot of uncertainty and risk that needs to be managed. Attitude, behaviour
and process are all key to this. Innovation Thinking is a process designed around people, whether
the end-users, clients or in Axiom's case circumstances that forced the company to seek sustainable
new business. It is about exploring new and better ways of doing things that deliver significant value
and then testing these through iterations and learning from feedback and user trails and making sure
it integrates with other existing procedures necessary in that industry or sector and ultimately delivers
business value and impact. The innovation process allowed a structured process to explore and
eliminate what would and would not work.

The practical application of Innovation Thinking is all about putting some order on an approach that many companies do in an ad hoc fashion. But under times of stress it is important to do it in a planned disciplined manner to manage the high-level risks involved. It also means accepting that many of the ideas will fail. The key is using the process to eliminate as much of this as early as possible.

Collaborative design – a way to make it all work

The fourth challenge design managers and leaders will need to face in the future concerns the role of collaboration in the design management process.

In all but the smallest design practice or design department, or with any but the smallest design project, designers do not work alone. The practice of collaboration, where the design activity occurs in many places at once is becoming well established. David Kestor of the UK Design Council cites many examples of collaborative design. The one that always appeals to me concerns Linux. He maintains we now live in an era where innovation and creativity frequently happens as the product of many hands in many places. He sites the fact that Linux, the open software program, is the work of a distributed collective of perhaps 120,000 registered developers.

James Berry, Design Director at Woods Baggot, makes a similar point when he says that 'creative capital is not just a collection of individual ideas, but also a product of interaction'. The point is not made by the specific examples but by the general trend that these examples illustrate. The role of design in business, in society and within the governmental organizations that enable society to work, is getting increasingly complex. Much of this book has been focused on reinforcing this point. Encouraging collaboration in the design and innovation processes is going to be key if we are going to successfully address the many, apparently insurmountable, problems we face – problems like global warming, global waste, crop shortages, sustainable energy and so on.

Of course the leadership or management of design is not going to solve all these problems but they can help, particularly in the way they can bring together expertise from all types of industry sectors, social sciences and ethnographic insights to create new scenarios that address audacious problems. Design leaders in particular have a responsibility to show how this collaborative approach can work and it is already an urgent need for today as well as the future.

Part Four – Further case examples

This fourth part consists of case examples that were too long to include in the general narrative without interrupting its argument, clarity and flow. These longer case examples illustrate many points although their principle focus is captured in the title of each. All case examples, whether the short ones positioned in the narrative where they best serve to illustrate the point being made, or the longer ones here, come from two sources. Either directly from my own experience working as a company design director or consultant in design leadership, or from the winners of the Design Business Association's Design Effectiveness Awards for which I was Chair of the judging panel for several years.

Each of the following case examples focuses on different aspects of leading design, such as selecting designers, design strategy, identity and design management, design integration, designing for future needs, manifesting new business and managing design in crisis. The cases have been chosen because they represent a variety of companies from different industries, each with significantly different challenges. Although the challenges described are particular to the company concerned there is much to be learned from them that is of a more general nature and this has been summarized at the end of each case.

Chapter 12
Roca: what next?

Roca is the world leader in the production of ceramic sanitary ware. It is profitable, family owned, hugely successful, based in Barcelona, manufacturing in 30 countries, selling in 135, has a production capacity of 40 million pieces per annum and has 22 brands. This case example examines the role of design leadership and innovation in extending Roca's business beyond the normal bounds of a production-led organization to one that is focused on creating new, consumer-based experiences.

Roca was established in 1917 by a family with a vision for success. In the 1920s they produced cast iron radiators, in the 1930s vitrified porcelain, in the 1950s taps and other bathroom hardware, from the 1970s to 2000s has experienced international expansion. They have engaged some of the most famous designers of today to develop new products and showrooms, including Giorgio Armani, David Chipperfield and Zaha Hadid. Roca is a great success story and has held a strong leadership position for many years. But the world is changing and so is the market in which they operate. The global commercial environment has caused Roca to consider its own future. They are already the biggest in their business, so 'what next'? This is a question they have asked many times from their earliest beginnings as a business.

Figure 12.1 Part of Roca's exhibition stand at ISH, the international trade fair for bathroom products

So far, success has depended on a business model based on:
- high-volume production;
- low reject rates;
- high efficiency;
- delivering customer expectations.

Although this approach has given them well-deserved leadership in many of the markets in which they operate none of these success criteria is unique – each of them can be copied. Roca's position in the market could be undermined by other companies doing exactly what they do, possibly better, possibly cheaper, and they are fully aware that this could happen. China has already declared its ambition to become 'the world's producer', and they are not alone in wanting to occupy this high ground.

Roca's strategic response to this situation has been in two parts:

- first, the imperative to build on its core strength of cost-effective volume production and thereby maintain current leadership position;
- second, to create the bathroom experiences of the future and so develop clear differentiation and a future leadership position.

This strategic response resulted in creating VISION2020, their internal transformation programme focused on managing a cultural change from being a producer of 'things' to becoming an innovator of 'experiences'.

At the heart of this shift has been a vision, a central idea that was for them to become....

'the global leader in defining bathroom experiences'

Although this simply stated vision is concise, it is packed with meaning – there is a lot behind these few words:

the the unquestioned

global local and international

leader recognized authority

in defining in anticipating, creating and offering

bathroom public washroom and private bathroom spaces,

experiences products and experiences for today
and the world of tomorrow.

This strategic intent meant:

- becoming the authority in bathroom thinking;
- delivering added-value products and services;
- defining quality bathroom experiences for today and the future;
- promoting an integrated vision of the bathroom experience, space and details, so that people in every part of the world know that Roca offers the bathroom that they need in their lives.

The vision was supported by a set of values that would underpin all that implementing this vision would mean:

- Innovation: vision, foresight.
- Design: style and fashion, technology and quality.
- Sustainability: efficiency, research, sustainable processes and products.
- Leadership: recognition, dynamism and orientation towards the future.
- Wellbeing: wellness, health and comfort.

The potential commercial benefits from this programme of change were clear. VISION2020 was to help build a more secure future for the business by helping it create:

- a more dominant position – the company that leads the thinking in any area is usually the one that dominates its market;
- additional or enhanced revenue streams through perceived value-market leadership with new and innovative products, and enhanced earnings and margins from existing operations;
- greater level of differentiation and positioning – the creator of products, spaces and experiences is positioned differently to the followers, the creator is the leader.

Statements of strategic intent are of little value unless they are used to direct work that will facilitate its delivery. Delivering VISION2020 was seen to be dependent on four key, interrelated, drivers for change. These drivers for change were:

- mindsetting, changing attitudes about what is possible and understanding what it means to shift from being a 'producer' to being an 'innovator';
- process development that would support innovation and sharing knowledge;
- research to better understand market differences and needs of ethnographic groups;
- to secure technical knowledge and inspiration to inform future developments;
- innovation in experience creation, product concepts, technical breakthroughs and business models.

With each of these drivers a small number of projects was developed that would 'pump-prime' that change. This was followed by a comprehensive plan of implementation that had three time horizons for change management and delivery.

At the heart of this transformation programme was Roca's vision. It was designed to inform every aspect of what the company was doing and was planning to do. It provided the focus to set about transforming its operation to compete better in markets where competition was increasing daily, prices were dropping and consumers were demanding better quality, choice and product desirability.

A key aspect of making this vision a reality was the need to innovate more comprehensively than before. It required an innovation process, structure and programme for delivery. This innovation programme was focused on changing working practices and culture. It required a different personnel structure and composition to that normally engaged in development work. These new innovation teams were to be cross-functional, staffed by people from different divisions and geographically dispersed parts of the organization. This combination of mixed skills and mixed loyalties brought new thinking and different perspectives to the innovation process and to the mindset of the teams involved. The teams were mentored by a small group of external consultants but, in essence, learned by practical, hands-on, application of a wide variety of tools and techniques on real projects and development programmes.

Other aspects of this transformation program included:
- greater internal communications and information sharing amongst the programme teams of the benefits each was achieving;
- exploring new innovative business programmes and opportunities, for future implementation;
- linking in with existing projects and programmes of work, communicating externally that Roca was transforming and wanted to be seen as the partner of first choice;
- bringing new skills in creativity and innovation management processes to teams that could then be inculcated further into the business;
- the role of design and innovation leadership in driving this process, thus empowering and motivating all involved;
- researching into new user and customer trends, and applying creativity techniques to generate new solutions and work programmes.

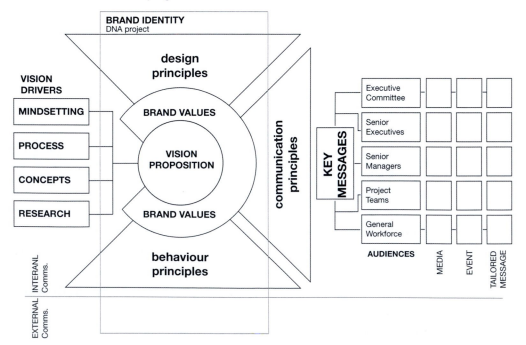

Diagram 12.1 *Template used to show how the work behind the vision drivers was informed by the vision proposition, its supporting brand values, and communication principles*

One of the underlying working principles of this transformation programme was integrated thinking, cross-pollination of ideas and the sharing of knowledge. An example of this was the way the company planned its communication about the progress of VISION2020.

The chart shown in Diagram 12.1 illustrates the template that was to be used to show how the work behind the vision drivers was informed by the vision proposition, its supporting brand values and communication principles. All this, in turn, would then shape the key internal and external messages about what the company was doing. Similar templates were prepared for the design and behaviour aspects of the programme.

Business model innovation

One important aspect of this design-led-innovation programme was to identify new market opportunities by utilizing existing technical processes and exploring new business models to create new opportunities for additional growth. The process used consisted of:

- defining project objectives;
- creating cross-discipline team and securing authorization for this activity;
- researching market trends and reviewing current best solutions and practices;
- training the team in tools and techniques to be used in the innovation process;
- undertaking competitor analysis and competitive options;
- interviews and group workshops with selected industry experts to identify current problems, constraints and challenges;
- exploring new product ideas and solutions and evaluating against existing solutions in the marketplace;
- developing a business feasibility case, linking all innovation drivers to create credible service offerings.

Although it is not possible to discuss the specific outcomes of Roca's work, there were a number of general points of learning that could be of value to other businesses in other sectors of industry. These include:

- thinking outside the current confines of existing business boundaries to explore the possible and, sometimes the unthinkable, can lead to the unexpected;
- technical solutions, using existing manufacturing and production knowledge, can lead to the creation of significant competitive differentials;
- new business models, and not just products or processes, can be identified through Innovation Thinking processes;
- once empowered within an agreed framework, Innovation Teams can uncover unmet stakeholder needs whether they are current or future customers, stakeholders, business partners, specifiers or suppliers.

More specific outputs from this kind of innovation work can be seen in the Case example of Axiom in Chapter 11. In their case Axiom developed completely new business models that enabled them to expand business horizons beyond the norms for their industry.

In Roca's case the company was courageous, being prepared to think differently about what it might do and how it might do it. It wanted to understand better what the bathroom experiences of the future could be like which in turn had to represent an exceptional step change beyond current ways of thinking and working. The work is extremely challenging and the time to do it is equally difficult. The operational reality for any in-house innovation team is that they still have to meet current demands and to deliver against their monthly targets.

Conclusion

World economic circumstances mean that programmes like Roca's VISION2020 are more difficult to focus on when trying to maintain revenue streams, yet are more critical than ever to address if companies are to survive.

Continuous improvement is always a good strategy but cannot be the only one. The management team at Roca could see that 'business as usual' was not going to sustain them forever. They could see that change was inevitable and for programmes like theirs to work required commitment to it, starting from the top of the company. The whole process is about leadership in exploring and envisioning new business models and innovative solutions to solve market challenges. Critical to this is being aware that the final decisions for change depend on many factors (tangible issues that are easy to measure, and intangible issues which are much more difficult to measure) like understanding future needs, market timing, creating acceptance and market readiness for change.

These ideas must be given time to develop properly because they will certainly be disruptive, challenging and easily dismissed before a proper evaluation of their feasibility, market potential and return-on-investment can be established.

Chapter 13
BAA: selecting designers

Figure 13.1 *BAA, is the Spanish-owned operator of airports in Britain, including Heathrow*

This case example looks at the role of design leadership in establishing a framework of design partners in a regulated environment. Although the case concerns a large multi-national company, the process and the learning from it could be of real value to many other sized businesses. The main content of this case was originally described in the *Design Management Journal*. Some changes to the text have been made in light of events since I wrote the original.

Design leaders are responsible for ensuring the design expertise employed by the company is appropriate. Sometimes selecting a consultant, or a short list from which to chose each time, is straightforward. Sometimes however it is not so easy as that. This case study is a good example of how one company, BAA, went about auditing the design industry with the view to selecting a range of preferred design suppliers that it could work with for a five-year period. The process was long, complicated and time consuming, largely as a result of two factors, the breadth of design expertise required and the restrictions imposed by EU legislation as to how they went about it. Despite this the results were extremely successful.

Although every company will have its own challenges as to which design consultancy to employ sometimes that choice is limited by legislation – particularly if you are based in Europe and have to conform to certain criteria laid down by Brussels. If, because of the industry you are in, the size of the design commission, whether you are a quango or a named business in its legislation, there may be international rules regarding how you go about selecting consultancy services (including legal, financial, management and design services). If any of this applies then the following Case example may be of value.

There are, of course, other ways of procuring design services than that described in the following case. Of particular value is the work the Design Business Association has undertaken in preparing an excellent process to help client companies select the most appropriate consultancy for their needs.

The design of a modern mega-project such as an airport is dependent on input from all manner of outside groups. In this process, having an efficient framework for selecting and managing consultants is essential. BAA, the private company that owned London's major airports, when this case was first prepared, had a team of design leaders, who with their procurement colleagues, devised a system for categorizing and pre-qualifying design suppliers, which improved quality while it permitted decentralized project management and saved significant time and money.

Some background

BAA – formerly the British Airports Authority – was privatized in 1988 and is amongst the world's largest privately-owned airport companies. It owns Heathrow Airport and Stansted and has management contracts with airports in several other countries around the world. In recent years BAA built the London-to-Heathrow high-speed express train and designed a fifth terminal at Heathrow which opened in 2005.

In an organization with the size and scope of BAA, design is an important and wide-ranging resource. Rigorous design standards are applied to the smallest piece of printed material and to the largest elements of its built environments, from a simple sign to a whole airport. This means that they use most of the recognized design disciplines – graphic, communications, environmental and product design. Also engineering, retail systems, infrastructure, signage and other information systems, architecture, master planning and transportation design. During the time of this procurement process they were spending £400–500 million every year on infrastructure development alone, that is a lot of design investment to be commissioned, directed and managed.

In response to this need for high-quality, business-focused design work, they created a designer selection and procurement process that ensured the creative and effective use of design throughout the business. Their corporate mission was to become the world's most successful airport operator. Key to achieving this was BAA's ambition to improve the quality, efficiency of production and cost of major infrastructure projects. It was critical to manage the selection and management of outside design consultants better and to give project managers more support and information in the process.

Inside or outside designers

Any organization that uses design to further its business has two or possibly three options to choose from to achieve its aim. It can use a team of in-house design specialists; it can source all its work from external consultants, leaving itself with the management responsibility; or it can combine both approaches.

Internal design teams come into their own when you are designing something industry specific. There was a time when BAA had a large internal architectural and engineering resource. Today it is much smaller, retaining only those people with specific technical knowledge not easily found outside their industry. When highly creative inputs are needed that benefits from a much wider base of experience than BAA can provide from within, outside design consultants are used. Come to think of it you have to question why a top-quality architect, say, would aim for his or her career to develop within the confines of just one aspect of one industry. But that is what an in-house designer does. He or she runs the risk of having only a narrow band of design experience to draw on. Consultants, on the other hand, are used to confronting a much wider variety of challenges in their work.

Like many companies on the client side of the design process, BAA is well aware of the value of the skills and advice from good consultants. Excepting a very small number of specific in-house services. the entire annual design output, which is enormous, comes from external design consultants. However, they do retain the responsibility to actively manage the design process.

The decision to procure design services from outside BAA rather than from inside was not difficult to make. There are plenty of excellent general and specialist practices covering the skills BAA demands. The problem was choosing from so many consultancies; it was an embarrassment of riches. But how do you maintain high design standards across the whole of a large company like BAA when there are so many suppliers involved? Which consultancy is selected to handle a particular project and why? More important, who is doing the choosing?

The opportunity

In the mid-1990s BAA's Management Committee formalized a process for doing this by establishing the Supply Chain Task Force to create 'Framework agreements' with a limited number of component suppliers, constructors and specialist consultants. The task was refining the selection and qualification process to reduce its core design suppliers to a smaller and more manageable base, at the same time not wanting to close off it's ability to source new creative skills as design practices start up or regroup.

BAA is essentially a project-driven company using projects, in many instances, to address major business issues. These projects are run by very experienced managers, who expect the processes they employ and the outputs they produce to be predictable and measurable. Design is part of that process. Devolved throughout the complex project process, it is guided by corporate design policies and strategies but managed locally by those project people empowered to deliver the final result. And this informed the way design consultants were selected.

BAA's skills are tangible. They build and manage airports and airport facilities; the projects are infrastructure projects. These run the gamut from a new range of check-in desks to a lighting scheme for a car park or the total planning, design and building of a multi-billion pound international air terminal complete with a high-speed rail interchange. Design has an impact on every project. As such it is an integral part of the project process rather than something tacked on as an afterthought. This means that project managers must be able to select and manage the design skills they need as they would any other specialization. Again, it is the project managers who are doing the hiring on behalf of the client. However, the business had to be confident that it was choosing from a list representing the most appropriate consultants for the work.

Up to the time of this procurement process BAA had too many suppliers with varying skills and capabilities. Although it might seem liberating to hire and fire design consultants at will, it also was the case that too many changes in design consultants resulted in a lack of coherence and mismatches in quality of facilities. Managing 100 specialists in one design sector is more complicated than managing ten; and having too many suppliers makes it harder for the people who commission design at the project level to make an informed choice.

BAA wanted an internal regime to select the professional design skills needed by the project managers, and to have the confidence that there was a base of designers to call on for those skills. For project managers to be able to operate without constant reference back to the corporate office they had to be sure that the consultant designers selected through this process understood the BAA culture as well as the project requirements. They also needed to be commissioned within a previously agreed-upon contract and fee structure.

Designing the design team

The first task was to determine the design skills needed on a regular basis. They found that eight broad categories of design were used on a regular basis, which could be broken down into many more subcategories. The list included design brief development; architecture and interior design; infrastructure, urban and environmental planning; retail and leisure (such as casinos, gyms and baby facilities); product design; structural and building services design; wayfinding; and a range of specialist engineering design skills in which BAA leads the world, for instance aircraft pavement design.

Before the list of consultants was reviewed the company had to decide exactly what they needed them to do. What was the business and project context in which they would have to work? What was the company's workload likely to be, now and in the future, in each of the specialist disciplines? This review was undertaken with the help of all parts of the business to ensure that there was a common understanding of where design could add real wealth to the company. Design works in BAA not because it is applied with a trowel, but because the line managers and project managers understand how it can help manifest BAA's strategic objectives through their management of it at an operational and project level.

Having decided what skills were needed and what type of work they were to do, a process for selecting the right type and number of design consultants for the work for the current and future workload was required. Here they did not have a totally free choice. The European Union (EU) has rules to ensure open competition among companies in member countries on projects over a certain value. BAA is one of the companies that had to comply with the EU process. Projects must be advertised openly across Europe with an auditable trail through the selection procedure to demonstrate that any qualified applicant had a chance to be considered equally. With the number of projects initiated each year, this process could have been onerous if each one has to be advertised and all replies evaluated, shortlisted and selected. Fortunately the rules allowed for other options including a preferred supplier list selected from appropriately set criteria. This is the route BAA followed. To avoid constant advertising, as well as the inherent problems of having to develop new relationships over and over again, they decided to set up framework agreements from a rigorously selected preferred supplier base in each design discipline. The only legal requirement was for a clearly auditable trail for fair selection.

Framework agreements allow companies like BAA to work with a design consultancy for up to five years before that agreement need be re-evaluated. The agreement can be reviewed at anytime, but the potential benefit is a partnership in which consultants learn with the client company to design effectively to meet objectives, reduce costs and waste from constant reinvention of design solutions, and produce a more intuitive working pattern that enables project managers to commission designers knowing that they understand and appreciate BAA's culture.

A secondary objective in creating a close-knit team of suppliers was to introduce a degree of design standardization, a phrase that sends shivers up the spine of some designers who think it means reducing creativity. That was neither the intention nor is it rarely the case.

Design standardization means, for example, avoiding using one of the, then current, 176 different design solutions of protective buffer to prevent luggage trolleys from damaging walls. That is one design of protective buffer every month for 14 years – and each one had to be designed, tooled up, manufactured, paid for and managed! The target was to end up using more than 50 per cent of standard components in any new building – without sacrificing the creative originality that has been the hallmark of BAA's major projects over many years. But to return to the selection of consultants.

Concentrating the search

The process was divided into six key stages.

1 Advertising

   Having identified the types of service required, BAA advertised them under the EU rules that permit any company anywhere in the world to respond. Small and large firms were eligible; in fact, any consultancy that employs at least two professionals. BAA looked for talent, not necessarily size.

2 Evaluation

   Then began the first evaluation stage, which was based on a detailed questionnaire asking for frank information about the company – financial status, technological investment, staffing, training policies, project and design management processes, quality assurance procedures, and so on.

3   Rationalizing

The responses to stage 2 were then rated by a multidisciplinary group of people from across BAA to narrow down the applicant base for each service skill, from perhaps 500 to 50.

4   Interviewing

This was still a large number, when the aim was to work with five to 15 consultancies, depending on the discipline. So stage 4 involved a two-stage interview process to assess the candidates' creative, technical and process management skills. It included a half day with up to 20 of the most likely applicants on their own premises.

5   Negotiation

From this the list of approved suppliers was selected and framework agreements negotiated. These took into account agreed fee rates, efficiency of operation and availability of key staff. It was far from buying on price alone. Great care was taken at this stage to issue only the number of framework agreements that could be honoured.

6   Induction

Work then started with the selected consultants, starting with an induction into BAA's business objectives, design policies and project methodology to ensure that their creative input worked at a strategic and project level. The interview and selection process involved all key users of design consultants at every stage. This facilitated complete 'buy-in' at the end of the day.

A Project Handbook of working practices was then developed for both consultants and project managers who commission design. It follows a schematic of seven events in the planning and commissioning of a project and eight management functions, including design management, used to complete the project, with detailed guidelines for each phase. See Figure 13.2.

Having affirmed an approved supplier list and established framework agreements, line and project managers could be confident about the quality of the final selection.

Structure, not straitjacket

This may sound like a heavy, system-based, process that might mitigate against new and lively creative solutions. However, this was not the case. As long as the design practice could handle the size of the job, any size of consultancy was considered potentially eligible.

It was not always assumed that every design project would be covered by this framework agreement structure. Specialized jobs could still be commissioned individually. However, up to 80 per cent of BAA's design work was commissioned under the new procurement process. It was not a perfect process of course. It would always be subject to adjustment. Once in place companies must prevent themselves from being too comfortable, losing that intellectual challenge. They must ensure not to miss out on new design thinking and talent by identifying special one-off-type projects that might benefit from a non-conventional approach.

Figure 13.2 *A Project Handbook of working practices was developed for both consultants and project managers who commission design*

The learning from developing this six-stage selection process was significant. Many consultancies did not apply to be on the framework, some of those were ones the company had worked with for many years. That was surprising. In some instances those companies were approached to see why they had chosen not to apply. Some felt uncomfortable with the process, and so BAA missed establishing a framework agreement with them. It was also surprising how the initial questionnaires revealed the true character of some companies, to a degree that meant they were not considered for a place on the shortlists. Some consultancies felt that the framework agreement would be financially restrictive, some revealed an attitude that BAA considered would not be conducive to long-term partnering. However, they did arrive at a position where there was a large, but manageable, pool of brilliant designers to choose from.

So, what next?

Finalizing the selection process was only the end of the beginning of working with the consultant designers. The next step was to start an ongoing dialogue with them regarding BAA's business and design vision and how this might affect the work they were to do on individual projects. This was seen as a two-way process. The company explaining what they were trying to achieve through the use of design, and the consultants explaining how it is working in practice on current projects. The plan was for an extensive programme of workshops with design consultants and suppliers in order to capitalize on the collective experience and creativity of them all. This programme included an annual conference of all framework design consultants to exchange views and ideas about how design could be used more effectively to achieve BAA's corporate objectives with consultants and key contractors interacting at the conference, exchanging ideas about improving the quality of service to airport passengers.

The real gain from this process is a supplier base of people who want to work together and who value their contribution to BAA as part of its, and their own, success. On a much larger scale, this approach to the design and construction of major facilities will help ensure that much more efficient processes are developed which will produce more cost-effective, better-quality, facilities for all users. The next stage was for BAA and its consultants and contractors to develop criteria to measure the effectiveness of the design investment at the project level.

BAA believed that in order to attain and maintain the high ground implicit in their mission statement, 'to be the best airport operator in the world' they had to manage the quality of customer experience better than its rivals. They also believed that the use of design could help achieve this above almost anything else. This was why it was so important that the designers used were selected for their total collective ability to contribute to this aim.

For a corporation the size of BAA, this selection process was a long and complicated one. However, for many years following there has been much evidence to show how well they have succeeded in choosing people who can work together to produce a quality of service that sets new worldwide benchmarks. In practice, you could say that what they undertook was an audit of an entire industry, the design industry, and from all accounts it was both sobering and exhilarating.

Chapter 14
Eurotunnel: design in a service industry

The management of design work is sometimes made particularly complicated when a new business, especially a new service business, is being created. Under these circumstances not only do you have the need to develop a new identity for the business that fully represents its strategic aims and values but also to manage a range of individual design projects that enable the business to become tangible – together with the added complication of managing the complex interface between these two disciplines.

Figure 14.1 *Eurotunnel, the organization that provides the rail link between England and France across the English Channel*

A good example of this relationship can be seen in the creation of the Eurotunnel service. Although this was a very big project, and is now about 20 years old, the challenges of using corporate identity and design management to help create a new service are still relevant today and are similar to those found in smaller projects and in other industries. Among the outcomes of this work are valuable lessons concerning distinctions between corporate identity and design management and their respective positions in an organizational structure. The original outline for this case was prepared in collaboration with a close colleague and mentor, Peter Gorb, (the pioneer of design teaching at the London Business School) and appeared in the *Design Management Institute Journal (Volume 3, Number 1)*. Since then this case has been revised to include some of the learnings from the service being in operation for about two decades.

Introduction

'Fog over Channel, Continent Isolated', an alleged headline from the *London Times* in the 1920s indicates that the problems to be overcome in building a tunnel and running a transport service between England and France are not limited to ones of geology, engineering and finance.

The history of the proposals to connect Continental Europe with its largest offshore island by a tunnel under the 20 or so miles of sea that separate them stretches back into the eighteenth century. They were defeated more often than not on psychological rather than technical grounds. However, with the advent of the European common market and the agreement of the French and British Governments, Eurotunnel was established to undertake what was (at the time) the largest civil engineering project in the world, and upon its completion to run a unique service business. Its purpose was to provide a transport service between England and France as an alternative to a sea voyage by ferry, hovercraft or hydrofoil. For the first time trains were to travel directly between the two countries.

The resources engaged in this project were enormous both in size and scope. Among them were the two main kinds of design resources with which this case is concerned. The first is the development of the corporate identity of this entirely new service business. The second is the design management of all the artifacts to be used by the service, many of which are were designed from scratch. This case explores how the two design activities relate and interact in an organization where history does not cloud the issues. When it was to start the Eurotunnel service would after all be a new concept.

Figure 14.2 *Le Shuttle, the Eurotunnel train service*

What this case sets out to do

Compared with other management disciplines, both corporate identity and design management are relatively new.

Although some confusion still exists as to the content and nature of the design management process, it is slowly becoming acknowledged that the effective use of design resources is a powerful weapon in the armory of managers. It is also increasingly recognized that the integration of those resources within the corporation requires a range of specialist management skills. With this acknowledged, and their training underway, a new profession is being established.

At the same time a similar growth in the importance of corporate identity management has taken place. Many worldwide corporations have begun to acknowledge the contribution that design-led thinking can make to their strategies in changing business circumstances, and to the consequent organizational changes that need to be made. This contribution is mainly concerned with the identity of the corporation under change and how corporate health can be maintained. The powerful visual skills of a handful of international design-led consultancies employing psychologists and behavioural scientists have dramatically changed our understanding of the nature of corporate identity work. It is now recognized that the external visual manifestation of a corporation constitutes only a small proportion of the work in the field of corporate identity and that it is in fact based on a much larger and more profound activity that takes place internally. Corporate identity management cannot be subsumed within one department like advertising, publicity or marketing. Like design management it is multidisciplinary, has a complex set of relationships with the rest of the organization, and needs to be formally managed by people with specialist skills. In spite of this progress neither discipline is as yet well established. Furthermore, because they are both design based, and because of their common points of contact with the organization, they are often confused with each other. So as a first step in defining their exact roles it is important to distinguish between them, not only to delineate their common ground, but also to demonstrate ways they work on it.

It is the purpose of this Case example to do just that. The frontiers between the two activities will be explored in order to understand more clearly their contribution to business performance and so help to make them more powerful management tools. In the process the differences between the two activities will become clearer. The case will show that they are in fact linked, that their work overlaps and can sometimes be managed from the same place in the organization, and sometimes not. However, to make the differences clear the two activities must first be artificially polarized.

The word 'management' is common to both functions, and our the task will be less complex if we put aside any discussion of the management aspects of each function for a while and concentrate on the relationship between the design activity and the corporate identity activity. Once the nature of that relationship has been established, we can consider whether the management process is common to both functions or whether it is conditioned and modified for each case.

Finally, in order to illuminate the arguments which follow only one organization has been referred to, Eurotunnel. It has been chosen because it is both large and complex, and both resources are used to help run an entirely new form of enterprise. What follows regarding Eurotunnel is, in large part, a description of the imaginative and exploratory design management work that was undertaken by a committed and enthusiastic management team within the organization.

Corporate identity at Eurotunnel

The work on corporate identity at Eurotunnel was to help establish and reinforce the proposition of an efficient transport service that moved people, cars and goods on trains through a tunnel under the channel between the UK and France.

To achieve this objective the corporate identity programme influenced a number of elements and activities of that transport service:

- Various engineering, architectural and related artifacts with particular reference to how they were to be used and seen by both travellers and employees. Key items included the terminal buildings and their related roads, amenities, control points, shuttles and signage systems.
- The communication devices used to describe, promote and manage the service – promotional and corporate literature, customer information, public address systems, computer terminals and management documents.
- The behaviour of the people providing the service and how they reacted with each other and to customers with particular reference to those things which influenced the way they acted, including uniforms, service counters and other transactional artifacts.
- The scope of the communication process and how it could efficiently support the transport service proposition to audiences other than employees and travellers. These included investors, local communities for whom environmental issues and local employment were key, all potential customers of the service in the UK, France and the rest of Europe, and governments, the media and other influential bodies.

Corporate identity at Eurotunnel was therefore a strategic process that touched many business functions like human resources, communications, marketing, public affairs and financial investments. Clearly it did not substitute for these functions, but it did help make all of them more coherent, explicit and efficient through a set of organized visual relationships deriving from the physical elements described above. It was possible to simplify and express the corporate identity function in a diagram that demonstrated the strategic issues affecting a range of artifacts through which the business worked. The right-hand side of the Diagram 14.1 suggests that if the corporate identity function activities are based only on the business strategy, they are inherently unstable. If they were to be effective, they needed the implementation skills of the designer. After all, without operational implementation, strategy is an armchair exercise.

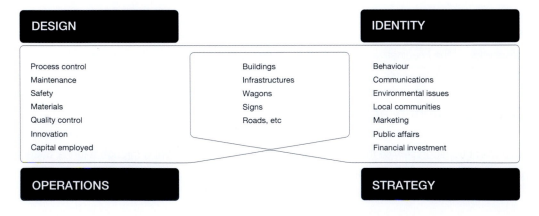

Diagram 14.1 *Overlapping interests of design and identity areas of focus*

Design at Eurotunnel

The design process was based not on strategy but on the operational activities which flowed from it – planning, process control, maintenance, safety, materials selection, quality control, innovation, finance, costs and capital employed. These activities were directly concerned with the same artifacts that concerned the business strategy, as the left-hand side of the diagram shows. However, by themselves these operational activities would have been directionless and so unstable. It is dangerous to operate without strategic objectives.

Consider one example of how strategic and operational considerations impinged on design – the terminal buildings and their surroundings in the UK and France. They were being designed in ways that respected the visual coherence demanded by the corporate identity whist also taking into account other factors which could have been in conflict with the corporate identity requirements, and which may have differed in the two countries. Examples of these factors were:

- political planning, legal and geographical constraints;
- maintenance and safety;
- materials requirements and modes of construction;
- quality control;
- the level of acceptable innovation in designing the terminals;
- operating costs and capital employment;
- process control and ease of manufacture.

These operational considerations had to be taken into account when designing everything from wagons to waste bins, which were also the concern of corporate identity, as is demonstrated in the diagram by the overlapped section. The real benefit of design and corporate identity working in tandem was that they brought greater stability to the business base.

How it works in Eurotunnel

Dealing with corporate identity and design issues at Eurotunnel was bound to be difficult, particularly as the enterprise had no significant operational history in which it could have developed its culture. That the idea of a channel tunnel had a long financial and political history was of little help in starting up an operation of this size and complexity, and design management as a resource was not part of the initial planning. As might be expected, it had developed from a consultancy assignment in corporate identity rather than one about design, with a concern for strategy before operations.

The corporate identity proposals for Eurotunnel, in common with many programmes of this kind, took as its starting point the identification of its central idea. This idea, and its expression in diagrammatic form, was first developed at Wolff Olins. Every successful company has a clearly defined central idea that dominates the physical, visual and cultural manifestations of the business. This central idea is communicated to all its audiences including customers, shareholders, employees, suppliers, competitors, government officials and opinion formers. One management task is to use design to make this central idea tangible because it has, in varying degrees, an impact on at least four manifestations that, as has been shown, are significantly influenced by business strategy and operations, namely:

- products or service which constitute the purpose of the organization;
- environments in which it operates to achieve that purpose;
- ways in which it communicates its purpose to each audience;
- behaviour of its people involved in producing its products or service.

When each of these elements is working in support of the others, and the organization is managing the manifestation of its central idea to maximum advantage, the whole then becomes greater than the sum of its parts.

Normally a central idea springs from the culture of an organization and has developed over a long period. But Eurotunnel had no operational history, and so needed to develop a vision of its central idea and then to turn that vision into reality. Of course the company had a clear view of what its objectives were in terms of general operations, commercial objectives and financial performance.

Less easy was the task of agreeing upon the vision for the service that was to be provided. A two-part vision for Eurotunnel's transport service was developed to provide a clear concept of its overall purpose, see Diagram 14.2. The first part described the idea behind the service and encapsulated the softer issues of how Eurotunnel wanted the service to act and to be described. The second part was concerned with the specific nature of the experience of using the service.

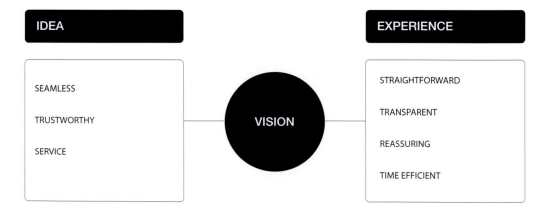

Diagram 14.2 *The two-part vision expressed in terms of basic experience and business idea.*

The idea behind the service was that it should be seamless; that the users should experience no holdups or bunching; that there would be an easy transition from one motorway to the other; that customers could trust it to be safe, reliable and regular; that the focus of the business would be service for the users and not an overt preoccupation with operational matters. The experience itself should be straightforward, with no complications of use, language or technique to confuse the passengers. It should be transparent, easy to understand and with no black-box mysteries, and reassuring, based upon traditional travel experience. Finally the service should be time efficient, allowing users to travel at their convenience rather than be a predetermined and limiting timetable.

The seven words grouped under these two headings of *idea* and *experience* encapsulated the concrete expectations that would be fulfilled through the transport service. Both the idea behind the vision and the experience which supported it could, it was agreed, be made manifest in four different but interrelated ways, see Diagram 14.3:

- its personality would enable people to understand the organization;
- service (a constantly reiterated word) would make the company good to deal with;
- appropriate identification would make the transport service recognizable and easy to use;
- design would provide visual coherence and integration, and thus pervade all the other manifestations.

This vision became the critical central link providing coherence, rationale and practical direction for each of the manifestations, and a programme of separate initiatives was developed for each of them, as is shown in the expansion of the Diagram 14.3 into Diagram 14.4.

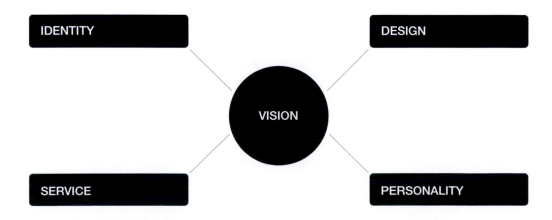

Diagram 14.3 *The four areas of vision manifestation*

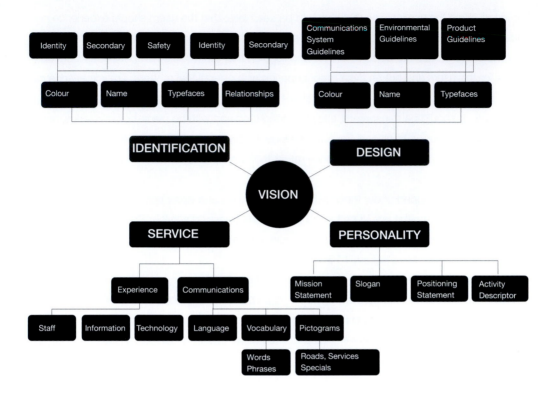

Diagram 14.4 *Expanding the vision into key areas of expression*

Personality

Just as no person is identical to another, so this transport service was to be different from any other form of crossing the channel – in the way it thought, the way it looked and the way it behaved. The personality of the transport service was described through four key communication tools, see Diagram 14.4:

- The mission statement defined the main purpose and core values of the transport service. It was for use by internal and external audiences and provided a common point of reference.
- The slogan is shorthand for the mission statement that distilled the core values into a single sentence. It would be used in advertising and promotional material to capture the spirit of the transport service.
- The positioning statement described how the transport service compared with other cross-channel operators. It provided information about what the company did, how it worked, and described its relationship with Eurotunnel, the parent company. This was primarily for external audiences who needed to understand the facts about the organization.
- The activity descriptor is a standard form of words, used in all communications like printed material, press releases, brochures, timetables, and much more, to ensure consistency in how everyone referred to the service.

Service

To manifest the vision by ensuring a good experience through service, the importance of people, and how they were to be treated, was emphasized over technology. In practical terms this meant the company had to be easy to understand and pleasant to deal with. This service strategy had practical implications for how customers were to be treated by staff, what information was given, how easy the technology was to use, which languages were spoken and written, the vocabulary that was chosen and how pictograms were used throughout the system.

Identification

The transport service needed to be made recognizable through its identification system, which was divided into four main parts:

- Relationships defined the position of the transport service with its parent company, Eurotunnel, and the position of the sub-services with the main service. For example, this part addressed such issues as whether both Eurotunnel and the transport service should appear to be the same thing, or separate but related activities, or completely different entities. Was the cargo division of the service to be differentiated from the rest or not?
- The name of the service and its constituent parts was clearly one of the most important decisions to have been made.
- The colours used throughout the system, both for safety and identification purposes, and for use throughout all architecture, rolling stock and hardware.
- The typefaces used in the identification of the service, traffic control, general customer information, safety and security messages.

Design

Finally the vision for the transport service was to be integrated and made coherent through design. This meant that every artifact, large or small, had to be selected or designed in accordance with a common set of criteria. Three different types were chosen:

- positioning criteria covered quality, the degree to which the artifacts should be contemporary, and the need for them to be unique;
- visual criteria described style, colour and materials; the degree to which similar artifacts used in the UK or France should have a common appearance; and their importance in contributing to the overall visual identity of the transport service;
- operational criteria described key user characteristics of each artifact.

Every artifact used on the system was described in terms of each criterion. For example, consider a freestanding lighting column. The quality of the lighting column was defined in terms that made it consistent with other similar types of structures, like road signs or wind-fence supports. The lighting column was not to be unique in appearance but certainly had to be contemporary rather than traditional. The style, colour, preferred materials, lighting levels and the colour of the light were also defined. It was agreed that the design should be common to both the French and UK terminals. Once described in this way, each artifact specification was incorporated into one of three guidelines which followed the traditional classification of design in business – communication system guidelines, product guidelines and environmental guidelines.

Size and complexities

The 'expanded' Diagram 14.4 shows how the activities were linked and informed by the same set of values, the central idea or vision. By linking them in this way the organization made a powerful and coherent statement about itself. What it does not demonstrate is how the activities, or the complex relationships among them, was to be managed using design as one of the integrating forces.

The scope and operation of Eurotunnel

Although corporate identity was a useful and powerful starting point for uniting the purposes of the organization, its implementation required many and varied design tasks to be carried out, often simultaneously. To do that effectively, and particularly because of the size of Eurotunnel, those tasks had to be managed in separate, but related, ways. Before describing how that management process worked, it is worth explaining something of the context in which these design tasks were coordinated and controlled.

Building the tunnel and its attendant roads, terminal buildings and related hardware was, at the time, the largest civil engineering project in the world. The project cost was about £8.5 billion, and spending was at the rate of £5 million a day. This was equal to the purchase of about 100 jumbo jets fitted out and ready to fly. The contractors removed 7.5 million cubic metres of earth, the equivalent in volume of three times the Great Pyramid. The system consists of 150 kilometers of tunnel and needed 700,000 tunnel lining rings, each weighing approximately as much as eight London buses. The service linked the UK with the rest of Europe for the first time in 10,000 years. Apart from a rail infrastructure for the UK, French and Belgium railways, the transport service was designed to take people, cars, freight, motorbikes and caravans under the channel on a shuttle train operating on a continuous loop between England and France. At peak periods a shuttle was to run every 15 minutes, and each shuttle is half a mile long; roughly equal in length to 200 family cars end to end.

The whole concept behind the transport system was for it to be a part of the motorways that exist on either side of the channel. To this end the system would be signposted like any other destination on either the UK or French motorways. The shuttles travel from one terminal through the tunnel to the other side, around a loop of track, and return after picking up passengers and their vehicles from one of the platforms. As drivers leave the French motorway system near Calais they will approach

Eurotunnel over a circular lake and under a semicircular celebratory arch, eventually arriving at the tollbooth where tickets are purchased. Tollbooths on both sites are the same because of the importance to customers of only having one set of transactional artifacts. The canopies covering the tollbooths, on the other hand, were to be different in the UK and France to reflect the overall style of architecture of each particular site. The driver could choose either to go directly to the shuttle or to the amenity building where all the facilities appropriate for a long journey are found. Frontier controls for both countries are the next step, thus ensuring no delay at the end of the trip. Drivers then head for the allocation area and then along the approach road, over one of a number of bridges, and down the ramp to their allocated shuttle. Driving down the platform, alongside the shuttle, brings them to the designated side entrance.

Once inside, vehicles are parked on the lower or upper deck and wait for the shuttle to move off. Tall vehicles, like campers or buses, use a specially designed single-deck carrier with a much loftier interior. Motorcyclists have their own accommodation close to their bikes. Truck drivers don't use the same shuttle as tourists. They park their vehicles in specially designed carriers and then are taken by minibus to an amenity coach. Once everyone is loaded, which takes about seven minutes, the shuttle moves off through its dedicated running tunnel, and 30 minutes later arrives at the other side. Information on progress across the channel is given via dot-matrix indicators and a public address system. When the shuttle arrives, the side doors open and drivers leave the shuttle for the open road.

Organizing for design at Eurotunnel

How was Eurotunnel organized to manage design in the creation of the transport service just described? Although Eurotunnel was to operate the service, and had commissioned its construction, it was not actually designing or building anything. That work was subcontracted to Transmanche Link (TML), a consortium of ten British and French construction companies. They divided the work into a number of separate projects of which the two main ones were the terminals and the shuttles. The others included tunnel construction and engineering infrastructure. Each separate project was the responsibility of a TML senior manager.

In turn, these two main projects subcontracted design development work. In the case of the terminal design, the responsibility for this was with London and Paris architects. The design-and-build responsibility for the shuttles was let to two separate consortia. Breda Fiat, based in Italy, was responsible for the freight shuttles and subcontracted the industrial design responsibility to Pininfarina. Euroshuttle Consortium in Belgium and France was to build the tourist shuttles and locomotives and they subcontracted the industrial design to DCA Design Consultants in the UK.

Diagram 14.5 shows these relationships and demonstrates that Eurotunnel, and its design advisers on corporate identity and design management, were a long way from where the design action was;

and these are only two of the many separate projects that went to make up the complete service. Each link on the diagram represents a separate relationship, and in many cases a separate legal contract. Design complexity needed to be managed. The fact that the locomotives, for example, had to be a common design compatible with both kinds of shuttle demonstrates the coordination difficulties, from both engineering and industrial design perspectives. Nor was the task made easier by the location of architects and designers in London, Paris, Warwick and Turin, or manufacturers in Italy, Belgium, France, Canada and the UK. In addition, designers did not have an open chequebook; every design solution had to take into account the economic feasibility of the solution.

Relationships between TML and Eurotunnel were complex and often difficult. Effective management of design required that those difficulties and complexities be resolved by diplomacy, tact and provision of firm authoritative direction with a light management touch. In addition to making design possible under the complex contractual situation described, it was also necessary to take into account the requirements of a number of regulatory bodies, for example the Inter-Governmental Commission. Clearly it was a great challenge to make the design of the system work as, and appear to be, one coherent and easily understood entity.

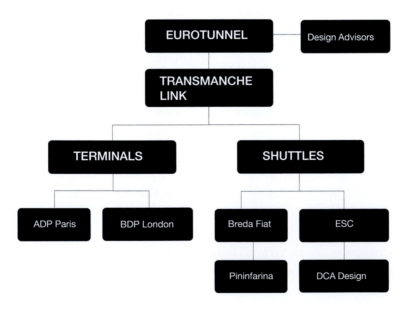

Diagram 14.5 *Organizationally Eurotunnel was not in direct control of design activity, this was the responsibility of Transmanche Link*

Different skills and attitudes for corporate identity and design

Different skills were required for the people tackling the design management and corporate identity problems. Those involved in design work need not necessarily be trained as production planners, or as development, maintenance, safety and process engineers, or as quality controllers, or as cost and financial accountants. However, a working relationship with, and some degree of working knowledge of, these fields were essential to successful design management. Similarly, those involved in the corporate identity work needed to relate to and understand the work of psychologists, communicators, environmentalist, marketing and public relations people, and financial analysts.

The cultural differences between the specialists involved were obvious as the differences in the knowledge bases. But there were also differences in attitude. Design-trained people, by their nature, are job and task dominated. In the spectrum between action and reflection they tend to deal with the how before the why. They try to make something happen and find out why it doesn't quite work, and then try again. They operate by the inductive rather than the deductive route to problem solving. This is a valuable and indeed inevitable way to work for people who are operationally biased.

On the other hand, people who work on corporate identity problems tend to follow the deductive route. Reflection and analysis precedes action; a broad, reflective and long-term view of problems is essential for people who are strategically biased and are dealing with the issues of continuity and differentiation with which at least part of corporate identity work must be concerned. Continuity and differentiation, in the literature of psychoanalysis, are the key issues that deal with the identity of individuals and their mental health as they interact within the various social groups of which they are a part. Work is going on in this field that suggests that these issues are also of direct relevance to corporate identity.

Having established these variations in the skills and attitudes demanded from the people involved, the next part of this case looks at how corporate identity and design were organized at Eurotunnel.

Management of design and corporate identity

Before design and corporate identity could be managed at Eurotunnel, its management had to be organized and a structure developed that would facilitate the work. The structure had to accommodate two major requirements. The first was the decision-making chain. It needed to provide for advice to be given, action to be agreed upon, approval to be obtained and a communication mechanism to keep the board informed when their approval was not specifically required. The second was a necessary flexibility of process as the project developed. Both the design management and corporate identity management needs were going to be different as time progressed, and the process had to be capable of adapting accordingly. The organization of these two requirements was in two phases as shown in Diagram 14.6 and Diagram 14.7.

PHASE 1

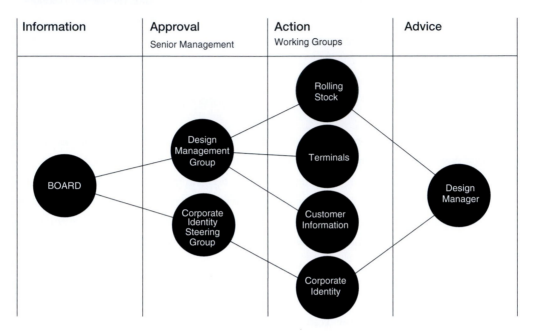

Diagram 14.6 *Organizing for design and corporate identity, phase 1*

Phase One was divided into four stages:

- Advice: authoritative design and corporate identity advice was provided by external consultants who attended a series of working groups. The advisers were retained by Eurotunnel, but had an informal professional contact with TML and their own design consultants.
- Action: working groups were established, each to look after the design management needs of discrete tasks. Membership consisted of people from Eurotunnel, TML, and the design and corporate identity consultants. Their task was to identify design gaps, agree upon design direction, and recommend to the project managers action that should be taken.
- Approval: where additional authority was needed to approve action agreed upon by the working groups, their chairpersons had access to one of two senior management groups, the Corporate Identity and the Design Management Steering Groups. These two groups were agents of Eurotunnel's Management Executive and as such were empowered to make top-level decisions. The Design Management Group was also empowered to establish new working groups as required, or to dissolve existing ones when they were no longer needed. This was not the case for the Corporate Identity Management Group, whose work was continuous, rather than divided into discrete elements.
- Information: it was necessary for the board to guide, and be kept informed about, major design and corporate identity decisions. In some instances the board approved the significant directions being taken by the two senior management groups.

In addition to this formal structure, there was also an informal one resulting from some common memberships in working groups and a free-roving commission that was allowed to the consultant advisers. As aspects of the project became completed, or at least the major design decisions were made, the initial complexity of the structure, as shown in Diagram 14.6, was simplified in Phase Two to that shown in Diagram 14.7.

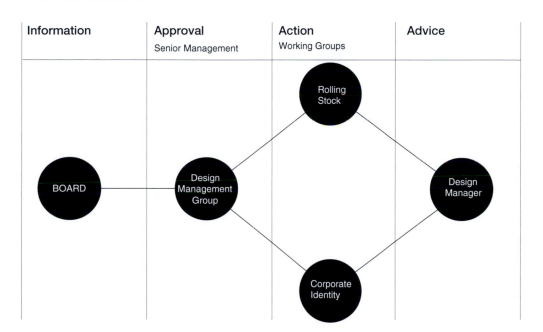

Diagram 14.7 *Organizing for design and corporate identity, phase 2*

By organizing in this way it was possible to manage effectively the multiplicity of projects, which were divided into five main groups:

- rolling stock, including locomotive shuttles and service vehicles;
- customer information;
- terminals, the architecture and artifacts including everything from phone booths to nine metre high wind fences;
- work wear for all tasks and weather conditions;
- corporate identity guide.

The customer information project

What follows is a brief description of just one of these projects, customer information.

In tackling customer information it was necessary to recognize the fundamental conflict between how each project was being managed and the need for cross-project consideration of the customer's information needs. Even though specific customer information needs were being accommodated in most individual projects (that is, on motorways, at toll booths, in terminals, on shuttles and so on), each endeavor was isolated from the rest, was largely operationally driven and was not influenced by decisions made elsewhere on other projects. It was agreed that a complete reappraisal was needed of the information required by all types of customers for each type of journey they might make.

Before these needs could be identified a number of general and strategic decisions had to be made. For example, which languages were to be used – English or French, or both, or any others? How much information was required and at what point in the system? Which words, terms and phrases were to be used that would be most suitable to multinational customers; and where should pictograms be used, if at all? What information was to be permanent and part of the regular operational needs of the system and what was only relevant to variable operational conditions, such as extremes in traffic congestion and adverse weather? What were the best media to employ for providing the information – by voice directly to individual customers or via a public address system, printed signage, dot-matrix indicators or simple variable signs? What were the different customer groups that needed the information in the first place – HGV drivers, tourists, travellers with mobility

USER TYPES										
Tourist car (non-disabled)										
Tourist car (with disabled)										
Motorcycle										
Disabled vehicle										
Tourist coach (non-disabled)										
Tourist coach (with disabled)										
HGV small										
HGV large										
JOURNEY PATHS	Tourist eastbound direct	Tourist eastbound via terminal	Tourist evacuation via tunnel	Tourist evacuation overground	Tourist westbound direct	Tourist westbound via terminal	HGV eastbound direct	HGV evacuation in tunnel	HGV evacuation overground	HGV westbound direct

Diagram 14.8 Matrix for passenger information needs by user types and journey paths

problems, motorcyclists? What types of information were likely to be needed – mandatory and informative traffic management information, safety, and descriptive, pedestrian related, general service, commercial and emergency?

A dedicated working group, consisting of members of both Eurotunnel and TML, was set up to identify all these general criteria and then determine the specific information needs of every potential user for each journey they might make. A matrix was developed that indicated the 11 basic journey variations and the eight customer types, see Diagram 14.8. Each intersection on the matrix indicates the need for a complete set of information for those specific circumstances. The working group produced a document called the Customer Information Guide that identified all the information needs of each of the junctions on the matrix.

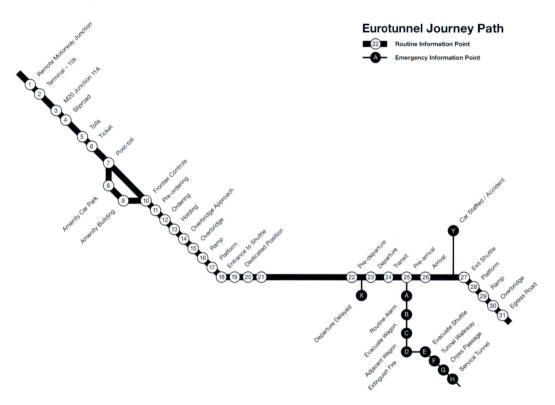

Diagram 14.9 Part of the Customer Information Guide

Diagram 14.9 shows part of the index of that guide and is one of the many maps designed to indicate the information points on a particular journey. In this case it shows the information points on a journey being made by a tourist in a car, travelling west to east. Diagram 14.10 shows the information needs at just one point of the map in Diagram 14.9, Pre-departure.

Pre-departure

User Group   Information Type

	Operational		Safety		Commercial
Operational	Please open window	☐	No smoking No naked flames	●	
	Engine off Handbrake on In gear Lights off	●	For your comfort please stay with your vehicle	🔊	
	Departing in ?? minutes	☐			
	Tune radio to xyz frenquency	☐			

☐ Fixed written

● Dynamic written

🔊 Audio

Diagram 14.10 *The information needs at one point of the map in Appendix Diagram 10, Pre-departure*

For the working group to be successful required that people from different departments within Eurotunnel, often found to have conflicting interests and priorities, sit down together and agree on a set of customer needs which extended beyond their own individual baronial concerns. In addition TML was also invited to make a non-contractual contribution to the debate. The resulting guideline was a single source of influence that informed the design of the whole project.

A design frontier

At the beginning of this case it was decided to put aside any discussion of the 'management' aspects of corporate identity management and design management in order to discuss the different skills, relationships and attitudes toward work required for each of these activities. Now is time to add back the 'management' aspect and look at the two activities to see whether they should be managed together or separately.

Consider just one of the working groups at Eurotunnel dealing with the design of the two terminals. The members of this group included the following:
- the UK and French operations managers were to eventually run the service;
- architects with specific skills in platform, building, wind fence, tunnel track and catenary design;
- the UK and French project managers with specific interest in contractual and commercial matters, logistical management, costings and timetables;

- commercial managers with specific interest in passengers and franchising;
- traffic flow engineers;
- maître d'oeuvre (government appointed assessors from France and the UK)
- safety engineering consultants;
- TML project managers operating in the UK and France for specific construction tasks;
- architects from the UK and France.

In addition were those people, both French and British, from TML and Eurotunnel, who were coordinating and managing this work.

With complexities of this sort it was clear that the management of both design, at least in part, and corporate identity, which has been demonstrated are both concerned with a common set of artifacts, needed to be approached in different ways. Not only did the skills and attitudes of the managers differ, but also so did their knowledge bases. Furthermore, the timescales and structure of the activities were different. Design work was divided into discrete projects, whereas corporate identity work was to be continuous. It was not likely, therefore, that corporate identity and design could be managed by the same person in an enterprise as large and complex as Eurotunnel.

Even in less complex businesses, the ways in which design and corporate identity are organized are unlikely to make them capable of being managed unilaterally. Organizing for efficient performance means the activities, and therefore the people, need to be placed in the organization in positions where their performance can not only be optimized but also be made accountable. For corporate identity work and its management this is clearly at the centre and near the top of the organization. With strategic issues as the mainspring of its work it can be nowhere else.

The position of design and its management is more complex, as this case has shown. In most large organizations, profit or cost responsibility is devolved to operating divisions or subsections. Design as an operational function must be managed within these operational centres. Consequently most product design management in the manufacturing industry reports in where the key profit measure of gross margin performance is determined and assessed. Similarly, in all businesses that invest significantly in plant, equipment, and building, the design activity, which is closely concerned with specifying, must be managed wherever that specifying takes place – in a purchasing department of a central project management division. In other words, from wherever the responsibility lies for improving that critical management ratio of return on capital employed,

Nevertheless, and in spite of the issues of accountability, in any but the smallest organizations it would be very unwise to forgo any central and strategic design overview. Otherwise that interlinking of purposes between corporate identity and design is likely to come unravelled. In organizations with developed accountability for design it is therefore wise to retain at the centre a strong advisory role on all design activities. In the interest of efficiency that role is likely to be undertaken by the team who are also directly responsible for corporate identity. As was explained in Chapter 9 with respect to all design work they will need to be given three important rights: the right to advise, the right of access to give that advice and the right to appeal on all design decisions, irrespective of where the accountability for the design project may lie.

Clearly there must also be some strong functional links between the central team and the operating design managers at profit or cost and capital centres. Furthermore, the central design team should also be responsible for the recruitment and training of all design people within the organization. They should ensure that design training is incorporated into the development training of the line manages to whom design people report. In this way the managers who run the business will eventually acknowledge the fact that design pervades every aspect of the corporation. As the work progressed on Eurotunnel this was increasingly the case.

The future – what needs to change?

With large projects like the one described here it is often necessary to set up corporate identity and design management systems that were not in place at the beginning. This was the case with Eurotunnel. But once a service or business is established, do these systems need to change? How does design and corporate identity get managed then? Not very differently from the way it is managed when the enterprise is being established. The corporate identity – the implementation of strategic purpose – usually requires an initial high level of activity which settles down into a continuous system of fine-tuning and adjustments. Major strategic change does not happen that often. Design work, on the other hand, as the Eurotunnel case has shown, is likely to take the form of a continuous stream of discrete projects. Their nature will change from major projects such as in the case of Eurotunnel, the rolling stock, to projects concerned with such subjects as safety modifications, the maintenance improvements and those that arise from increasing operational sophistication. And there would be similar types of continuous development programmes in all businesses.

The nature of the resources to make all this happen does therefore change. The outside consultants who provide it may be different people, but the management activities are unlikely to change. For the foreseeable future Eurotunnel will need a central management person or team to control the corporate identity and coordinate and advise on all design projects. However, the projects themselves, and their capital cost, are likely to be managed through the line management structure. National and geographic boundaries as well as the investment in areas as diverse as architecture, information systems, rolling stock and the wide variety of operational hardware, are all likely to drive design down the line-management route.

What this implies is that however well advised by design professionals, whether as employees or consultants, the ultimate decisions on design matters will be made by men and women who are not designers, and who are likely to have had little or no design training. The key words are 'well advised'. To make good use of advice in any professional field, some awareness and familiarity with the field is always desirable. This is especially true of design and corporate identity; which as professions are relative newcomers. In Eurotunnel's case the working relationships among managers and the design professionals were very close and complex enough to ensure that design and corporate identity were managed effectively at the beginning.

This was essential, since the social, economic and political significance of Eurotunnel is profound; and the decisions made by a few people will be having an impact on the lives of millions for a long time to come. Design is one of the main ways by which this impact can be made and modulated. That is why managing design, corporate identity and the sensitive frontiers between them is so important to Eurotunnel's continuing success and the opportunity it gives to dissipate 'fog over the Channel' forever.

Chapter 15
Glohealth: rethinking health insurance

GloHealth

Clearly different. Clearly better. Clearly great cover.

Figure 15.1 *Courage, conviction and commitment to challenge the status quo brought this new health insurance provider into the market with great acclaim*

This Case example describes the process behind the creation of a new business, its positioning in the marketplace, competitive differentiation, values, product and identity. It is a story of creating an alternative offer where it appeared there was little room for more.

Introduction

Bringing a new product or service into an already crowded market is never easy – but it can be done. Orange did it for mobile phones; First Direct did it for telephone banking; Ryanair did it for air travel; Sony and then Apple did it for music; Virgin did it for just about everything they were involved with. Each has been successful; each changed the industry they were in and in doing so changed themselves. Above all this they changed the subsequent expectations of all stakeholders.

In each of these cases, as with many others, success was dependent on three key factors:
- the leaders of the business had a clear idea of what they wanted to achieve in the long term;
- the courage, conviction and commitment to challenge the status quo;
- a belief in a core proposition that could be of immeasurable worth. In other words, something that would become such a vital part of their corporate DNA that it would inform everything the company stood for, become a force for loyalty, high levels of service and exemplary behaviour towards customers, and symbolize the long-term values of the business, internally and externally.

Experience teaches that when these three key factors are addressed with creative and rigorous thinking they can provide a rite of passage to create change. If undertaken in a half-hearted way, a lot of time, money, physical and emotional energy will inevitably be wasted.

GloHealth

In this particular case there were many challenges for this new entrant to entering a market where there was space but that was dominated by three large established companies. It was a market with one significant insurer that did not need to be regulated, where customers were confused over the differences between the products on offer, regulatory restrictions and a lot of inertia due to complexity of market.

A small group of industry experts had the conviction that there was a need to deliver a step change in value for customers wanting private health insurance in Ireland. They were convinced it was all about rethinking what were the norms in the industry and shaping a new business around it. Almost 50 per cent of people in Ireland have private health insurance and for a long time, until 2012, three large companies dominated the market. The fact that there had only been three was, in part, due to the regulatory environment that became a barrier to entry. Government policy towards health insurance was changing but remained unclear, costs to consumers were rising, and the products and services of each provider had become virtually indistinguishable from each other. Competition had become reliant on promotional offers and gimmicks. In 2011 it was considered timely for a new entrant with a clear proposition, a strong consumer and cost focus, with the technical expertise and the desire to become the insurer of choice by delivering real and recognized value – by doing things differently. The idea behind GloHealth was born.

The alternative way

GloHealth, from the beginning, wanted to be a business that provided the alternative way to private health insurance. The desire to differentiate itself from the rest of the industry had been fundamental to the creation of this business – how it looks, how it feels to work with, its product differentiation and the manner by which it does things.

Defining the brand

To resolve the many questions it had about the nature of what their offering would be the company engaged in a rigorous process that was designed to identify opportunities for differentiation and distinction. Diagram 15.1 shows the roadmap they used to define their brand, identify its differentiating qualities and answer why customers would buy what they offered.

At the centre of GloHealth was a team of highly respected experts from the field of health insurance. From the beginning they had the creative skills and determination to do things differently, better and with the needs of the consumer being an integral part of the company's DNA.

Jim Dowdall, GloHealth's Chief Executive says, 'We know what makes us different and what this means to the products and services we offer. This difference is born out of a clear understanding of our strategic intent, vision, values, product design and quality of delivery. Collectively these summarise who we are and what we stand for.'

These relationships are illustrated in the roadmap and expanded in the text below. Each part of the roadmap was the subject of one-to-one discussions and an iterative series of workshops that interrogated every part of the brand definition. The result was a well thought through structure upon which the subsequent presentation of the brand, its differentiating features and the full character of what made this business unique, was built. The members of the core management team, who had

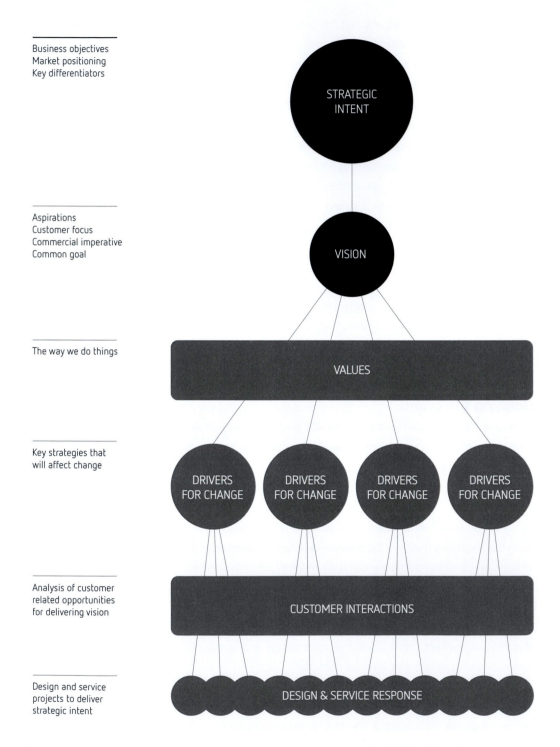

Business objectives
Market positioning
Key differentiators

Aspirations
Customer focus
Commercial imperative
Common goal

The way we do things

Key strategies that
will affect change

Analysis of customer
related opportunities
for delivering vision

Design and service
projects to deliver
strategic intent

STRATEGIC INTENT

VISION

VALUES

DRIVERS FOR CHANGE   DRIVERS FOR CHANGE   DRIVERS FOR CHANGE   DRIVERS FOR CHANGE

CUSTOMER INTERACTIONS

DESIGN & SERVICE RESPONSE

Diagram 15.1 *The roadmap for developing the GloHealth brand. This 'how/why' diagram can be read from top to bottom, or bottom to top, to ensure all design and service responses are delivering the vision and strategic intent*

worked together from the beginning, developed this solution and in the process became the owners of the brand and everything it stood for.

Strategic intent

At the core of GloHealth's business is the strategic aim to be the private health insurance brand of choice for its market segment and to profitably provide relevant health insurance solutions for underserved markets. As was explored more fully in Chapter 7, strategic intent does not go far enough in defining differentiation. It is, after all, an inward-looking set of ambitions – an end result. GloHealth needed to define what it was that would give it the means to attain and then maintain the high ground implicit in its statement of strategic ambition. This was provided by their vision.

Vision

To successfully achieve their strategic intent they developed a vision that would guide all they were to do in creating and managing the business. It was:

'to become our customer, to stand in their shoes'

This would enable them to:
- understand their customers needs;
- challenge the status quo;
- represent customer interests;
- create relevant solutions that work;
- deliver brilliantly.

This vision was supported by a brand proposition, a brand promise, of being:

'clearly different and clearly better'

Values

To manifest the vision they also needed a set of values that were not generic but particular to their business and which summarized the way they were to work and behave. These values were to be critical in setting GloHealth apart from competitors. They were to be key to winning new customers and retaining them. There are five and are written in the 'first person' making it easy to relate to and own on an individual as well as corporate basis.
- Clarity because we believe it is important to make everything for our customers easy to understand and simple to use. When dealing with each other and with our business partners, we will be clear, straightforward and direct. We don't like jargon, we don't like inventing long and complex ways of describing things if there's an opportunity to do it more simply.

Courage because we will deliver what is right even though it will not always be the easiest to accept or do. We are always prepared to challenge the status quo, when it is in our customers best interest.

- Smart because we are always in-tune with our customers needs and respond accordingly. It means being innovative and forward thinking. It means giving customers the confidence that they were smart to join us and feel comfortable knowing we are the best fit for their health insurance needs.

- Integrity because being true and honest to ourselves will reflect positively in all our relationships. It means we will be consistent and open in our dealings. It means being ambitiously engaged and dedicated, emotionally as well as intellectually, because this will ensure exceptional contributions in achieving our business objectives and delivering our vision.

Drivers for change

GloHealth is different from its competitors. These differences are evident in the type of products they offer and the way they offer them. They represent the high ground that will help enable success and help change the industry. These differences are effectively the drivers that will create differentiation. There are four:

1   High value, low cost

Delivering the best value health insurance in Ireland. This is achieved through effective distribution channel selection and management, rigorous efficiency with no unnecessary internal costs. In this way the customer pays the least for the best insurance that their money can buy.

2   Digital technology, personalized communications

Creating a significant competitive edge through digital operations platform by:

- using digital technology to personalize communications, and utilizing all social network channels, to connect with the target market segment, and to develop a better communications infrastructure;
- creating greater levels of economies of scale;
- innovative data management;
- greater process efficiency.

3   Product clarity, process simplicity

Products are clearly and simply described. They are delivered in a simple, straightforward way. There are three basic products, simply named Good, Better and Best. See Figure 15.2.

4   Voice of the customer

Talking regularly to customers, seeking advice and opinion on matters that concern them, and where necessary becoming their voice to the Regulator and opinion formers. Championing change in the industry by actively evolving the role of the health insurer, helping and empowering customers to take more control of their health and long-term wellbeing, reflecting the national psyche of Irish people.

Design and communications

Their belief is that the tone of voice and the design of all communications are guided by their vision and values – they are key to manifesting them. For example the:

- vision of GloHealth has understanding human needs at its core together with a human face;
- value 'COURAGE' means they will challenge the status quo and their communications should reflect this;
- value PRODUCT CLARITY, PROCESS SIMPLICITY has an overt implication for the visual manifestation of all communications as well as the words used and the tone of voice adopted.

The name GloHealth is different in kind from others used in the industry – there are no initials, it is 'to the point', easy to say and remember. It has two meanings and suggestions:

- 'glo' health is good health in mind and body, radiant, an experience of wellbeing or happiness, as from an intense emotion;
- 'glo' health means a sense of satisfaction or enthusiasm from having taken the intelligent option.

Their design approach is honed to the point where it has a memorable clarity and distinction. It is conspicuously different from the competitors. It says, 'We are different, authoritative, approachable and above all else are perfectly aligned with our customers needs.' Communications are direct, simple to understand, using no jargon, and with a tone of voice that is to the point without being aloof. Their attitude is apparent and important. Being prepared to challenge the status quo means they do not follow industry convention unless it is in their customer's best interest. They speak up for customers to those who need to listen.

Conclusion

From the start of this process the GloHealth team were determined to create a valuable alternative for people needing health insurance. GloHealth's conviction and diligence in finding the best values, strategies, products and means of communicating them were all driven by a certainty that their vision was right. Creating a new business, with a different sort of name and completely different type of brand was never going to be easy, and it was not. However the determination to redefine an industry was strong enough to launch the company in the summer of 2012 to great acclaim and initial success.

Figure 15.2 GloHealth product range

Chapter 16
DAA: design integration

Figure 16.1 *DAA, the airport management company in Ireland*

The Dublin Airport Authority (DAA) is an airport management company with 3,000 employees and a turnover in 2010 of €558 million. Headquartered at Dublin Airport, the DAA's principal activities include airport management, operation and development, domestic and international airport retail management, and airport investment. The company's domestic operations include the running of Dublin, Cork and Shannon airports.

This case looks at the role of design leadership in integrating design into the organization to improve the quality of experience of everyone using Dublin Airport. DAA's vision is to deliver a quality airport travel experience to the best international standards. This is a profound statement in the sense that it puts the nature of the customer experience at the centre of the company's strategic intent. To explore the opportunities for delivering this vision DAA developed a number of 'customer journey' maps that examined in detail what it was like to use the airport as a passenger. In parallel with this they did a comparative study of similar sized airports elsewhere in Europe to see how well the DAA experience compared with the others. These maps showed what elements of the journey worked well, which ones did not, what improvements could be made and what design work was needed to deliver the quality of experience demanded by DAA's vision. The output from this work has not only been used as a critical component in the brief for the development and refurbishment of Terminal 1 at Dublin Airport but also as a set of key benchmarks for the development of Terminal 2 opened in 2010.

DAA, believe that design integration is key to delivering their vision because it takes a holistic view. This then enables them to create a continuity of customer experience, in line with best practice. Diagram 16.1 shows the essence of the Design Integration Plan that was in six parts, and shows the connections between the DAA vision and delivering a better customer experience.

1 Vision

In the world of airports it is rare to find a vision statement that puts customer and quality of experience central to what it does. This is despite the fact that airports are all about doing just that! Airports are about managing three things – planes coming and going, bags and people. Bags don't care where they go but people do, yet this simple fact seems to escape the corporate consciousness in so many instances.

DAA's Design Integration Plan clearly linked the strategic intent of the company with the investment projects that provided it with a key mechanism to deliver that intent.

2 Design response

DAA's vision, 'to deliver a quality airport experience to best international standards', section 1 of Diagram 16.1, provides the overriding aim for design integration. In response, to this a design vision, or design response, was developed. This was to focus the use of design 'to create a sense of place, a place of sense', see section 2 of Diagram 16.1 and further explanation in Diagram 16.2

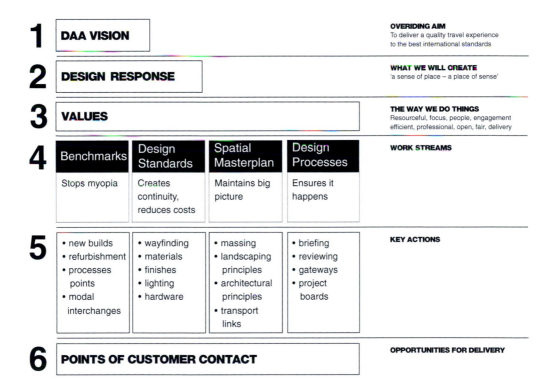

1 DAA VISION
OVERIDING AIM
To deliver a quality travel experience to the best international standards

2 DESIGN RESPONSE
WHAT WE WILL CREATE
'a sense of place – a place of sense'

3 VALUES
THE WAY WE DO THINGS
Resourceful, focus, people, engagement efficient, professional, open, fair, delivery

4 WORK STREAMS

Benchmarks	Design Standards	Spatial Masterplan	Design Processes
Stops myopia	Creates continuity, reduces costs	Maintains big picture	Ensures it happens

5 KEY ACTIONS

• new builds • refurbishment • processes points • modal interchanges	• wayfinding • materials • finishes • lighting • hardware	• massing • landscaping principles • architectural principles • transport links	• briefing • reviewing • gateways • project boards

6 POINTS OF CUSTOMER CONTACT
OPPORTUNITIES FOR DELIVERY

Diagram 16.1 DAA design integration strategy showing the progress from vision to points of customer contact

3 Values

The Design Integration Plan referenced the company wide values as these made very clear the approach that was to be taken in making the plan a real work experience. Everything the business did was conditioned by these values that have been reproduced in section 3 of Diagram 16.1.

2

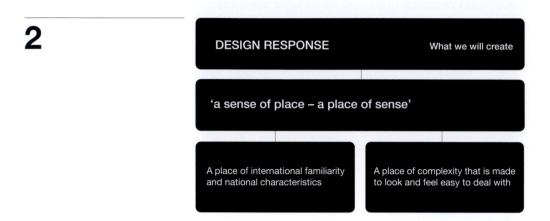

Diagram 16.2 Statement of design response to corporate aims

4   Work streams

Based on the Design Response and the company wide values, a comprehensive design plan was then developed to show the practical ways that this response could be created and delivered. The design plan had four work streams, or areas of activity, that created the foundation for subsequent design integration, see section 4 in Diagram 16.1.

These work streams were:
- benchmarking;
- design standards;
- central area masterplan;
- processes.

Benchmarking

In order to deliver a quality airport experience to best international standards it was important to understand how customer experience at Dublin Airport compared with international best practice. This insight, or benchmarking, could then be used to guide improvements to the design of the airport. It had the added benefit of counteracting the tendency to be myopic, or inward looking all the time – so often a characteristic of specialist industries, especially leaders in that industry.
A benchmarking brief was developed to compare the key steps on customer journeys to and through the airport in Dublin with nine other European airports of a similar size to Dublin, and three other major airports worldwide. A set of benchmarks was produced to gauge how well Dublin's current facilities compared with international best practice, see Figure 16.2.

An outline plan and cost estimates were then developed to upgrade where necessary. This benchmarking study then formed an element of the brief for the new terminal that was, at the time, in the process of being designed.

Design standards

These provided common design solutions for aspects of airport facilities that are repeated across the campus and so establish continuity of customer experience whilst reducing duplication of design effort, build and management costs for projects. Five basic design standards were produced in the initial programme of work. They were Passenger Signing; Materials, Finishes and Colours; Lighting; Hardware and Furniture; and Baby Changing Rooms.

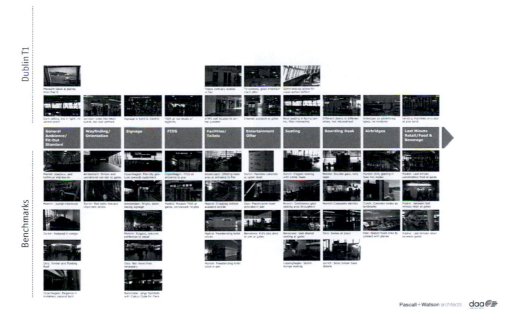

Figure 16.2 *Part of a customer experience benchmarking study*

Central area masterplan

This was an overview of the development of the central operating area of the airport that provided the direction for architectural style; planning and building massing; landscaping; and passenger movements between buildings. It covered requirements of customers, staff and business partners.

Processes

These are a set of management systems and resources by which design integration was to be implemented in practice. They included approaches and templates to design briefing; reviewing of design work; design project management alignment with corporate gateway approval processes; job descriptions of design management staff; and assessment criteria for design projects.

One process that was particularly important to establish was the Design Approval Process, see Diagram 16.3. It is similar to that used by many companies making a significant capital investments and shows the basic design approval process together with the associated steps in the creation of design proposals. Depending on the complexity of the project this approval process would be

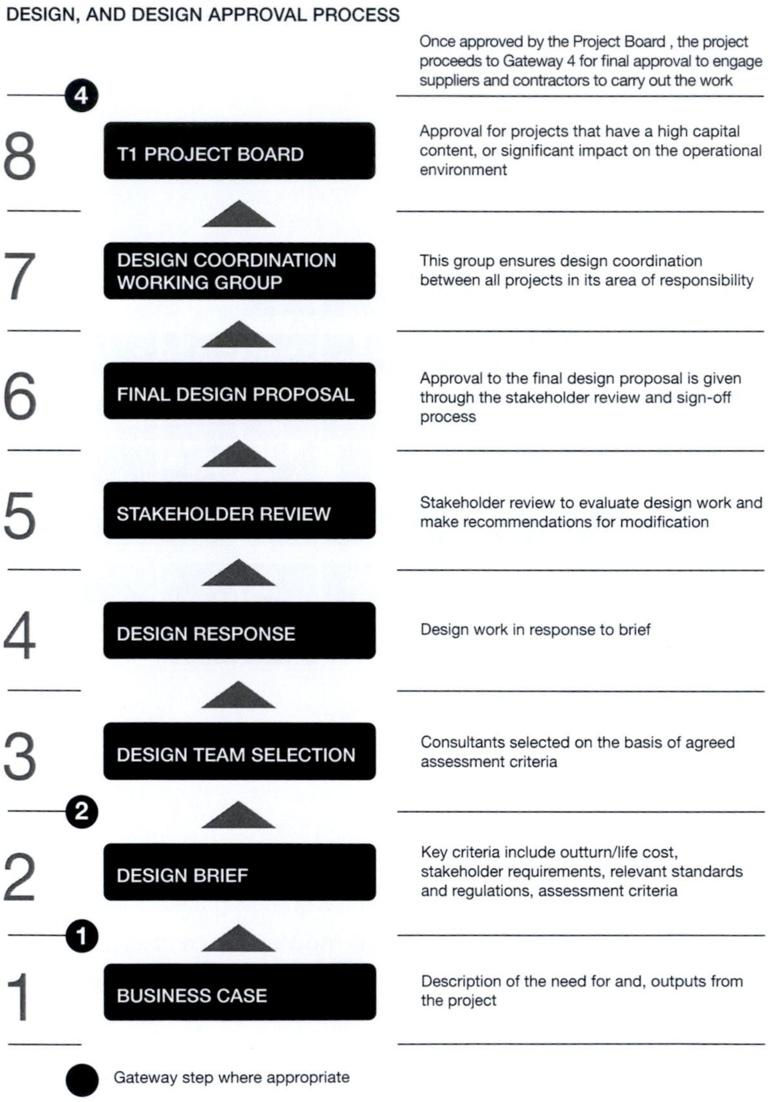

DESIGN, AND DESIGN APPROVAL PROCESS

4

Once approved by the Project Board , the project proceeds to Gateway 4 for final approval to engage suppliers and contractors to carry out the work

8 — T1 PROJECT BOARD

Approval for projects that have a high capital content, or significant impact on the operational environment

7 — DESIGN COORDINATION WORKING GROUP

This group ensures design coordination between all projects in its area of responsibility

6 — FINAL DESIGN PROPOSAL

Approval to the final design proposal is given through the stakeholder review and sign-off process

5 — STAKEHOLDER REVIEW

Stakeholder review to evaluate design work and make recommendations for modification

4 — DESIGN RESPONSE

Design work in response to brief

3 — DESIGN TEAM SELECTION

Consultants selected on the basis of agreed assessment criteria

2

2 — DESIGN BRIEF

Key criteria include outturn/life cost, stakeholder requirements, relevant standards and regulations, assessment criteria

1

1 — BUSINESS CASE

Description of the need for and, outputs from the project

● Gateway step where appropriate

Diagram 16.3 *Basic design approval process*

supplemented by additional steps. A variety of inputs could be made into the 'design brief' stage – including the design standards and guidelines.

5 Key actions

These are the list of key activities, together with the business case, timetable and budget requirements, that constitute the detail of the 'work streams'.

6 Points of customer contact

The final part of the Design Integration Plan was identifying the opportunities for delivering the practical connection with the DAA's overall business aim and the design vision. This is section 6 in Diagram 16.1.

The opportunities for creating facilities inline with the Overriding Aim of the business were originally mapped in the study of three customer journeys to and through the airport – outward-bound, inward-bound and transferring between flights, see Figure 16.3. These maps highlighted every step, and annotated what worked well and what did not. They were very revealing. Together with the results of the Benchmarking Study they formed one of the pillars for future development. They enabled capital investment to be planned on the basis of its short, medium and long-term benefit to customers. Another of their key benefits is that they can be prepared periodically, say every six months, to see what changes have been achieved since last time and to what degree are the changes assisting in achieving the overall aims of the business. Which is where this case started!

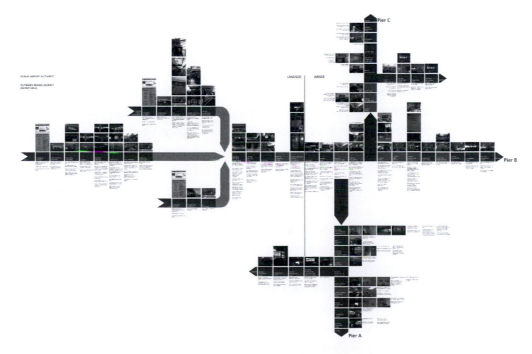

Figure 16.3 *Customer journey map analysis showing each step through the airport on the outward-bound route*

Chapter 17
Design for future needs

Figure 17.1 Terminal 5, Heathrow, a design concept informed by a study into the world of tomorrow

This Case example looks at the role of design leadership in helping with the requirement to understand future needs (referred to as Foresight in this Case example) when making significant investment in infrastructure development. It also illustrates how a clear vision can help shape that investment and the design responses that they depend on. It shows how by putting received wisdom to one side a new attitude of mind can be created in the design team and how this enabled a new benchmark in airport terminal design to be developed. The UK's Design Council closely followed the role of design in this project and the case that follows was documented in close collaboration with them.

Introduction

Terminal 5 (T5) at Heathrow Airport, London, was the biggest construction project ever undertaken by BAA, the owner and operator, both in terms of physical size and financial investment. The overall site is equivalent to 22 football pitches and the development budget was estimated to be £3 billion but was nearer £4 billion by the time the project was finished. The new terminal was designed to supplement Heathrow's existing four passenger terminals, improving the airport's ability to utilize existing capacity and accommodate the world's most advanced larger generation aircraft. It also provided a new facility to serve an additional 30 million domestic and international passengers per year. After 13 years of planning and the UK's longest public inquiry, of almost four years, construction started in 2002. The first phase of the terminal became operational in 2008.

When Managing Director of the Terminal 5 project, Eryl Smith maintained, 'The biggest challenge for all of us concerned with this exciting project is to consider these key factors in a truly open-minded manner, to ensure that T5 remains both a relevant and refreshing experience for travelers for decades beyond its launch. To achieve this we must employ not only our intellectual capacity, our logical reasoned thought, but also our imaginations.' The planning of T5 presented significant challenges for design and Foresight. In particular:

- Designing a terminal that would still be relevant and continue to meet its purpose for at least 25 years. How can changes in climate, lifestyle, technology and regulations be anticipated and accommodated?
- Ensuring that teams from different disciplines in the project have shared goals and a collective vision that enables them to respond creatively to future requirements.
- Managing the needs of over 50 stakeholders, including government, local communities, regulatory bodies and public interest groups, making sure that their requirements are represented and satisfied in order to secure approval, agreement and involvement in the project.

Figure 17.2 Terminal 5, Heathrow, transparency into and through the building was key to intuitive wayfinding

The case example describes the role design played in the 'front end' of the design process, this is the early phase of development where visions are formulated and the strategic direction for the brief is defined. Only once this is established, can the design and production aspects of structures and interior environments begin. Focusing on this early part of the process, the case example describes the importance of design leadership in defining a strategic vision, sets a creative direction and creates a framework in which to interpret and use Foresight information.

The challenges of the T5 project were not just technical but also cultural and emotional. Managing the emotional tension that connected many different stakeholders to the project as well as creating a shared vision for both British Airways (BA) and BAA, made the project even more complex and set expectations high. The case example briefly charts the history of the project then examines in turn, the events and design activities over the period leading up to construction, that relate to design and Foresight. Finally, it considers how specific tools and techniques used in design leadership may be relevant to Foresight activities in general.

Background

BAA, formally British Airports Authority, employs over 11,000 people through international operations. At the time of this case it owned and operated seven airports in the UK and also had management contracts or stakes in 12 airports overseas. In total BAA serve around 200 million passengers worldwide, including over 120 million in the UK.

The original proposal for building a fifth terminal at Heathrow was put forward in the early 1980s, when it became apparent that a steady growth of air traffic, amounting to a 60 per cent increase in passengers per year indicated that soon Heathrow would no longer have capacity to deal with the volume nor the sophistication of design and technology to be efficient. By 1989, BAA and BA had agreed to a joint venture to build T5, what would be the UK's largest airport terminal, completely unaware that construction would not start for another 13 years. The timeline shown in Diagram 17.1 illustrates the key steps in the planning, design, development and construction of the project.

Time Line for the development of Terminal 5

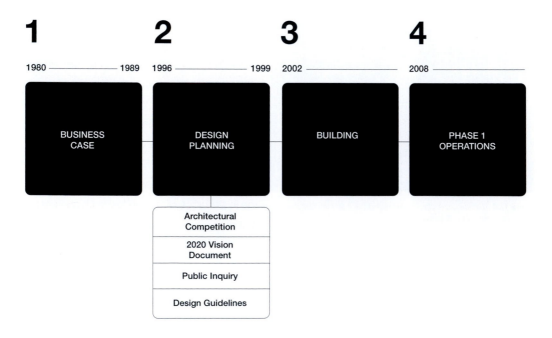

Diagram 17.1 *The overview of time for the development of Terminal 5*

The project was launched with an architectural competition, to which leading architects were invited to pitch for the design concept work. Architects, Richard Rogers Partnership, now known as Rogers Stirk Harbour and Partners, won the competition with a distinctive building design that challenged the conventions of existing airports and the use of materials.

The UK Government required that all major developments must be approved through a formal consultation process, whereby stakeholders had the opportunity to comment and reject the proposal if they wished to. Stakeholders ranged from government bodies to local community groups, each with different and often conflicting interests that had to be resolved before approval is given. Finally, after about four years, the longest public inquiry in UK legal history, T5 was given approval by the Government. It then took approximately five years to build.

Design and development process

The context for the design process in its development is unusual in a number of ways:

- T5 involved the design of a building and infrastructure in addition to service products and passenger experiences.
- The expected lifespan of T5 is around 50 years, very much longer than is the case for most products that have a consumer interface.
- The amount of financial investment required was very high.
- The complexity and therefore risk of the development was equally high.

Figure 17.3 *Building the longest unsupported single span building in Britain was just one of the challenges facing the team responsible for designing for future needs*

Beyond the construction of the terminal itself, further investment was required in order to develop transport links with Heathrow Airport. As well as plans to provide a bus and coach station at T5, plans were in place to link the terminal to a widened orbital road around London, the M25, extend the Piccadilly underground tube line into T5 and develop six multi-storey car parks to accommodate new traffic.

As a consequence of the project's size and scale, accurate and realistic interpretation of Foresight was critical in order to design an airport infrastructure that would stand the test of time; advances in technology, changes in politics, demographic and climate, and also shifts in lifestyle and consumer behaviour.

I joined the T5 team in 1997 as Design Director having previously worked for BAA as Group Design Director with overall design responsibility for their major projects including the Heathrow Express. As such I was well placed to review progress and reassess the design proposals against the strategic objectives. Before joining, the design input into the project had taken the form of a detailed and technical specification document largely based on engineering and operational constraints together with the visualization model from the architects.

I saw the main challenge being to reconnect the design concept of the project with strategic objectives and ensure that the final solution had the right criteria for success. Working with the design and engineering teams of both BAA and BA, the intended principal tenant, I encouraged employees to re-evaluate existing plans and generate improved solutions which were more future focused and responsive to user.

A new design strategy was developed in order to refocus and energize the many parts of the design team, extend thinking horizons beyond standard airport practice and integrate activities and thinking into the whole project.

'The world's most refreshing interchange' became the vision statement for the T5 project, a sentence which embodied ambitious objectives, encouraged future-focused solutions and delivered the business objectives of both BAA and BA. T5 would aim to be an international benchmark for airports and set a future standard and ethos for BAA operations that would anticipate and accommodate future change and provide a user-experience that exceeded expectations. This vision was more than just a smart slogan, it was packed with meaning as elaborated in Diagram 17.2.

a multi transport interchange	that leaves passengers positively refreshed

The world's most refreshing interchange

stimulating a change in thinking and attitude	creating a world benchmark in airports

Diagram 17.2 *The vision of Terminal 5 that was to set a new benchmark for all airport terminals*

First it captured the strategic ambitions of both companies, BAA's to be the world's most successful airport group and BA's to be the world's favourite airline. Additionally it captured the essence of what was going to differentiate this airport terminal from all others. This meant a facility that:

- was more than just an airport terminal, in fact a multi-transport interchange, that accommodated the needs of everyone moving between road, rail and air transport at T5;
- left passengers positively refreshed;
- stimulated a change in thinking and attitude by the people designing,building and running it;
- created a world benchmark in airports.

This was a profound moment. Suddenly, after several months of re-examining what the investment in T5 was trying to achieve, here was something that both organizations could subscribe to and something that could be used to motivate the several hundred members of the design team.

A four-part strategy, or drivers for change, supported that vision, to:

- improve sustainability by making sure T5 was going to be future proof and able to adapt to change;
- integrate passenger journeys by making the transition from one mode of transport, or one part of a journey, to another easy and trouble free;
- improve the experience of travel by making T5 more pleasurable to use than anywhere else;
- enhance value by making the facility commercially viable for both BA and BAA.

Strategic brief

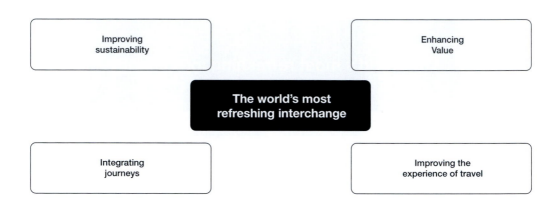

Diagram 17.3 *The strategic brief for change that helped ensure that the design of Terminal 5 was not based on 'business as usual'*

This vision and strategic brief were presented to the key decision makers in both companies in a vivid way that brought the vision to life by illustrating the differences it would make for the people using T5 and for those running it. They agreed that this was the way forward and all future design work would be assessed against this vision and strategic brief.

2020Vision: a view from the future

Long-term planning projects can be extremely vulnerable to external changes in technology, society and the economy and during the 13 years of planning T5 the context for design had already changed. It was certain that over its expected life many more changes would occur that could potentially have an impact on the design of the terminal and how it would work. The design challenge was to understand the nature of these changes and the impact on the airport of the future, then respond with solutions that would be flexible to accommodate these changes should they occur.

For example, it was expected that refinement in technology would make ticket-less travel standard meaning that many fewer check-in desks would be needed. Also new larger aircraft carrying 800 people would soon to be introduced and would require terminals capable of handling both the aircraft and the number of passengers arriving and departing at one time. In addition there were other, less clear, changes to take into account. For example, how do airports prevent the impact of airborne diseases, the requirements of a changing demographic population and climatic shifts?

To communicate the implications of future change on the design process, a magazine-style report called 2020Vision, see Figure 17.4, was compiled to examine the major issues, trends and changes that might affect the design of airports in years to come. The report drew on other work undertaken in BAA called 'Airports of the Future' which explored how an airport might function in the future and mapped out the likely future changes given the information and opinions of experts in different fields. The distinctiveness of the 2020Vision report was in the way it translated Foresight knowledge and made it accessible. Interpreting information and opinion on future change into possible scenarios and challenges, which then presented new constructs for the T5 design brief. The document was a significant step to connect up the macro issues and strategic objectives to the micro context, defining 'the everyday airport experience'. The 2020Vision document triggered discussion and extended the teams thinking horizons to the future. This thinking was later taken forward by the teams to explore and present potential solutions.

Figure 17.4 *A view from the future, part of the study into the world of tomorrow*

The chart shown in Diagram 17.4 highlights some of the issues raised by the 2020Vision document and also a selection of inferred challenges for the design of airport infrastructures.

Issue	Challenges for design
Global concerns	What would it would it take to achive containment of airbourne hazard?
Technology	What would hydrogen fuels mean for aviation?
	When everything is instantly locatable, how will this change airport process?
Lifestyle	What is needed for group travel? Prevalent in Asia?
	If people want to travel light and switch planes at a moment's notice, can we cope?
	What type of experience would tempt passengers with their heads in cyberspace to give you their attention?
	What sort of lifestyle brand would an aiport an aiport be a part of?
Personal security	In a world of pervasive invisible security scanning, what does 'airside' mean?
	Who will own access to what information about the passengers?
	What do concerns for personal security mean for the design of car parks?
	How can airports serve the confused passengers and those in need of reassurance?
Transport futures	Are there any new models for surface access? Hybrid taxi-buses?
	In a 24-hour world with few night flights, how is the terminal utilized at night?
	What does it mean to have no queues anywhere?
	Could airports develop into 'trunk' interchanges with separate satellities for private cars and local transport?
Climate change	How will buildings, aprons and operations cope with flash floods?
	Is it worth safeguarding for water recycling?

Diagram 17.4 *Some issues raised by the 2020Vision project and selection of inferred challenges for design of airport infrastructures*

Sharing the vision

In parallel to distributing the 2020Vision report, workshops were held at a senior level and with key teams in order to develop understanding and commitment amongst employees from both BA and BAA and encourage them to think beyond what they knew or were comfortable with. Sharing the vision and getting the project teams to believe in the changes presented a cultural challenge. In addition to unifying two organizational cultures and visions, there were also 60 different suppliers involved in the design process.

The next step was to share the vision with the rest of the employees. For this a presentation was created for a larger audience to communicate the vision, demonstrate where the vision had improved current solutions and underpinned the thinking behind it. The presentation explained:

- Why a vision was necessary in T5.
- What that vision was.
- What kind of culture was needed to help deliver this.

It was important to excite the design team to ensure that they wanted to be part of creating and delivering the 'most refreshing interchange.' The design leadership team coined the phrase 'motivating proposition' to describe the way in which employees could be inspired and encouraged to deliver the vision. Examples were used to illustrate how and where this type of approach was used, for instance in improving the design of the roof structure to allow maximum interior space and flexibility for changes in the floor layout, and also cost savings and improved intuitive wayfinding that came through moving the passenger drop-off-area to the roof of the car park building.

After the presentation, their enthusiasm was sustained by conducting smaller workshops with eight–ten different teams which renewed energy for the programme and offered support to help them move beyond traditional ways of working. The teams responded well to the workshops and the challenge set, offering many suggestions and creative solutions once they felt they had a supportive and creative environment. To enable this a comprehensive communications campaign was developed that helped motivate the workforce to think differently and share the same vision.

Figure 17.5 *Part of the internal communications campaign to change mindset of the team working on Terminal 5*

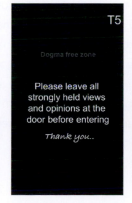

Owning the vision

Through the workshops the various design teams also began to own the 'vision' and started to redefine their work and expectations of themselves in the context of it.

In order to demonstrate this 'new thinking', the teams had to understand more fully passenger behaviour. Product teams were created, consisting of designers and engineers from different disciplines and from both BA and BAA. Their brief was to look at the different types of passenger journeys likely to be experienced at the airport. There were nine different types of journeys, for example, from train to plane, from car to train, from train to plane, from bus to train, from plane to bus and so on. The product teams were responsible for investigating different aspects of each of these passenger journeys to and through the total terminal campus, like checking in, leaving, going through security. Observational methodologies were used to follow passengers through other terminals at Heathrow and comparative reports were written on international airports. One aspect of this research examined 'wayfinding' and explored the visual cues and zoning strategies that would make an airport easier to navigate and a more pleasant environment to be in.

The product team's research was communicated visually via a uniquely designed passenger journey map that showed every step on the outward-bound, inward-bound and connecting journeys. Each step was represented by a coloured box and described the experience to be created at that point. This information then became an integral part of the design brief. For instance, on arriving at the airport, how might the design of information, layout, signage and environment help provide the most 'refreshing experience'? What information does the passenger need to know? Want to know? How easily is the information currently displayed? How do passengers feel on arrival? Apprehensive? Excited? Reassured? What experience should they have? This approach to mapping customer experience was subsequently used by DAA, the Dublin-based airport authority as explained in the case example previously.

Each product team produced a final report that was shared amongst the relevant design teams and fed into the design brief and development process. Product team thinking not only offered a rich insight into user behaviour and an indication of where to improve, but also challenged their assumptions of users, discovered new and emerging patterns of behaviour and helped them analyze the likely impact of their design responses on people using the airport. From a design leadership perspective the outcomes of the product team programme were not just about product and process improvements but more critically about finding sustainable ways to challenge and change the way employees think. To give them the confidence to set more ambitious boundaries from which to design and create within, and develop a more future focused yet realistic criteria for success.

Implementing the vision

Through these activities design leadership instigated a cultural shift in the way the design team viewed the T5 project. The new vision, future thinking and renewed focus on the user led to the design of T5 being seen as a total experience as opposed to a technical solution to bag and people handling housed in a large built structure. Information and insight from the 2020Vision work was actively being used to challenge the longevity and quality of ideas and solutions in terms of how they would meet the needs of users at that time and into the future.

Significant changes were made as a result of this new perspective, for example, the number of check in desks was reduced to anticipate the introduction of ticket-less travel, flows through the buildings became much more intuitive, innovative ways of integrating unsightly plant into the superstructures of the buildings were developed that improved the overall appearance of the buildings, and a new wayfinding strategy was introduced to aid navigation.

To support this work and ensure the design solutions proposed had been rigorously reviewed before implementation, advisory panels of internationally recognized experts from different areas, for example sustainability and product design, were used to maintain a critical perspective and create a dialogue to help develop the most effective solution. Every two months the teams would review and present their work to the expert panels for feedback. This process reduced the risk of failure, made the designers challenge and improve their ideas and also helped make the decisions more quickly and more effectively.

Protecting the vision

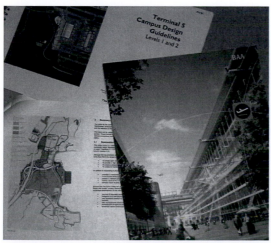

Protecting the vision over time and ensuring the learning and insight gained through the research, development and design was actually used and not compromised is a significant design leadership challenge. To help ensure these ideas survived the long design gestation period and the subsequent construction timetable, work soon began on preparing the 'Campus Design Guidelines', see Figure 17.6, which outline a 'how to' deliver the vision through a defined design strategy and summarizes the outcomes of all the research.

Figure 17.6 Part of the documentation that made up the long- term design guidelines used during the design implementation phase

These guidelines proved to be an essential part of protecting the overall vision and preventing any unauthorized changes. They communicate how design specifications directly relate to delivering strategic objectives, and emphasize how critical it was to follow the guidelines when producing and delivering the final design solution.

Design and Foresight

The nature of the T5 Case example illustrates the broader role of design beyond, products or services. T5 shows how design activity and in particular design leadership can be instrumental in redefining strategy, creating shared vision, changing behaviour and interpreting and using critical Foresight information in order to sustain commercial success in the long term.

Design and Foresight are intrinsically linked. Design is typically about making something that does not already exist, either to meet current needs more effectively or meet new or emerging needs. Designers work within varying timeframes designing solutions with different life spans. At one extreme, where the longevity of the product is relatively short, design can be very reactive and fashion led. Here the value of future thinking is less obvious, however in the design of products and services with a longer lifespan, for instance, cars or public transport systems, Foresight information is critical and needs to be comprehensively integrated into the design process. As clients and companies take a more long-term perspective in business planning, the value of Foresight information increases. In T5, design helped to make this information accessible and useable.

Through the planning journey of T5, four key observations have been made to illustrate how design leadership and design activity have addressed this challenge:
- translating Foresight information;
- capturing Foresight information;
- communicating Foresight information;
- shaping and framing Foresight information;

These are briefly examined in turn with respect to how they worked in practice in the T5 project.

Translating Foresight information

Designers routinely gather and incorporate different types of Foresight information depending on what is being designed. In this case Foresight information was based on three main criteria:
- expected life span of the solution;
- needs of the user during this time and;
- strategic objectives of the business.

These three constructs provided the designer with a framework to find relevant information. Once this information has been identified, they then use it to inform the brief and explore a range of possible solutions. A brief outlines the requirements of what is to be designed and is used to provide the boundaries for the project in terms of target market, user benefits, as well as finance and deliverables. Designers consider the brief as a 'problem-solving' activity and use visualizing and intellectual skills to develop different solutions. During this early part of the design process, known as 'conceptual prototyping', designers often have the opportunity to look further than the brief, challenge what is known and as a result, often reveal unexpected solutions.

The non-linear process of design can add value to Foresight activity. Instead of following a step-by-step process, designers make intellectual leaps between the intangible 'what if?' and the tangible. They continually investigate and inform their decision-making to optimize the final solution. This iterative way of working is critical in understanding changes in requirements and anticipating the future. It also encourages continual review and modification of ideas then translates and represents this visually to communicate these ideas. This is a low-cost strategy that can identify potential problems and risks very early on in the process before finances are committed.

Designers prioritize and synthesize information to generate real user-focused solutions which connect ideas to the needs of the user and align these to business objectives. Evidence of this can be seen in T5:

- translation of the 'airports of the future' research into the 2020Vision document;
- defining the criteria for success to incorporate user benefits, longevity and experience, as well as business objectives;
- team workshops which explored future-focused solutions and ideas that pushed boundaries of the, then, current thinking.

Capturing Foresight information

Designers use a hybrid of tools to gain insights into future needs. Some tools, for example, scenario building, ethnographic techniques which are taken from other disciplines like social sciences, are then adapted or modified by designers to suit their needs. Other tools are more associated with the design process like visualization, prototyping and characterization scoping, sometimes called 'mood boards'. Designers have a particular way of combining different types of tools and adding a visual dimension. This not only aids communication but also offers invaluable insights into the future, for example, the likely reaction of the user to change, and an understanding into the drivers behind consumer adoption, adaptation and rejection. Examples of design approaches that combine tools in this way are evident in:

- product team research;
- wayfinding research;
- customer experience mapping.

Communicating Foresight information

One of the most accessible arguments for design's role in Foresight activity is the way in which designers use a visual language to express ideas and represent information from different sources. Visuals provide a common reference point and can be used to explain complicated concepts.

Two-dimensional images and three-dimensional models offer a more realistic way of exploring future scenarios. They provide a platform for stakeholders to comment on the tangible outcomes rather than abstract concepts, and these are more likely to reveal the latent and unarticulated needs and concerns of users. Errors may be avoided by gathering stakeholder opinions as early as possible in the process. Images and models are invaluable communication tools. In the T5 project, visuals were critical to establishing and sharing the vision internally and in getting approval from stakeholders externally. In particular it used:

- 2D Computer Aided Design drawings and models to visualize and 'bring to life' the possible solutions;
- communication campaign to motivate staff and remind them of the overall vision;
- campus design guidelines that helped to capture and manage stakeholder requirements.

Shaping and framing Foresight information

The design process can also generate unexpected insights into emerging trends and can help companies monitor reactions to change in 'real time'. This is particularly important when trying to understand the impact of events that cannot be predicted. Design research is also particularly effective in identifying trends that emerge from the user and from the behaviour of early adopters. Through the design process ideas are continually presented, tested and evaluated. This learning process helps designers to describe future needs and take into account small changes in users requirements as well as the impact of socio-economic trends. In the Terminal 5 example there were many including the following ones:

- design provided early and continual testing of solutions that were challenged and subsequently improved the brief;
- design leadership was key in developing the Airports of the Future work and then introducing the findings into the design process. This in turn helped create the 2020Vision document that filtered and prioritized Foresight information and made it visible to employees and critical to the project's success;
- a multidisciplinary approach in the form of the design advisory panel ensured that during the design process experts were consulted and used to test and evaluate future scenarios and solutions;
- product teams engaged in researching specific passenger journeys were used to find latent user need, for example, the creation of 'quiet zones' where people with impaired hearing could go to listen to announcements. Creating the 'Campus Design Guidelines' to protect and ensure that the vision was delivered and the learning was fed into new design standards for future projects across BAA.

Conclusions

Terminal 5 illustrates how a design-led approach to strategic thinking can improve long-term decision making. This in turn can be used to create a vision that could accommodate future requirements and reduce risks of designing the wrong thing. It could also help organizations, in this particular case BAA and BA, to focus on the future, challenge their existing ways of working and set new benchmarks for other design teams to build on. In this instance, the 'design approach' encompassed design skills, design methodologies and design perspectives. In the development of Terminal 5 there were three distinctive levels of design input that proved critical to success.

Design activity
Design teams used practical skills and manipulation techniques to conceptualize, visualize, create and make products, services and environments or communicate ideas and messages.

Design management
Project managers had a comprehensive understanding of the mechanics behind the design process and aimed to deliver on deadlines and fulfill the brief efficiently.

Design leadership
This was concerned with representing design at a strategic and board level. A small team of design leaders from the client and the consultant teams helped to create an overall 'vision' which provided the context for design work and also the constructs by which to measure success.

Figure 17.7 Terminal 5 interchange plaza from BAA's 2002/03 Annual Report' investing for the future'

T5 presents a credible case for the value of a 'design-led approach' in Foresight. It illustrates the relationship between design and Foresight with respect to:

Translating Foresight information
How design was used to frame and translate foresight information through the 2020Vision report and make it relevant to the project teams.

Capturing Foresight information
How design added an extra dimension to Foresight by offering new and adapted tools to capture foresight information, for instance design team workshops, product teams and user experience mapping.

Communicating Foresight information
How design helped explore and communicate potential solutions and open up a dialogue

both internally to change the employees ways of working and externally to engage stakeholders and identify their requirements.

Shaping and framing Foresight information

How design deepened BAA and BA's understanding of user needs and experiences, and the implications of future change to create solutions that would evolve with time. Amongst the next challenges is to explore how design and Foresight tools and approaches may be most usefully integrated to improve longer-term planning decisions and inform policy makers.

Chapter 18
London Transport: design in crisis

The first significant point in the integration of design and business is reached when a company recognizes that design is out of control, and particularly when it is considered to be a cost rather than an investment. This first milestone is called 'design in crisis'. This case looks at that particular period in the history of London Transport when this became the reality and what the signs were that it was happening. It is a critical first step in the management of design and could be of real value to any company wanting to understand the state of design in their situation.

The starting point

The starting point for this Case example is the early years of the twentieth century in London. Underground the Victorians had built the Metropolitan Railway, opened in 1863. It was the first of its kind in the world. The steam locomotives had special condensing apparatus to get rid of the smoke. Overground, public transport relied on horse-drawn buses on the roads and steam trains. During the early years of the twentieth century a number of companies providing public transport amalgamated into a larger privately-owned organization called the Underground Group. They established a trading mark comprising a tramcar in the centre, and underground railway lines leading to it. The Underground Group also developed an architectural style for their new stations and tube lines which opened in 1906. The buildings all followed the same architectural theme and used a consistent approach to materials, colour and lettering style for signage. Being extremely publicity conscious they were soon handing out free maps to the public.

Transport operators amalgamate

In 1933 the Underground Group amalgamated with all other underground railways, bus and train operators in London and formed one new monopoly public body, responsible to the local government authority. The company was called the London Passenger Transport Board, soon known to everyone as London Transport.

This transition from private enterprise to public service was marked by the gradual development of a trading mark that was finalized in 1933 and is still in use today. With the creation of a single public authority responsible for all bus, tram and underground railway operations in the capital, it was possible to develop a design ethic for the whole organization. London Transport was eager to promote the public image of a progressive, efficient, caring and style conscious company. According to Frank Pick, their Chief Executive, they were committed to using design as a means of 'harnessing commercial methods to the achievement of large social objectives'.

A design strategy

London Transport believed that good design could mean good business. It represented a major opportunity for them to contribute to the creation of a civilized and well-planned urban environment. They used the best designers of the day to help achieve that objective.

With product design their buses and underground trains were the most advanced and sophisticated in the world. Bus development culminating in the custom designed Route Master bus, and train development culminating in the fully automatic one that is running today. Other hardware specifically designed for them included ticket machines, notice boards, rubbish bins, light fittings, seats, sign systems, bus stops and shelters, and much more.

Figure 18.1 *London Transport Design Manual, mostly concerned with the management of its graphic system*

With environmental design they created what was termed 'a new architectural idiom', consisting of two modern design concepts appropriate for central London and suburban stations. Both design concepts set the familiar house style of London Transport for the years to come and were capable of considerable variation for different sites and structures. Innovative design solutions were also developed for rebuilding ticket halls like Piccadilly Circus and the dramatic new headquarters for the company at St James Park. Even bus garages were treated as part of their public identity and were used to give greater street presence to the company.

As far as information design was concerned London Transport soon acquired an international reputation for patronage of modern graphic art by commissioning colourful pictorial posters to publicize the company's services. Throughout the interwar years the London underground station had become a popular showcase for avant-garde poster design. A particularly significant development in the company's publicity was the redesign of the geographical underground map in the early 1930s into the familiar, easy to read, diagram, an extended version of which is still in use today. This same idea has been copied the world over.

Figure 18.2 Design of passenger information, product and interior design had lost its way in being an integral part of what made London Transport a benchmark for city travel

Design coordination

Through its product, environmental and information design, London Transport was able to present, to the travelling public, a consolidated and unified message that every care had been taken to provide them with the best possible service that was both easy and convenient to use. Each area of design was treated with the same sense of priority, and even earned the, somewhat surprising, compliment from Nikolaus Pevsner that 'this was the most efficacious centre of visual education in England.' This coordinated design approach culminated in two discrete major projects, the development of the Victoria and Bakerloo lines between 1969 and 1979. In both cases all aspects of design were made to work in support of each other to reflect a new image of clinical efficiency appropriate to the world's first fully automated underground railway. And to top it all they even produced a design manual, see Figure 18.1.

Figure 18.3 *Transport for London, the most recent reincarnation of London Transport, an integral part of modern life in the city*

Design collapse

As a result of many complex factors there followed a degeneration of design throughout the organization. Underground platform designers became preoccupied with superficial decoration, particularly in their attempt to emphasize the geographical sense-of-place of each location. Passenger information on both trains and buses became sloppy, unclear and uncoordinated. Much of the hardware in use became treated as though it had nothing to contribute to the public perception of the company. And there was even gross disrespect for the one thing that the company had developed and established as representing all that was good in public transport, and in London, the symbol. It was redrawn in a variety of comic ways, often degenerating into advertising gimmicks for such things as the London Transport health plan or annual carol service. See Figure 18.2. It would be oversimplifying the situation to say that all this happened as the result of one incident. During the 1970s plans were made to move the control of London Transport away from local government to central government. Perhaps these political issues diverted everyone's attention away from their integrated design policy, it is difficult to be sure.

London Regional Transport

However, in the early 1980s, with the passing of an Act of Parliament, a new authority was created, London Regional Transport, often referred to as LRT. After that London Transport as a company ceased to exist.

This new body was charged with providing the most cost-effective passenger service within Greater London. Part of its task was to make the main businesses of underground and bus services profitable so they were not so dependent on public financial support. In 1982 major transport subsidiaries were created, one called London Underground Limited and the other London Buses Limited. The creation of these wholly-owned subsidiaries, which were operationally independent, presented LRT with the problem of formulating its own design strategy for the future.

These changes led to an ironic situation. Whereas design was once used to draw together the activities of a number of different companies at the turn of the century and unite them into an integrated transport service during the mid-century years, the company was now faced with using design to help it handle precisely the reverse situation. That is to allow the controlled separation of the main business units on the one hand, and still to present a coordinated transport service to the public on the other.

However, long before this, and despite the early commitment to a coordinated design approach, and similarly later regarding the two newer underground lines, design had lost its way both in terms of purpose and focus. London Transport had experienced a major crisis. Design was no longer coordinated, nor was it fulfilling a strategic purpose – worse, design was out of control. Almost without noticing that anything had happened it had reached the first milestone in the relationship of design and business. Design was in crisis.

From this point on considerable effort and investment has been made to reinstate the public transport services in London into one of the best in world. See Figure 18.3. However, as this Case example shows, it is all too easy to lose grip on the use of design to such an extent that reputation and service quality can suffer badly.

Summary of reflections

I have written this section for two reasons. The first is to act as a summary of what has gone before, to be a convenient reminder of some of the key issues raised through out the book. The second is for those people (and I number myself as one of them) who invariably start at the end of a book and read the conclusions or summary to decide whether the book is worth reading in the first place. It is to both audiences that this section is directed.

The subject of design leadership is one that is evolving. Understanding its role in business and how to use it effectively and comprehensively is the challenge for all those interested in maximizing shareholder return and creating a better society. In writing this book I have tried to set out some of the issues and responses that have been useful, and lessons learned from them, during my career. This chapter starts with mantras of learning, or the 13 things you should never forget about design leadership and then, without wishing to repeat myself unduly, it summarizes some of my key arguments which have been detailed more fully in the preceding pages. And finally, a thought to leave the reader with.

Mantras of learning – 13 things you should never forget!

The following mantras are not intended to reduce the critical role of design in business, society and government to a series of sound bites. Rather they provide the means of focusing the discussion around a number of key issues, and subsequent points of learning. These will be of practical value to every design leader and design manager and of particular relevance as well to business leaders and managers. I put them here, near the end of the book, as much for the reader to find them easily in one place as well as to act as a reminder of them. They are, by their nature, focused on the beneficial, practical and future-shaping role of design. But that is what this book has been about – arguing the case for an inclusive place for design in our commercial and social worlds, a place that will help shape a better future. The mantras have been grouped under three broad headings.

Leadership and management

1   Design leadership helps define the future, design management provides the tools for getting there.
2   Persuade by the authority of your argument, not the argument of your authority.
3   Design is a process, not a thing.
4   Design management is a commercial imperative.

Strategy and implementation

5   Design provides a clear and practical link between the strategic decisions of the boardroom and the day-to-day activities of the business.

6   Design is a business tool that makes strategy visible.

7   Corporate reputation is built on customer experience, design helps create it.

8   A good idea doesn't care who has it.

Cost or investment?

9   Investment in design increases shareholder and brand value.

10 The amount spent on design is the largest single sum most company boards know the least about.

11 Design's impact on a business can be measured.

12 Putting design into the DNA of the company is the only way to maximize shareholder value from the investment.

13 Investment in design reduces development costs and time to market.

A summary of key arguments

Creating visibility and meaning for business strategy

Design no longer belongs to designers. It is a process by which every aspect of an organization including, but not just, its products and services, look and feel. Often 'design' is narrowly defined as graphic, corporate identity, signage and packaging design. In turn, the job of designers is even more narrowly defined as guardians and implementers of such identities, focusing on the detail of guidelines rather than the reality of the customer's experience. Design is much more a way of doing things, rather than of just 'things'. Too rarely does design encompass every visible and experiential aspect of an organization's interaction with all its stakeholders. The exceptions to this sweeping generalization are notable and are the much cited proponents of 'good' design including Lego, Apple, Orange, Heathrow Terminal 5, Innocent and Green & Black's.

A process to create quality earnings

Today's global business world is a fast-moving and complex one. Given that any organization today, no matter how small, has multiple stakeholders, how the organization is presented to and interacts with all of them across many channels adds to this complexity. Stakeholders include, at a minimum, staff, customers and shareholders. The active management of the design process to affect their experiences is now more important than ever. And as if things weren't complicated enough already, customers and journalists the world over have access to market, company, corporate reputation and customer service stories in an instant – witness the speed with which the markets have reacted to the current financial crises whilst corporate spin strongly rebutted, for longer than was credible, any suggestions that all was not well.

All this means that design is no longer limited to an intermittent logo blitz. It has to be an ongoing process ensuring that the organization and what it offers are always as good as they can be. And when things are as good as they can be, customers reciprocate. Consider for a moment the fervent loyalty of Virgin business class customers, Apple Mac users, specific car marques, Starbuck's coffee drinkers or any number of fashion brands. Such loyalty is hard to earn but, once earned, it protects margins and generates high-quality earnings. It can also influence the markets and insulate quoted companies from otherwise volatile staff, customer and even analyst loyalty.

Design for the good times?

In good times, and where they exist in the first place, design budgets tend to rise along with optimism and forecasts. In bad times, 'design' may end up fighting for its very survival in marketing (or the more fashionably titled mar-comms) departments. In very bad times, these same departments can end up fighting for their own survival with their contribution to profitability challenged and their budgets scrutinized for all possible savings. In such straitened circumstances, it is easy to see how a quick slash of design budgets with a commitment to review the situation when things 'pick up again' immediately improves the bottom line.

So how often is design perceived as a means to enhance the value of the business in good times as well as bad? And is this real value even greater in risky and challenging times such as these? The honest answer to both of these questions is usually no. Some businesses can answer with a qualified yes and just the few exemplary design leaders such as Nintendo and First Direct can nod in full agreement. The relegation of design to Any Other Business on the management agenda becomes especially prevalent in difficult, recessionary times. There is a strong case to be made that investment in design enhances the value of a business, especially in tough market conditions. The key question is how?

Making business strategy tangible

History teaches us that strategy becomes more critical in the unforgiving times than it does in the good ones. Experience also teaches that design can make strategy not only visible but also tangible in very many ways. And for busy people living and working in a world where there is ever more information and ever less time, the quickest and most effective means to manifest business strategy is of particular interest.

As we now confront the harsh economic realities of a global, medium-term, recession, intensified by the peculiarities of the many European micro-economic climates, making business strategy tangible is a compelling argument for design investment. As organizations confront the challenges of reduced competitiveness and increased costs, what really is the role of design? More importantly, what is its potential to contribute to the future development of the business? Design is much more than a nice-to-have in the good times. It is a valuable tool that lets a company communicate its strategy effectively by making it visible and tangible in a relevant and powerful way at every organizational touch point.

Increasing return on investment

The fundamental challenge facing every business, irrespective of size, customer base, location or sector, is how to increase their return on investment whilst at the same time reducing the costs of making that investment. In relation to the ROI ratio, accountants and management consultants forensically examine costs and look to reduce them wherever and however possible. Cost reduction, containment, savings, efficiency and now 'The Recession' and its close companion 'The Crisis' is the vocabulary of senior management and the boardroom.

In these circumstances it is easy to view design as a cost and not an investment. The inevitable consequence of considering design a commodity is that the cheapest, rather than the best, prevails. Once it is commoditized to the extent that the one and only measure of its value is cost, design stops being a wealth-creating tool to realize business potential.

Serving business better

It is instructive to step back from the subjective debate of 'what is good design?' and consider 'how design might serve business better?' There are a number of factors worth considering here. The first is the design brief and the extent to which it is aligned to resolving business issues. The second concerns the connection between the objectives of a particular design project and the wider context of the strategic intent of the business. The third is concerned with using the measures preferred by business to evaluate design proposals. And the fourth factor is the connection between design and corporate reputation.

The brief

Design can provide a clear and practical link between the discussions of the boardroom and the day-to-day activities of the business. This is a unique and powerful argument and one that is at the heart of the case that design makes business strategy tangible. But how can a mere design brief achieve this?

The design brief is akin to a single text agreement. It may be the first time that a business has to summarize and define what it is setting out to do so as to enable others to interpret its requirements. A good brief is clear about what is to be done and what success looks like, both qualitatively and quantitatively. A good brief clearly articulates the requirements of all stakeholders and focuses on business objectives that are shared by all. It sets out the company's strategic intent or ambitions but, critically, indicates how they should be realized. For example, the brief for the development of the Heathrow Express is succinct yet contains all of these elements: 'Bringing Heathrow to London in 15 minutes for a budget of £350 million'. Of course there was more to it than that, as the case example in Chapter 7 describes, but as a short statement this does say a lot!

Strategic context

The essence of a good, inspirational brief is that it clearly articulates business objectives, the requirements of all stakeholders are clearly understood and taken account of and they subscribe to the design parameters. In short, the brief reflects a deep understanding of the strategic context in which the business, product or service operates. Once a brief reflects the strategic intent of the business, clarifies a vision of the project at hand and reflects the values of the organization commissioning it, then an effective design response is likely. Clarity and shared understanding at this stage are most likely to produce a response that is at minimum, acceptable and at best, exceptional in realizing business need. And design that makes strategy tangible and brings it to life is vastly more effective in both cost and communications terms than one that merely decorates a business card or the home page on the company's web site. Look at how Innocent has taken account of consumer concerns regarding traceability, ethics and sustainability but have leveraged them to create very drinkable smoothies, a strong brand and exceptionally popular consumer promotions.

Applying business measures

Business success is measured by relatively few financial ratios, critically gross margin, net margin and ROI. In relation to gross margin, design can impact in two ways: it can reduce the cost of sales by reducing the cost of production and it can also create value in the marketplace by making the product more widely appealing. With respect to ROI or ROCE, design can help get the most out of the capital spend on plant, premises and people. Today, especially in service businesses, payroll costs are often the single biggest cost on the revenue statement. Thus improving productivity and effectiveness dramatically impacts on profitability. Design can contribute to the creation of more efficient and better working and sales environments, improve staff retention levels and, in turn, the customer's service experience. Consider how the revenue commissioners have designed processes to turn attention from tax avoidance and evasion to making pre-emptive prompt returns online. In strictly capitalist terms, unleashing the potential of the human capital in an organization is key to profitability and design is often used to make this possible.

Enhancing corporate reputation

Today, in a world where the customer is king, the king has endless choice. So shaping customers' experiences is pivotal to success. Consider the link between customer experience and corporate reputation: the better the experience, the better the reputation of the company in the mind of that customer. And a brand is simply the sum of these collective perceptions and experiences. When they are good, they lead to further sales and when they are bad, they don't.

Design has a critical role to play as it shapes experience. For instance, it can be used to heighten excitement for a product launch, create calm and order in an airport or hospital waiting room, provide clarity around travel information or reassurance in the realm of financial services. As people get busier, less time will be spent rationally analyzing a brand's product and service offering – life is just too short. Reputation influences decision-making and affects customers' propensity to choose one brand, service or product over another.

A final thought

The overwhelming conclusion from my experience is this: design can be managed to serve business and society well. At one level it can ensure that managers create efficient systems and behaviours for the customer experience to be the best possible and to help the business work well. On another level it can enable a business to achieve more as design creates visibility and meaning for its strategic intent. And any business strategy that is both visible and meaningful is one that is much more likely to succeed.

No matter how much money is spent on design, no matter how many designers are employed when spending it, no matter what sort of business you are in, design leadership is all about recognizing three irrevocable truths:

The first is that design is a commercial and social imperative if we want all that it can offer.

The second is that without business direction design will have no lasting effect, and business direction without design will fail to deliver its full potential.

Coming to terms with these two truths and taking the actions proposed in this book will help companies, governments and social structures to maximize their potential to provide financially sound, comfortable and secure futures for all.

I have been lucky enough to have had many thought-shaping influences in my professional life. One of them was meeting Peter Gorb, my mentor and friend for many years. I unashamedly borrow from him my third irrevocable truth and final thought to leave you with, and it is this...

'put aside the idea that design is just for designers, it is infinitely more important than that'

Figures and Diagrams

Figures

Diagrams

References

Best, K. 2010. *The Fundamentals of Design Management*. AVA Academia.

Berger, W., Mau, B. 2009. *How Design Can Transform Your Life and Maybe Even the World*. Penguin Group USA.

Carlzon, J. 1989. *Moments of Truth*. Harper Collins.

Cooper, R., Press, M. 1994. *The Design Agenda*. Wiley.

Cortada, J.W. 1998. *Rise of the Knowledge Worker*. Elsevier.

D'Arcy, G. 2010. Bord na Móna Annual report 2010/2011.

Duffy, F. 1998. Working at Waterside – conduciveness as a workplace of the British headquarters in Harmondsworth, England. The Architectural Review, August.

Gorb, P. 1979. Design and its use to managers, *Journal of Royal Society of Arts*, vol. 128, no. 5283.

Gorb, P., Dumas, A. 1987. Silent design, *Design Studies*, vol. 8, no. 3.

Law, J. ed. 2009 *Oxford Dictionary of Business and Management*. Oxford University Press.

Lawrence, P. 1998. Egan interview, *Corporate Design Foundation*, vol. 4, no. 2.

Lindstrom, M. 2005. *Brand Sense*. Kogan Page.

Lockwood, T. 2008. Design Value: A Framework for Measurement, *Design Management Review*, vol. 18, no. 4.

Mott, G. 2008. *Accounting for Non-Accountants*, Kogan Page.

Olins,W. 1985. *The Wolff Olins Guide to Design Management*. The Design Council.

Peters, T. 2003.   *Re-imagine-Business Excellence in a Disruptive Age*. DK Publishing.

Pevsner, N. 1942.   Patient progress – The life work of Frank Pick. *Architectural Review*.

Philips, P. 2004.   *Creating the Perfect Design Brief*. Allworth Press.

Pick, F. 1916.   From an address given on design and industry at an exhibition of design workmanship in printing. Edinburgh.

Pine, B., Gilmore, J. 1999.   *The Experience Economy*. Harvard Business Press.

Ratner, G. 1991   Speech to Institute of Directors, 22 November.

Topalian, A. 1980.   *The Management of Design Projects*. Associated Business Press.

Topalian, A. 2002.   Promoting design leadership through skills development programmes. *Design Management Journal*, vol. 13, no. 3.

Turner, R. 1996.   Selecting designers: one client's way of auditing an entire industry, *Design Management Journal*, vol. 7 no. 2.

Turner, R., Gorb,P. 1992.   A design frontier: corporate identity and design management at Eurotunnel. *Design Management Journal*, vol. 3, no. 1.

Turner, R., Topalian, A. 2002.   Core responsibilities of design leaders in commercially demanding environments. Design Leadership Forum.

Wolff, M. 2012.   In conversation with Mike Dempsey, http://mikedempsey.typepad.com/graphic_journey_blog/2012/01/michael-wolff-in-conversation.htmlIndex

Index